Deborah C. Fisher was born in 1955 and educated in Port Talbot and St Hilda's, Oxford, where she obtained a degree in French and Latin. She is an Associate of the Library Association. Having worked in the civil service for a number of years, she is now a computer systems analyst in Swansea. A keen amateur archaeologist, she is married and has two daughters.

WHO'S WHO
IN
WELSH HISTORY

Deborah C Fisher

CHRISTOPHER DAVIES

Published in 1997 by
Christopher Davies (Publishers) Ltd.
P.O. Box 403, Swansea, SA1 4YF

Printed and bound in Wales by
Dinefwr Press
Rawlings Road, Llandybie
Carmarthenshire, SA18 3YD

Front cover illustrations: Aneurin Bevan (by kind
permission of the *Western Mail*); Hywel Dda, Edgar
Evans, Saunders Lewis, David Lloyd George (by kind
permission of the *National Library of Wales*); Dylan
Thomas (by kind permission of *Llew Thomas*).

Back cover illustrations: Henry VII (*Cardiff Castle*);
Ivor Novello (*National Library of Wales*); William Price,
Thomas Pennant, Dr Joseph Parry, William Williams,
Pantycelyn (by kind permission of the *Museum of Welsh
Life*).

Cover design: Llew Thomas Design, Swansea.

CONTENTS

INTRODUCTION

This is not a work of historical scholarship. It is a simple alphabetical index designed to aid the would-be student of Welsh history, or anyone with a passing interest in the subject. The biographical notes are brief; for more information on the people mentioned, the reader must consult the history books. However, the length of each entry is intended to reflect the relative importance of its subject.

Nor is the list exhaustive. The scope is admittedly wide, in that it goes back as far as possible in time, and includes not just the major players in Welsh history, but lesser-known figures, and some whose contribution has been to the cultural and religious life of the nation, as well as the political. However, it stops short of the present day, in that no one still living is included in the list. This has resulted in the exclusion of a number of men and women who have already made a significant contribution to Welsh history, but whose ultimate influence cannot perhaps yet be seen in context.

Not all the subjects listed are of Welsh birth, or even of Welsh ancestry. The criterion for inclusion is the degree of influence on Welsh history (which may be for better or worse). For example, all the English "Princes" and "Princesses" of Wales are included, but Kings and Queens of England, with few exceptions, are not present unless they come into this category. Conversely, persons of Welsh birth or parentage are included even if their sphere of influence was outside Wales. However, in the interest of balance, I have deliberately limited the number of references to the prolific Welsh royal families of the Middle Ages, when infighting and family feuds caused as much damage as wars with foreigners. In fact, the further back one goes in time, the harder it is to say what constitutes Welsh blood, or indeed what constitutes Wales. My definition is based on present-day boundaries which were not even thought of in the earliest times.

The author is aware of many names which have been omitted for reasons of space, but the publishers welcome readers' views on any inclusions for consideration in preparing future editions.

NOTES

First Names and Surnames

Subjects are listed in alphabetical order of surname, where possible. This is difficult to achieve up to the Middle Ages, prior to which most people were known by a forename and perhaps a nickname. In Wales, the patronymic form **"ap"** was commonly used; in these cases and all other cases where there is nothing immediately recognisable as a surname, the forename is generally used (I have also limited the use of **"ap"** to one generation: for example, Cadwaladr ap Gruffydd ap Cynan is listed simply as **CADWALADR ap Gruffydd**). However, the question of what constitutes a surname is not easily resolved, and this is most noticeable with some of the Norman names. Where the place of origin (eg. **CLARE**) developed into a recognisable surname over a long period, it is used as such from the beginning; but where the only entries are from the earlier period, the first name is used, eg. **ROBERT of Belleme**. As a general rule, entries under first name precede surnames: for example, **GRUFFYDD Hiraethog** comes before **GRUFFYDD, Elis**. Entries are cross-referenced where confusion is likely.

Dates

The dates of birth and death of all subjects are given where possible. In many cases, these dates can only be approximate, and these are indicated by the usual "c." (circa). However, note that, where this information is not available and historians are unwilling to commit themselves to a likely date, I have in some cases made my own, non-scientific, estimate, in an attempt to assist the reader.

Families

The separate list of family names concentrates on those families where more than one family member or generation of a family has excelled in a particular field or been well known in a community. In many cases, there will also be entries in the main biographical list for individual family members; as far as possible, these are easily recognisable. Families mentioned in the biographical entries for which a separate entry occurs in the family list are identified by means of an asterisk, eg. **BULKELEY***.

The Welsh language

Although this book is written in English, practicality forces us to assume that the reader, whilst not necessarily being familiar with the Welsh language, will be able to tell Welsh and English apart. I apologise to Welsh speakers for any impurities in the use of the language, eg. the use of the more common spelling, "Gruffydd", in preference to "Gruffudd".

References to place names, which are sometimes necessary, give rise to problems. In recent years there has been an increasing tendency to refer to Welsh towns by their original Welsh names instead of the English variant, eg. Llanelli (Llanelly), Cydweli (Kidwelly). Where the risk of misunderstanding is small, I have listed the Welsh name only. In other cases, the more familiar name (to English speakers) is given first, followed where helpful by the alternative.

I would like to thank Mr Ray Woodward for his assistance with translation.

Publishers' Note

No volume is comprehensive and no doubt many a reader will claim that some figure has been omitted from the book and is deserving of an entry. The publishers welcome any suggestions in writing and these can be sent to Christopher Davies (Publishers) Ltd., PO Box 403, Swansea, SA1 4YF.

A

AB
Alternative form of **AP**.

ABERDARE, 1st Baron
See **BRUCE, Henry Austin**.

ABLETT, Noah
(1883-1935)
Left-wing politician, founder of the Plebs League at Rhondda (1909) and a leading figure in the Central Labour College movement.

ABRAHAM, William (Mabon)
(1842-1922)
Liberal and Labour politician, MP for Rhondda 1885-1920 and first president of the South Wales Miners' Federation. A great public speaker, he was also a prominent member of the Eisteddfod movement.

ADAM OF USK
(c.1352-1430)
Cleric, supporter of King Henry IV of England. His "Chronicle", covering the period up to 1421, is a useful historical source.

AIDAN or AIDUS
(6th century; exact dates unknown)
Saint of Irish origin, brought up in Wales; also known as Maidoc or Madoc.

ALEXANDRA OF DENMARK
(1844-1925)
Princess of Wales by her marriage in 1863 to "Bertie", later King **EDWARD VII**. Unlike most of their predecessors, they made official visits to Wales, and the anthem, "God Bless the Prince of Wales", was written to commemorate their marriage. As Queen, she founded Queen Alexandra's Nursing Corps (the Q.A.s) and the Alexandra Rose Day.

AMBROSIUS AURELIANUS (Emrys Wledig)
(5th century; exact dates unknown)
British leader, possibly a grandson of **MAGNUS Maximus** and **ELEN (1)**, and a predecessor of **ARTHUR**. He is mentioned by **GILDAS** and **GEOFFREY of Monmouth** as having defeated **GWRTHEYRN** (Vortigern) and rebuilt the city of Winchester.

ANARAWD AP GRUFFYDD
(c.1115-43)
Prince, son of **GRUFFYDD ap Rhys (1)**. He became ruler of Deheubarth in 1137, and, with his brother **CADELL ap Gruffydd**, joined **OWAIN Gwynedd** to attack the Normans at Cardigan. He was murdered in 1143 by Owain's brother, **CADWALADR ap Gruffydd**.

ANARAWD AP RHODRI
(c.850-916)
Prince, eldest son of **RHODRI Mawr** and **ANGHARAD (1)** and brother of **CADELL ap Rhodri**. He succeeded to Anglesey and Gwynedd on his father's death in 878, allying himself first with the Danes, then with Alfred of Wessex, with whose help he attacked his brother's lands of Ceredigion and Ystrad Tywi in 895.

ANEIRIN or ANEURIN
(6th century; exact dates unknown)
Poet, sometimes identified (probably incorrectly) with **GILDAS**. He was nicknamed "Mechdeyrn" (Great King). His poem, "Y Gododdin", which deals with the Battle of Cattraeth (possibly Catterick), revealing him as a native of Manaw Gododdin (Strathclyde), is preserved in a 13th century manuscript known as "The Book of Aneirin".

ANGHARAD (1)

(9th century; exact dates unknown)
Princess of Ceredigion, sister of **GWGON ap Meurig** and wife of **RHODRI Mawr**. Through this marriage, Rhodri acquired the territory of Seisyllwg. She gave birth to six sons, three of whom jointly inherited their father's lands.

ANGHARAD (2)

(10th–11th centuries; exact dates unknown)
Princess of Deheubarth, daughter of **MAREDUDD ab Owain**. She married, firstly, **LLYWELYN ap Seisyll**, and secondly, Cynfyn ap Gwerstan. Her children from these marriages included **GRUFFYDD ap Llywelyn (1)**, **BLEDDYN ap Cynfyn** and **RHIWALLON ap Cynfyn**.

ANGHARAD (3)

(c.1080-1162)
Daughter of Owain ab Edwin of Gwynedd and wife of **GRUFFYDD ap Cynan**, to whom she bore eight children.

ANGLESEY, Marquess of

See **PAGET, William**.

ANIAN (1) (Einion ap Maredudd)

(c.1200-1266)
Bishop of St Asaph from 1247 until his death. He supported **LLYWELYN ap Gruffydd**, and acted as an intermediary in his dispute with the Bishop of Bangor.

ANIAN (2)

(c.1230-1293)
Bishop of St Asaph from 1268, and an opponent of **LLYWELYN ap Gruffydd**. Under the treaty of Aberconwy (1277) his diocese came under the control of the English Crown, but he nevertheless refused to participate in the excommunication of the Welsh leaders in 1282.

ANIAN (3)

(c.1250-1306)
Bishop of Bangor from 1267; confessor to **LLYWELYN ap Gruffydd**. He fled to England in 1277 and again in 1282, and swore fealty to the new Prince of Wales (later **EDWARD II**) in 1301.

ANTHONY, Jack

(1890-1954)
Jockey, three times the winning rider in the Grand National steeplechase.

ANWYL, Edward

(1866-1914)
A founder member of Cymdeithas **DAFYDD ap Gwilym** at Oxford in 1886, later Professor of Welsh at University College of Wales, Aberystwyth 1892-1913; knighted 1911.

AP, AB

Welsh patronymic form. See under first name, eg. **CADWALADR ap Gruffydd**.

ARMSTRONG-JONES (formerly JONES), Robert

(1857-1943)
Psychiatrist, Director of the pioneering Claybury asylum 1893-1916; knighted in 1917.

ARNOLD, John

(1634-98)
Protestant activist, MP and Sheriff of Monmouthshire, who persecuted local Catholics in the wake of the "Popish plot".

ARTHUR

(c.470-520)
King of Britain mentioned by **NENNIUS** and **GEOFFREY of Monmouth**, the subject of innumerable legends. He is said to have fought twelve important battles against the Picts, Irish, and English, includ-

ing that of Mount Badon in about 516. Though he may not have originated from Wales, he was allied with Brythonic Celtic leaders. There is no definite evidence concerning his dates of birth and death or the location of his court.

ARTHUR OF WINCHESTER
See **TUDOR, Arthur**

ASAPH
(c.600; exact dates unknown)
Saint, a pupil of St Kentigern; founder of the bishopric in Flintshire. *Gave his name to:* St Asaph.

ASHLEY (née MOUNTNEY), Laura
(1925-85)
Designer, famous for a range of colourful fabrics for clothes and home furnishings, produced by her factory in Newtown.

ASSER
(c.850-909)
Scholar of St David's and Bishop of Sherborne; biographer of King Alfred of Wessex, to whom he reputedly taught Latin. He was influential in persuading the Welsh rulers to pay homage to Alfred.

ASSHETON, Thomas
See **SMITH, Thomas Assheton**.

AUBREY, William ("The Great Civilian")
(c.1529-95)
Anti-Puritan lawyer and judge, who officiated in important cases such as those of Lady Catherine Grey (1552) and the Bishop of Ross (1571). Related to both **John PENRY**, whom he helped condemn, and **John DEE**, he was the great-grandfather of the writer John **AUBREY***, the last of the family to hold their Welsh estates.

AUGUSTA OF SAXE-GOTHA
(1719-72)
Princess of Wales by her marriage to **FREDERICK Lewis Augustus** in 1736; mother of King George III, on whom she exerted considerable influence.

AUGUSTUS, William (Wil Awst)
(18th century; exact dates unknown)
Author of "The husbandman's perpetual prognostication" (1794), one of the first published works on meteorology, written partly in English and partly in Welsh.

AVRANCHES, Hugh of
See **HUGH d'Avranches**.

B

BACON, Anthony
(1718-86)
Industrialist who brought Merthyr Tydfil to its prominent position as an industrial centre by establishing a large iron-works and building roads; MP for Aylesbury 1764-86.

BAGLAN
(6th century; exact dates unknown)
Saint, originally from Brittany. Various legends connect him with Wales. *Gave his name to:* Baglan, West Glamorgan.

BAILEY, Crawshay
(1789-1872)
Iron-master, brother of **Joseph BAILEY** and nephew of Richard **CRAWSHAY***; MP for several South Wales constituencies 1852-68. He expanded the railway network in the area, purchasing the Aberaman estate from the **BACON*** family. A popular song, "Cosher Bailey's engine", commemorated him.

BAILEY, Joseph
(1783-1858)
Iron-master, elder brother of **Crawshay BAILEY**; MP for Worcester 1835-47 and Brecknock 1847-52, created a baronet 1852. He was co-owner of Cyfarthfa ironworks 1810-13, then successfully took over the Nant-y-glo works. His estates in Brecon, Radnorshire, Herefordshire, and Glamorgan included the family seat at Glanusk Park.

BAKER, Charles
See **LEWIS, David (2)**.

BAKER, David or **Augustine**
(1575-1641)
Benedictine priest, a leading Catholic figure; author of works on history, law, and theology.

BAKER, Stanley
(1928-76)
Actor and film director, best known for his appearances in British films of the 1950s and 1960s, especially "Zulu" (1964); knighted in 1976.

BALLINGER, John
(1860-1933)
First librarian of the National Library of Wales at Aberystwyth (1908); knighted for his services to librarianship in 1930.

BARHAM (née MIDDLETON), (Lady) Diana
(1763-1823)
English Baroness, resident at Fairy Hill, Gower, 1813-23; builder of chapels in the district on behalf of the evangelical Methodists.

BARLOW, William
(c.1499-1568)
Protestant Bishop of St Asaph and St David's (1536-48), who won the favour of Thomas Cromwell and Queen Anne Boleyn, but spent the years 1555-58 in exile in Europe; founder of Christ College, Brecon.

BARRI, Gerald de
See **GERALD OF WALES**

BAXTER, William
(1650-1723)
Antiquary, associate of **Edward LHUYD**; an early proponent of the idea of a national university for Wales.

BAYLY, Lewis
(c.1570-1631)
Bishop of Bangor from 1616 and author of "The practice of piety" (1611), translated

into Welsh by **Rowland VAUGHAN (2)**; opponent, and later friend, of Sir **John WYNN**.

BEBB, William **Ambrose**
(1894-1955)
Author of historical works, editor of "Y Wawr". Influenced by the Breton national movement, he co-founded Plaid Cymru (1925), and stood as a Parliamentary candidate in 1945.

BECK or **BEK, Thomas**
(c.1230-93)
Bishop of St David's from 1280, by the patronage of King **EDWARD I** of England; previously Chancellor of Oxford University (1269), Keeper of the King's Wardrobe (1274), and Royal Commissioner in Wales (1280)). He founded collegiate churches at Abergwili and Llanddewibrefi and hospitals at Llawhaden and St David's, and probably built Llawhaden Castle.

BEDLOE, William
(1650-80)
Petty criminal, involved with Titus Oates in concocting the "Popish Plot".

BELL, Harold **Idris**
(1879-1967)
Scholar, author and translator, employed as a Librarian at the British Museum.

BELL, Richard
(1859-1930)
MP for Derby 1900-1910, an early supporter of the Labour Party; President of the Trades Union Congress 1904-10.

BELLEME, Robert of
See **ROBERT OF BELLEME**.

BERAIN, Katheryn of
See **KATHERYN OF BERAIN**.

BERNARD
(c.1080-1148)
Bishop of St David's from 1115, builder of the large cathedral demolished in 1182. A former chaplain of King Henry I of England, he was an unpopular choice, but carried out reforms in the diocese. Despite winning his argument with Bishop Urban of Llandaff over which diocese should have jurisdiction over the Welsh Church, he failed to obtain metropolitan status for St David's, but may have achieved the canonisation of St **DAVID**.

BERNARD OF NEUFMARCHE or **NEWMARCH**
See **NEUFMARCHE, Bernard de**.

BERRY, James (1)
Puritan military leader, placed in charge of Wales and Hereford by Cromwell after a Royalist rebellion in 1655.

BERRY, James (2) Gomer
(1883-1968)
Journalist, brother of **William Ewart BERRY**; baronet 1928. He became chairman of Kemsley Newspapers Ltd in 1937, and was created Viscount Kemsley in 1945.

BERRY, William Ewart
(1879-1954)
Journalist; brother of **James Gomer BERRY (2)**, with whom he founded "Advertising world" (1901). In 1915, they acquired the "Sunday Times", followed by several other newspapers. After a period as editor of the "Daily Telegraph", he was created Viscount Cambrose in 1941.

BEUNO
(6th century; exact dates unknown)
Saint born in North Wales, member of the royal family of Morgannwg, founder of a monastery at Clynnog Fawr. The Bronze Age stone, Maen Beuno, at Aberriw (Berriew) is reputed to have been his first pulpit.

BEVAN, Aneurin ("Nye")
(1897-1960)
Labour politician rejected by the establishment. An ex-miner, he was MP for Ebbw Vale from 1929 until his death, founded the journal, "Tribune", in 1942, and served as Minister of Health and Housing 1945-51, being instrumental in the creation of the National Health Service. Later he became deputy leader of the Labour Party. Though he neither favoured independence for Wales nor cared for the Welsh language, his loyalty to Wales and to Socialist ideals ensured the continued support of his constituents.

BEVAN (née VAUGHAN), Bridget
(1698-1779)
Philanthropist, wife of Arthur Bevan (MP for Carmarthen) and daughter of **John VAUGHAN (5)**. She acted as trustee for schools on behalf of **Griffith JONES (1)**, whose correspondence with her has been published, and carried on his work after his death.

BEVAN, Edward
(1861-1934)
First Bishop of Swansea and Brecon, appointed in 1923.

BIRCH, Evelyn Nigel Chetwode
(1906-81)
English-born economist; Conservative MP for Flintshire and Secretary of State for Air in 1955-7. The post of Economic Secretary to the Treasury was created for him in 1957, but he resigned in 1958, along with Lord Thorneycroft and Enoch Powell. He was created Baron Rhyl (life peer) in 1970.

BLACK PRINCE
See **EDWARD OF WOODSTOCK**.

BLACKMORE, Richard Doddridge
(1825-1900)
English-born novelist, best known for "Lorna Doone" (1869). He was related to the **KNIGHT*** family of Nottage Court, where he was resident when writing "The maid of Sker" (1872).

BLEDDYN AP CYNFYN
(c.1030-75)
Son of Cynfyn ap Gwerstan and **ANGHARAD (2)**; thus half-brother of **GRUFFYDD ap Llywelyn (1)**. He ruled Powys for twelve years, at first as a vassal of Edward the Confessor, and upheld the laws of **HYWEL Dda**. A ruthless warrior (with his brother **RHIWALLON ap Cynfyn**, he defeated Gruffydd's sons at the Battle of Mechain (1070)), he was assassinated by **RHYS ab Owain**.

BLEDRI AP CYDIFOR
(c.1080-1120)
Supporter of the Normans during the revolt of 1116. He acted as their interpreter, and may be the "Bledhericus" mentioned by **GERALD of Wales** and the author of the legends of Tristan and Iseult and the search for the Holy Grail.

BLEGYWRYD
(c.900-945)
Scholar and legal expert who assisted **HYWEL Dda** in his attempt to standardise Welsh law.

BOHUN, Humphrey (de) (1)
(c.1220-65)
Lord of Brecon, Hay and Haverfordwest through his marriage to Eleanor de **BRAOSE***; son of the 2nd Earl of Hereford. He was killed at the Battle of Evesham, supporting Simon de Montfort.

BOHUN, Humphrey (de) (2)
(c.1249-98)
3rd Earl of Hereford and 2nd Earl of Essex; son of **Humphrey de BOHUN (1)**. He maintained possession of Brecon, in opposition to **LLYWELYN ap Gruffydd**.

BOHUN, Humphrey (de) (3)
(1276-1322)
4th Earl of Hereford and 3rd Earl of Essex, son-in-law of King **EDWARD I** of England; killed at the Battle of Boroughbridge.

BOHUN, Mary (de)
(c.1369-94)
Heiress to the earldoms of Hereford, Essex and Northampton through her direct descent from **Humphrey de BOHUN (3)**; first wife of Henry Bolingbroke (later King Henry IV) and mother of seven children, including King **HENRY V**.

BORROW, George
(1803-81)
English traveller, author of "Wild Wales" (1862).

BOWDLER, Thomas
(1754-1825)
English doctor, censor of the Bible and Shakespeare, whose activities gave rise to the term "bowdlerisation". He died at Swansea and is buried at Oxwich.

BOWEN, Ben
(1878-1903)
Miner, poet and author, associated with the "Bardd Newydd" school, surrounded by religious controversy.

BOWEN, Hannah
(1729-1805)
Sister of **Sarah LLOYD**, whom she succeeded as "matron" of the Trefecca family, leaving in 1771 to become matron of Lady Huntingdon's college at Trefecca.

BRACE, William
(1865-1947)
Vice-president of the South Wales Miners' Federation, "Lib-Lab" MP for South Glamorgan 1906-18, and Labour MP for Abertillery 1918-20.

BRANGWYN, Frank
(1867-1956)
Artist, painter of the "British Empire panels" (1925), which were rejected by the House of Lords and are now displayed at Swansea's Guildhall. *Gave his name to:* Brangwyn Hall, Swansea.

BRAOSE, Isabella or **Isabel de**
(early 13th century; exact dates unknown)
Daughter of **William de BRAOSE (2)**, wife (1229) of **DAFYDD ap Llywelyn**. Their marriage was childless.

BRAOSE, Reginald de
(c.1170-1228)
Son of **William de BRAOSE (1)**, he seized control of his father's former territories in 1215. He was an ally of **LLYWELYN Fawr**, whose daughter, **GWLADUS Ddu**, he married, but later changed allegiance and supported King Henry III of England, until forced into submission by Llywelyn.

BRAOSE, William de (1)
(c.1150-1211)
Ruthless Norman Marcher lord, the most powerful of his day, frequently in conflict with native Welsh rulers. As Sheriff of Herefordshire 1192-99, he was in favour with the English Kings Richard I and John, but rejected the Crown's authority in the Welsh Marches in order to justify his military offensives and brutal acts such as the murder, in 1175, of Seisyll ap Dyfnwal and other local leaders whom he had lured to Abergavenny Castle. At the height of his power, he was lord of Elfael (1191), Gower (1203) and Three Castles (1205), but was disgraced in 1207 and exiled to France. His wife and son, imprisoned at Windsor, were starved to death on the orders of King John.

BRAOSE, William de (2)
(c.1190-1230)
Lord of Brecon, Builth, and Abergavenny; son of **Reginald de BRAOSE**. While a prisoner of **LLYWELYN Fawr** in 1228, he

contracted a marriage between Llywelyn's son, **DAFYDD ap Llywelyn** and his own daughter, **Isabella de BRAOSE**, creating an alliance which brought territorial and other benefits to both sides. However, in 1230 he was executed for an alleged affair with Llywelyn's wife, **JOAN (1)**.

BRAOSE, William de (3)
(c.1215-90)
2nd Baron of Gower and Bramber; a grandson of **LLYWELYN Fawr**. His three marriages enabled his family to obtain possession of various territories through his descendants and their marriages.

BRAOSE, William de (4)
(1291-1326)
Lord of Gower who granted a charter of liberties to his tenants. His lordship was disputed by the powerful **DESPENSER*** family.

BROCHWEL YSGYTHROG
(6th century; exact dates unknown)
Prince of Powys (sometimes called by poets "the land of Brochwel"), possibly the father of **TYSILIO**. He may have had a palace at Shrewsbury.

BROUGHTON, Rhoda
(1840-1920)
Prolific and popular novelist, with a reputation for free speech. *Gave her name to:* Mount Rhoda, Antarctica.

BRUCE, Henry Austin
(1815-95)
Liberal MP for Merthyr Tydfil 1852-73, later MP for Renfrewshire. He was Home Secretary and Lord President of the Council under Gladstone (1868-73), and was created 1st Baron Aberdare in 1873. He was the first Chancellor of the University of Wales (1895).

BRUCE, William Napier
(1858-1936)
Educationist, younger son of **Henry Austin BRUCE**. He had considerable influence on the organisation of secondary education in Wales.

BRYCHAN
(5th century; exact dates unknown)
Legendary ruler and saint, of Irish origin. His large number of descendants are one of the three "tribes of the saints". *Gave his name to:* Brycheiniog (Brecon).

BRYNACH
(5th-6th century; exact dates unknown)
Saint associated with Pembrokeshire, founder of a settlement at Nevern (Nanhyfer); sometimes known as "Wyddel" ("the Irishman").

BUCKLAND, William
(1784-1856)
English archaeologist who, in 1823, discovered the "Red Lady of Paviland" (a human skeleton now believed to date from about 25,000 B.C.) in a cave on the Gower peninsula.

BULKELEY, Richard
(1533-1621)
MP for Anglesey, a favourite of Queen Elizabeth I; knighted in 1577. He founded the **BULKELEY*** family seat at Baron Hill in 1618.

BULKELEY, Thomas
(1585-1659)
Royalist commander during the Civil War, son of **Richard BULKELEY**; created Viscount **BULKELEY*** of Cashel 1644.

BURGES, William
(1827-81)
English architect, son of a partner in the East Bute Docks company. He was commissioned by the **3rd Marquess of BUTE** to rebuild and decorate his residences at Cardiff Castle and Castell Coch, which he did in a pseudo-medieval style fashionable during that period.

BURGESS, Thomas
(1756-1837)
English Bishop of St David's 1803-25; founder of several schools and St David's College, Lampeter (1822).

BURGH, Hubert de
(c.1180-1243)
Earl of Kent, Justiciar of England under King Henry III; a leading opponent of **LLYWELYN Fawr**. He held the Three Castles, and Montgomery 1223-8, and controlled most of South Wales until his downfall in 1232.

BURNE-JONES, Edward Coley
(1833-98)
English-born painter of the "Pre-Raphaelite" school; created a baronet in 1894. He was noted for his designs for tapestries and stained glass. Celtic romance is a strong theme in his work, reflecting his ancestry.

BURTON (formerly JENKINS), Richard
(1925-84)
Successful and influential stage and screen actor. He took the surname of his teacher and adoptive father, Philip H Burton. Though nominated seven times for an Academy Award, he never obtained it, instead gaining notoriety for his lifestyle and his marriage to the actress Elizabeth Taylor. His most successful films included "My cousin Rachel" (1952), "The spy who came in from the cold" (1965), and "Equus" (1977).

BUSHELL, Thomas
(1594-1674)
English entrepreneur who carried out silver mining activity in Cardiganshire from 1611 to 1646. A Royalist supporter during the Civil War, he set up a mint at Aberystwyth, but was forced into temporary exile on Lundy Island.

BUTE, John, 2nd Marquess of
(1793-1848)
Industrialist, largely responsible for the growth of Cardiff, where he established the West Bute Dock in 1839. He continued the renovation of Cardiff Castle which had been begun by his father, the 1st Marquess, through whose marriage to Charlotte Windsor he inherited the **HERBERT (2)*** estates in South Wales.

BUTE, John, 3rd Marquess of (John Patrick Crichton Stuart)
(1847-1900)
Scholar and amateur historian, reputedly the richest man in the world, largely as a result of the business investments of his father, **John, 2nd Marquess of BUTE**. He was responsible for excavations at Cardiff Castle and Castell Coch, and their renovation under the direction of **William BURGES**. His conversion to Roman Catholicism is depicted in Disraeli's novel, "Lothair" (1870).

BUTLER, Eleanor
(1739-1829)
Irish lady, originally of Kilkenny Castle, who lived at Plas Newydd with her companion, **Sarah PONSONBY**, from 1780 until her death. They drew around themselves a coterie and became renowned throughout Britain as "the ladies of Llangollen", with admirers including Wellington, Wedgwood, Wordsworth, and Queen Charlotte.

BUTTON, Thomas
(c.1570-1634)
Sea captain who attempted to find the North-West passage in 1612, and succeeded in exploring Hudson Bay instead. Knighted by King James I, he was created an admiral, and in 1620 joined **Robert MANSEL**'s mission against piracy.

BYFORD, Lewis
See **LEWIS AP IEUAN**.

C

CADELL AP RHODRI
(c.850-910)

Prince, son of **RHODRI Mawr** and **ANGHARAD (1)**. On his father's death, he inherited Seisyllwg, which he ruled for twenty-three years, frequently warring with his brothers, **ANARAWD ap Rhodri** and Merfyn ap Rhodri.

CADELL AP GRUFFYDD
(c.1120-75)

Son of **GRUFFYDD ap Rhys (1)**, who ruled Deheubarth after the murder of his brother **ANARAWD ap Gruffydd**. He campaigned successfully against the Normans, but in 1147 allied himself with the Fitzgerald family. When his military career was at an end, he entered the abbey of Strata Florida.

CADFAN (1)
(6th century; exact dates unknown)

Saint of Breton origin, founder of several churches, including a monastery on Bardsey Island. *Gave his name to:* Llangadfan, Powys.

CADFAN (2)
(c.550-625)

Prince of Gwynedd, mentioned by **GEOFFREY of Monmouth**.

CADOG
(5th century; exact dates unknown)

Saint, subject of the "Life of St Cadog" written by **LIFRIS of Llancarfan**; son of **GWYNLLYW**, whom he reputedly converted to Christianity, and possibly grandson of **BRYCHAN**. He founded the monastery at Llancarfan *Gave his name to:* early churches in Wales, Cornwall, Scotland, and Brittany.

CADWALADR AP GRUFFYDD
(c.1110-1172)

Prince, younger brother of **OWAIN Gwynedd**. At first they fought and ruled together, but he lacked Owain's princely qualities. Having allied himself with the Normans by his marriage to Alice de **CLARE***, he caused a diplomatic incident by sanctioning the murder of **ANARAWD ap Gruffydd**, for which he was exiled in 1143. Returning with a force of Danes from Dublin, he was reconciled with his brother, but was exiled again in 1152, and restored in 1157, by the intervention of King Henry II of England.

CADWALADR FENDIGAID (Cadwaladr the Blessed)
(c.620-680)

Prince of Gwynedd, son of **CADWALLON (1)**; mentioned by **GEOFFREY of Monmouth**. He defeated the usurper Cadafael ap Cynfedw to regain his father's kingdom of Gwynedd. His standard, the red dragon, was adopted by **Henry TUDOR**, who claimed descent. *Gave his name to:* Llangadwaladr, Anglesey.

CADWALADR, Beti
See **DAVIES, Elizabeth**.

CADWALADR, Dilys
(1902-79)

Poet and author, the first woman to win the Crown at the National Eisteddfod, which she achieved in 1953 with her poem, "Y llan", in the "pryddest" form.

CADWALLON (1)
(c.590-634)

Son of **CADFAN (2)**, ruler of Gwynedd from 625. Having defeated the Irish immigrants in the region, he allied himself with Penda, King of Mercia, in order to drive out Edwin of Northumbria, whom they defeated and killed at the Battle of Meigen or Heathfield in 632. Before he could return to Wales, he was himself defeated and killed at Hefenfelth near Hexham by Edwin's brother, Oswald.

CADWALLON (2) (AP GRUFFYDD AP CYNAN)
(c.1100-1132)
Prince, son of **GRUFFYDD ap Cynan**. In 1124 he conquered Dyffryn Clwyd, adding it to the territories of Gwynedd which he ruled with his brothers, **OWAIN Gwynedd** and **CADWALADR ap Gruffydd**. He himself was defeated and killed by the ruler of Powys.

CADWGAN AP BLEDDYN
(c.1070-1111)
Prince of Powys and Ceredigion, son of **BLEDDYN ap Cynfyn**. With two brothers, he drove **RHYS ap Tewdwr** into exile in 1088; his brothers were both killed in battle on the latter's return. He strengthened his position with a castle at Trallwng Llywelyn and a marriage alliance with the Norman SAY* family. The scandalous conduct of his son, **OWAIN ap Cadwgan**, caused his dispossession in 1109, and he was later ambushed and murdered by a nephew.

CAIN
See **KEYNE**.

CAIN, Rhys
(c.1550-1614)
Poet and herald, who took his name from the river Cain; best known for an elegy for his teacher, William Llyn, whose library he inherited. His own manuscripts passed into the hands of the **WILLIAMS-WYNN*** family. His son, **Sion CAIN**, carried on his work as a genealogist.

CAIN, Sion
(c.1575-1650)
Herald and poet, son of **Rhys CAIN**. His manuscripts became part of the Hengwrt collection.

CALLICE, John
(16th century; exact dates unknown)
Pirate of the Glamorgan and Monmouthshire coast, eventually captured in 1567.

CAMBROSE, Viscount
See **BERRY, William Ewart**.

CAMPBELL, Frederick Archibald Vaughan
(1847-1911)
Viscount Emlyn and 3rd Earl of Cawdor (from 1898). He served as Conservative MP for Carmarthenshire 1874-85, and was later a member of the Committee on education in Wales chaired by **Henry Austin BRUCE**. He held the post of First Lord of the Admiralty in the Balfour government of 1905.

CARADOG or CARA(C)TACUS
(c.10-54)
Chief of the Catuvellauni and Trinovantes; son of Cynfelin (Cymbeline). Defeated by the Romans, he led the Silures and Ordovices (tribes dwelling in South and North Wales respectively) in continued resistance. In AD 51, during the reign of the Emperor Claudius, he was captured and taken to Rome, where he won the admiration of the citizens for his dignified conduct and was spared from execution.

CARADOG AP GRUFFYDD
(1040-81)
Prince of Deheubarth, son of **GRUFFYDD ap Rhydderch**. In 1065, he attacked the property of Harold Godwinson at Portskewit, and by 1078 had eliminated two rulers of Deheubarth, including **RHYS ab Owain**, as well as taking possession of Glamorgan. He was himself defeated and

killed at the Battle of Mynydd Carn by **RHYS ap Tewdwr** and **GRUFFYDD ap Cynan**.

CARADOG AP IESTYN
(c.1078-1148)
Prince, son of **IESTYN ap Gwrgant** and an ally of **ROBERT Fitzhamo(n)**. He was granted the lordship of Nedd and Afan, and constructed a castle on the banks of the Afan.

CARANNOG
(6th century; exact dates unknown)
Saint associated with places in Cardiganshire, Somerset, Cornwall and Brittany; possibly the son or grandson of **CUNEDDA**. *Gave his name to:* Llangrannog, Dyfed.

CARA(C)TACUS
See **CARADOG**.

CARNE, Edward
(c.1500-61)
Lawyer and leading Catholic, a diplomat under **Mary TUDOR** and her successors, despite having been involved in her father's divorces from **KATHERINE of Aragon** and Anne of Cleves, as well as the dissolution of the monasteries. A member of the distinguished **CARNE*** family, he became the first Sheriff of Glamorgan (1542), a member of the Council of Wales (1551), MP for Glamorgan (1554), and Ambassador to Rome (1554-59).

CAROLINE OF ANSPACH
(1683-1737)
German princess who gained the title Princess of Wales when her father-in-law became King George I of England in 1714, and her husband, later **GEORGE II**, became Prince of Wales. She became popular with Welsh expatriates in London because her birthday fell on March 1, St David's Day. As Queen of England from 1727, she wielded considerable political influence.

CAROLINE OF BRUNSWICK
(1768-1821)
Granddaughter of **FREDERICK Lewis Augustus**, Princess of Wales through her marriage in 1795 to her first cousin, later King **GEORGE IV**. They soon separated, and their only child, Princess Charlotte, died in 1817. She lived abroad until her husband's coronation, but was rejected by him and by the British public on her return.

CARTER, Isaac
(c.1690-1741)
Printer, proprietor of the first permanent press in Wales, at Adpar, Cardiganshire (1718). His publications included works by **Alban THOMAS**.

CARTER, John
(c.1620-76)
Colonel in the Parliamentary army during the Civil War, who married into the **HOLLAND*** family of Kinmel in 1647. Following the siege of Denbigh, he was made Governor of Conway Castle and commander in North Wales. He was knighted both by Cromwell and later by King **CHARLES II**.

CATHERINE OF ARAGON
See **KATHERINE OF ARAGON**.

CATHERINE OF VALOIS
See **KATHERINE OF VALOIS**.

CATI, Twm Sion
See **JONES, Thomas (1)**.

CATRIN OF BERAIN
See **KATHERYN OF BERAIN**.

CHADWICK, Nora
(1891-1972)
English scholar, a specialist in Celtic and Germanic literature and history, whose

books include important studies of medieval Welsh culture.

CHALONER, Thomas
(c.1550-98)
Herald, appointed Ulster King of Arms on the day of his death; also a painter, poet, antiquary, and actor.

CHAMBERLAIN, Brenda
(1912-71)
Painter, also a poet of the "Anglo-Welsh" school, and a prose writer in English. During World War II, she collaborated with her husband, John Petts, on the "Casey Broadsheets", an anthology including works by **Dylan THOMAS**.

CHAMBERS, William (1)
(1774-1855)
Industrialist and High Sheriff of Carmarthenshire (1828). Having inherited the estate of Sir John Stepney (1824), he played an important role in the industrial development of Llanelli, establishing the South Wales Pottery in 1840.

CHAMBERS, William (2)
(1809-82)
Industrialist, son of **William CHAMBERS (1)**; co-founder of the Llanelli Reform Society (1839) and first chairman of the Llanelli Board of Health (1850). His involvement in putting down Rebecca riots at Pontarddulais in 1843 made him unpopular locally.

CHARLES I
(1600-49)
King of England, who became Prince of Wales in 1616, following the death of his elder brother, **Henry STUART**. He was one of the most infamous English kings, throwing Britain into civil war by his arrogance and intransigence, and was afterwards executed by order of Parliament.

CHARLES II
(1630-85)
King of England, eldest son of **CHARLES I** but never formally invested with the title Prince of Wales. After his defeat at the Battle of Worcester (1651), he spent fifteen years in exile in various European countries, but was recalled to Britain to take the throne after the death of Oliver Cromwell. The Duke of Monmouth, his illegitimate son by **Lucy WALTER**, unsuccessfully claimed the throne after Charles' death.

CHARLES, David
(1762-1834)
Methodist minister and hymnist, brother of **Thomas CHARLES**, who helped to establish the "Home Mission". Hymns include "O fryniau Caersalem ceir gweled" and "O Iesu mawr".

CHARLES, Thomas ("of Bala")
(1755-1814)
Pioneer of Methodist/Anglican Sunday schools in Wales. A minister himself, he trained peripatetic teachers, and later supervised the publication of a new Welsh Bible by the British and Foreign Bible Society (1814). His own works include a Scriptural dictionary, "Geiriadur ysgrythyrawl" (1805-11).

CHARLTON, Edward
(1371-1421)
Lord of Powys, Commissioner for the Defence of the Marches; leading opponent of **OWAIN Glyndwr**.

CHRISTINA
See **CRISTIN**.

CLARE, Eleanor de
(1292-1337)
Heiress to Glamorgan, daughter of **Gilbert de CLARE (3)** and sister of **Gilbert de CLARE (4)**. She married, firstly, **Hugh le DESPENSER**, and second, William, Lord Zouche.

CLARE, Elizabeth de
(1295-1360)
Heiress to Clare and Usk, daughter of **Gilbert de CLARE (3)** and sister of **Gilbert de CLARE (4)**; founder of Clare College, Cambridge. She married, firstly, John de Burgh; secondly, Lord Theobald Vernon, and thirdly, Lord Roger Damory.

CLARE, Gilbert de (Gilbert fitz Gilbert) (1)
(c.1100-48)
Lord of Strigoil (Chepstow), created Earl of Pembroke and Cilgerran by King Stephen (1138).

CLARE, Gilbert de (2)
(c.1180-1230)
1st Earl of Gloucester (1217) and Lord of Glamorgan through his mother; one of the barons involved in the signing of Magna Carta (1215). His marriage to Isabel, daughter of **William MARSHAL (1)**, brought him the lordship of Usk and Caerleon.

CLARE, Gilbert de ("The Red") (3)
(1243-95)
3rd Earl of Gloucester, whose conduct of affairs in the Welsh Marches was mainly responsible for the rebellion of 1294, led by **MADOG ap Llywelyn** and **MORGAN ap Maredudd**. He had been a commander of King **EDWARD I**'s forces in 1282-3, and accompanied his father-in-law, the King, on his subsequent tour of Wales, but finally fell from favour after a quarrel with his neighbour, **Humphrey de BOHUN (2)** over the siting of Morlais Castle. He also built Caerphilly (Caerffili) Castle.

CLARE, Gilbert de (4)
(1291-1314)
4th Earl of Gloucester; son of **Gilbert de CLARE (3)**. Popular with his Welsh subjects, he placed trust in the local leader,

LLYWELYN Bren. He died in the service of King **EDWARD II** of England, at the Battle of Bannockburn; his property was divided among his three sisters, **Elizabeth de CLARE, Eleanor de CLARE** and Margaret de Clare.

CLARE, Richard de (Strongbow)
(c.1130-76)
Earl of Pembroke, son of **Gilbert de CLARE (1)**. His successful campaigns in Ireland resulted in the preservation of the family name. On his death without a male heir, his titles passed to the **MARSHAL*** family, through the marriage of his daughter, Isabel. *Gave his name to:* County Clare and River Clare, Ireland.

CLARK, George
(1809-98)
Engineer who worked on the Great Western Railway under Brunel, later controller of the Dowlais ironworks (1852-97). He co-founded the Royal Archaeological Institute.

CLEMENT, Geoffrey
(c.1250-94)
Deputy Justiciar of South Wales, murdered during the rebellion of 1294.

CLENOCKE, Maurice
See **CLYNNOG, Morys.**

CLIVE, Edward
(1785-1848)
Viscount Clive (grandson of "Clive of India"), who took his mother's name of **HERBERT (2)*** in 1807 and inherited the Earldom of Powis in 1839; MP for Ludlow 1806-39, and Knight of the Garter 1844. He sponsored the Welshpool eisteddfod of 1824, founded Powis Exhibitions at Oxford and Cambridge for Welsh students, funded public buildings in Montgomery and Welshpool and built additions to Powis Castle.

CLOUGH, Richard
(c.1530-70)
Knight of Denbigh, merchant and agent for Elizabeth I in Europe. He was instrumental in the publication of the maps of **Humphrey LLWYD**, and began a project to make the River Clwyd navigable. Having amassed great wealth, he built two mansions in Denbigh (Plas Clough and Bachygraig), and was on his way there with his wife, **KATHERYN of Berain**, when he died suddenly in Hamburg. The descendants of their marriage included **Hester THRALE**.

CLYNNOG, Morys (Maurice Clenocke)
(c.1525-81)
Catholic theologian and lawyer, appointed Bishop of Bangor in 1558. He went into exile immediately on the death of **Mary TUDOR**, and became warden of the English Hospital in Rome in 1577, but was forced to resign in 1579, supposedly for showing favouritism towards Welsh students.

COFFIN, Walter
(1784-1867)
One of the first mine-owners in the Rhondda valley, a director of the Taff Vale Railway and MP for Cardiff 1852-57; also a leading Unitarian.

COKE, Thomas
(1747-1814)
Methodist minister, historian and author, appointed by John Wesley in 1784 as Superintendent of the Methodist Church in America. He became a bishop in 1787.

COLLEN
(6th-7th century; exact dates unknown)
Saint, a hermit associated in legend with King **ARTHUR**. *Gave his name to:* Llangollen.

COMBERMERE, 1st Viscount
See **COTTON, Stapleton**.

CONWAY, Charles
(1820-84)
Painter and engraver, many of whose studies of nature and Welsh scenes are held by the National Museum of Wales.

CONYBEARE, William
(1787-1857)
Clergyman and geologist, one of the first to study the formation of the South Wales coalfield. As Dean of Llandaff, he was responsible for restoration of the cathedral.

COOK, Arthur James
(1884-1931)
English miner who became a trade union leader at Rhondda, and eventually General Secretary of the Miners' Federation of Great Britain. He was one of the main leaders of the General Strike of 1926, and the author of its motto, "Not a penny off the pay, not a second on the day" as well as of the important 1912 document, 'The miners' next step'.

CORY, James
(1857-1933)
Younger son of John Cory (the founder of "John Cory, Sons & Co", based in Cardiff); Conservative MP for Cardiff South 1918-23, created a baronet in 1919.

CORY, John
(1828-1910)
Industrialist, eldest son of **Richard CORY**. With his brother, Richard, he acquired collieries in the Rhondda, Ogmore, and Neath valleys to supply steam coal for shipping. A staunch Wesleyan, he donated large sums to religious and charitable causes, co-founded Barry dock and railway, and served as a Glamorgan County Councillor and President of the British and Foreign Sailors' Society.

CORY, Richard
(1799-1882)
Devon-born owner of a shipping business, established in Cardiff in 1838, which became known throughout the world.

COTTON, James
(1780-1862)
Dean of Bangor 1838-62, having previously held other appointments in the diocese. In 1810 he started a Sunday school in the cathedral, and later opened several National Schools locally, himself serving as both teacher and inspector. He was a leading critic of the Education Commission Report of 1847 (the "Blue Books").

COTTON, Stapleton
(1773-1865)
6th baronet Cotton, descended from Sir **John SALUSBURY (1)**. He served with distinction as a cavalry officer under Wellington, and was created 1st Viscount Combermere in 1827 after the capture of Bhartpur in India, eventually rising to the rank of Field-Marshal in 1855.

COX, Leonard
(c.1510-80)
Scholar and teacher, translator and author of works on grammar and rhetoric; friend of Erasmus.

CRADOC or CRADOCK, Walter
(1610-59)
Puritan preacher, leading supporter of Parliament in Wales during the Civil War. Under the act of 1650, he was one of the examiners appointed to choose suitable preachers for Wales, and supported Cromwell against the criticisms of **Vavasor POWELL**.

CRADOCK, Mathew
(c.1468-1531)
Steward of Gower and Constable of Caerphilly (Caerffili) Castle under **Henry TUDOR**. His daughter by his first marriage (to a member of the **MANSEL*** family) became the mother of **William HERBERT (2)**. His second wife was Katherine Gordon, widow of the pretender Perkin Warbeck.

CRAWSHAY-WILLIAMS, Eliot
(1879-1962)
Poet and novelist, secretary to Winston Churchill and **David LLOYD GEORGE**; Liberal MP for Leicester 1910-13.

CRISTIN or CHRISTINA
(12th century; exact dates unknown)
Daughter of Gronw ab Owain, and second wife of **OWAIN Gwynedd**. Because she was his first cousin, their marriage was not recognised by the Church; Owain's refusal of Pope Alexander III's command to divorce her resulted in his excommunication. Following Owain's death, she encouraged her sons, **DAFYDD ab Owain** and **RHODRI ab Owain**, to attack his eldest son, **HYWEL ab Owain**, and is condemned by contemporary writers.

CUDLIPP, Hugh
(1913-90)
Journalist, editor of the "Sunday Pictorial" 1937-40. He was Chairman of Mirror Group Newspapers 1963-8 and of the International Publishing Corporation 1968-73. Knighted in 1973, he was created a life peer in 1974.

CUDLIPP, Percy Thomas James
(1905-62)
Journalist, brother of **Hugh CUDLIPP**. At the Evening Standard in 1933, he became the youngest editor of a British national newspaper. He was later editor of the Daily Herald 1940-53 and founder editor of the "New Scientist" (1956).

CUNEDDA (Cunedda Wledig, "Cunedda the Emperor")
(c.370-430)
Legendary ruler of North Wales. A Christian immigrant from Manaw Gododdin (Strathclyde), of the Votadini tribe, he is said to have migrated to Anglesey in about 400 and expelled the Irish settlers, eventually ruling half of Wales. His eight sons included **EINION Yrth**, Ceredig, and Rhufon.

CURIG
(6th century; exact dates unknown)
Saint, sometimes known as "Curig Lwyd" (Curig the Blessed) or "Curig Farchog" (Curig the Knight). *Gave his name to:* Llangurig, Capel Curig.

CYBI
(6th century; exact dates unknown)
Saint, supposed founder of a monastery at Holyhead; probably of Cornish origin. He was nicknamed Cybi Felyn (Yellow), because of his tawny colouring. *Gave his name to:* Caergybi (Holyhead).

CYFFIN
See **KYFFIN**.

CYNAN
See **EVANS-JONES, Albert**.

CYNAN AB OWAIN
(c.1125-1174)
Prince, son of **OWAIN Gwynedd**. At first he fought with his brother, **HYWEL ab Owain**, but was imprisoned by Owain in 1150, and later joined in an attempt to capture **RHYS ap Gruffydd (1)**. On his father's death, he inherited Eifionydd, Ardudwy, and Meirionnydd.

CYNDDELW BRYDYDD MAWR
(c.1140-1200)
Poet of Powys, court poet to **MADOG ap Maredudd**, **OWAIN Gwynedd**, and **LLYWELYN Fawr**, among others.

CYNGEN
(c.800-55)
Prince of Powys, brother of **NEST (1)**. He erected the monument known as "Eliseg's Pillar", as a memorial to his great-grandfather. On his death, his lands were inherited by his nephew, **RHODRI Mawr**.

CYNOG
(5th-6th century; exact dates unknown)
Saint, son of **BRYCHAN**. His torque was still an important religious relic in the time of **GERALD of Wales**. *Gave his name to:* Defynnog, Llangynog.

CYNWAL, William
(c.1550-88)
Poet and genealogist, great rival of **Edmwnd PRYS**.

CYNWRIG HIR (The Tall)
(11th century; exact dates unknown)
Folk hero, reputed rescuer of **GRUFFYDD ap Cynan** from his imprisonment in Chester.

CYSTENNIN or CONSTANTINUS
(4th-5th centuries; exact dates unknown)
Legendary figure, associated with **MAGNUS Maximus** and sometimes referred to as the grandfather of **ARTHUR** . He is mentioned by **GEOFFREY of Monmouth**

D

DAFYDD AB EDMWND
(c.1430-90)
Bard, a leading authority for contemporary poets, winner of a silver chair at the Carmarthen Eisteddfod held about 1450. He devised the "cadwynfyr" and "gorchest y beirdd" verse forms.

DAFYDD AB OWAIN
(c.1140-1204)
Prince, son of **OWAIN Gwynedd** by **CRISTIN**, heir to a share in Gwynedd on his father's death in 1170. To improve his chances of dominating his brothers, he married Emma, half-sister of King Henry II of England. Having lost half of Gwynedd to his brother, **RHODRI ab Owain**, in 1175, he was expelled from his remaining territory by his nephew, **LLYWELYN Fawr** in 1197, and exiled to England.

DAFYDD AP BLEDDYN
(c.1280-1346)
Bishop of St Asaph from 1314. During his episcopate, the Llyfr Coch Asaph (Red Book of Asaph) was compiled.

DAFYDD AP GRUFFYDD
(c.1235-1283)
Prince, a younger son of **GRUFFYDD ap Llywelyn (2)** and **SENENA**. Though during his career he continually switched allegiances between his elder brother, **LLYWELYN ap Gruffydd**, and King **EDWARD I** of England, it was his rash attack on Hawarden Castle in March, 1282, that caused the final conflict with Norman England. The last Prince of Gwynedd and Wales, he ruled only for a few months after Llywelyn's death. Seeking refuge from the English forces in the mountains of Gwynedd, he was eventually captured and executed at Shrewsbury (some sources identify him as the first victim of hanging, drawing and quartering).

DAFYDD AP GWILYM
(c. 1320-80)
Generally regarded as the greatest Welsh poet of all time. His work was progressive, showing a wider European influence, and he popularised the metre known as "cywydd". Belonging by birth to a noble Ceredigion family, he was not a professional bard, but travelled widely. His main theme is love, and many of his love poems are addressed to a woman called Morfudd.

DAFYDD AP IFAN
(c.1420-70)
Lancastrian commander during the Wars of the Roses, famous for his defence of Harlech Castle in the years 1460-68.

DAFYDD AP LLYWELYN
See **GAM, Dafydd**.

DAFYDD AP LLYWELYN
(1208-1246)
Only legitimate son of **LLYWELYN Fawr**, by his wife **JOAN (1)**. Recognised as Prince of Wales by the English King Henry III in 1220 (the first to hold this title officially), he ruled Gwynedd following his father's death in 1240, despite the rival claims of **GRUFFYDD ap Llywelyn (2)**. His revolt of 1244 against the Crown was only a temporary success, and his sudden death led to disorder, his marriage to **Isabella de BRAOSE** having failed to produce an heir.

DAFYDD DDU
(14th century; exact dates unknown)
Poet and priest, author of a bardic gram-

mar; identified by some sources with the English scholar Roger Bacon.

DAFYDD GAM
See **GAM, Dafydd**.

DAFYDD LLWYD
See **LLWYD, Dafydd**.

DAFYDD, Edward
(c.1600-78)
Glamorgan bard, associated with the **MANSEL*** family of Margam. His importance is largely based on the later inventions of **IOLO Morganwg**.

DAHL, Roald
(1916-90)
Cardiff-born author of Norwegian parentage, best known for his phenomenally successful children's books, such as "James and the giant peach" (1961) and "Charlie and the chocolate factory" (1964).

DALTON, Edward **Hugh** John Neale
(1887-1962)
Labour politician, a nephew of Sir **Hugh EVAN-THOMAS**; MP for Peckham 1924-9 and Bishop Auckland 1929-31 and 1935-59. As Chancellor of the Exchequer 1945-7, he was responsible for nationalising the Bank of England, but resigned over the leaking of Budget information. He was created Baron Dalton of Forest and Frith (life peer) in 1960.

DANIEL, **Glyn** Edmund
(1914-86)
Archaeologist, editor of "Antiquity" 1958-86 and Professor of Archaeology at Cambridge 1974-81. He gained wider fame as the chairman of the popular BBC programme, "Animal, vegetable, mineral".

D'ARCY, William Knox
(1849-1917)
English industrialist, who made his fortune in the Australian goldfields and was later involved in obtaining oil concessions from the Shah of Persia. *Gave his name to:* Llandarcy in Glamorgan, built for workers in his oil refinery established there during World War I.

DAVID (Dewi Sant)
(c.515-588)
Patron saint of Wales. According to **RHIGYFARCH**, he was the son of Sant, king of Ceredigion. Unlike most contemporary "saints", he was actually canonised by Rome (1120). An ascetic, reputed to have drunk only water, he founded the monastery at St David's, and made a pilgrimage to Rome and Jerusalem, accompanied by **PADARN** and **TEILO**. March 1st, as the presumed date of his death, is Wales' national day.

DAVID, Tannatt William Edgeworth
(1858-1934)
Geologist who took part in Shackleton's expedition to Antarctica 1907-9, reaching the magnetic South Pole in 1909, and led expeditions to other parts of the world. He was knighted in 1920.

DAVIES, Aneirin Talfan (Aneurin ap Talfan)
(1909-80)
Poet, broadcaster, and literary critic; founder of the periodical, "Heddiw". With his brother, Alun Talfan Davies, he founded the publishing firm, Llyfrau'r Dryw. He was also responsible for and produced the first poetry readings by **Dylan THOMAS** on BBC Radio.

DAVIES, Clara Novello
(1861-1943)
Singer and choir-mistress, who travelled world wide with her choir and raised funds for the British forces in World War I. She is chiefly remembered, however, for the influence she had on her son, **Ivor NOVELLO**.

DAVIES, Clement
(1884-1962)
Liberal MP for Montgomeryshire 1929-62, leader of the Liberal Party 1945-56.

DAVIES, David (1)
(1714-1819)
Clergyman, author of "The case of labourers in husbandry" (1795), an important social document.

DAVIES, David (2)
(1763-1816)
Independent minister and hymnist, the greatest preacher of his day.

DAVIES, David (3) (Dai'r Cantwr)
(c.1812-74)
Singer and poet, a leader of the "Rebecca" movement, for his role in which he was transported to Australia. He remained there from 1843 to 1854, returning to live as a tramp in Wales.

DAVIES, David (4) (Llandinam) ("Top Sawyer")
(1818-90)
Coal-owner largely responsible for the industrialisation of the Rhondda Valley and the construction of Barry Docks, founder of the Parc and Maendy pits; Liberal MP for Cardigan 1874-86.

DAVIES, David (5) Christopher
(1827-85)
Self-educated geologist and mining engineer, director and developer of quarries in France, Germany and Norway.

DAVIES, David (6)
(1880-1944)
Philanthropist, grandson of **David DAVIES (4)**, brother of **Gwendoline DAVIES** and **Margaret DAVIES**; Liberal MP for Montgomeryshire 1906-29, and founder of the New Commonwealth Society (1933).

DAVIES, David (7) James
(1893-1956)
Socialist and Nationalist politician, architect of Plaid Cymru's economic policy for the first twenty-five years of its existence. Works include "The economic history of South Wales" (1933) and "The economics of Welsh self-government".

DAVIES, Edward ("Celtic" Davies)
(1756-1831)
Clergyman, poet and schoolmaster, author of works on Celtic history, one of the first to suspect the integrity of **IOLO Morganwg**.

DAVIES, Elizabeth (Beti Cadwaladr)
(1789-1855)
Nurse, daughter of the preacher and poet, Dafydd Cadwaladr. She left home after her mother's death, went into service and changed her name. After the death of her fiance, she travelled widely and eventually served in the Crimean War under Florence Nightingale, at the age of 65. Her autobiography was published in 1857, by the efforts of **Jane WILLIAMS**.

DAVIES, George Maitland Lloyd
(1880-1949)
Christian Pacifist and Labour sympathiser imprisoned during World War I; grandson of **John JONES (7)** and brother of **John DAVIES (4)**. After serving as MP for the University of Wales 1923-4, he became a Calvinistic Methodist minister. As President of Heddychwyr Cymru (1939), he continued his anti-war activities.

DAVIES, Gwendoline
(1882-1951)
Granddaughter of **David DAVIES (4)**. With her sister, **Margaret DAVIES**, she lived at Gregynog Hall and was a patron of the arts. Their valuable collection was left to the National Museum of Wales ("the Davies bequest").

DAVIES, Gwilym
(1879-1955)

Baptist minister and peace worker, Honorary Director of the League of Nations Union 1922-45. He opposed Plaid Cymru, but made the first radio broadcast in Welsh (1923).

DAVIES, Idris
(1905-53)

Socialist poet, a coal-miner. Works include the collections "Gwalia deserta" (1938) and "Angry summer" (1943).

DAVIES, John (1) ("of Hereford")
(c.1565-1618)

Welsh-speaking poet from the Border area. He wrote mostly in English, but his "Cambria" is a poem of national pride.

DAVIES, John (2) ("of Mallwyd")
(1567-1644)

Scholar, the publisher of a Welsh grammar (1621), a Welsh-Latin dictionary (1632), and "Bishop Parry's Bible" (1620).

DAVIES, John (3)
(1795-1861)

Philosopher, author of "The estimate of the human mind" (1828) and several theological works.

DAVIES, John (4) Glyn
(1870-1953)

Poet and translator, best known as a children's writer; grandson of **John JONES (7)** and brother of **George Maitland Lloyd DAVIES**.

DAVIES, John (5) Humphreys
(1871-1926)

Principal of the University College of Wales, Aberystwyth, 1919-26. A historian and bibliographer, he campaigned for the establishment of a National Library of Wales, to which he bequeathed his collection of Welsh books and manuscripts (the Cwrt-Mawr collection).

DAVIES, James Kitchener
(1902-52)

Nationalist poet and playwright. Works include the controversial play, "Cwm glo" (1935), and "Sŵn y gwynt sy'n chwythu" (1953), a poem in the "pryddest" form.

DAVIES, Margaret
(1884-1963)

Granddaughter of **David DAVIES (4)**. With her sister, **Gwendoline DAVIES**, she lived at Gregynog Hall and was a patron of the arts. Their valuable collection was left to the National Museum of Wales ("the Davies bequest").

DAVIES, Mary
(1855-1930)

London-born singer, wife of **William DAVIES (3)**. She became Principal Soprano Vocalist at the London Ballad Concerts. At the National Eisteddfod of 1906, she co-founded the Welsh Folk Song Society, and was its first President.

DAVIES, Mutton
(1634-84)

MP for Flintshire 1678-81, creator of beautiful Continental-style gardens at his Llanerch Park estate.

DAVIES, Philip
(1645-79)

Jesuit priest and martyr, imprisoned in 1678 as a result of the activities of **John ARNOLD**, and executed the following year; beatified by the Catholic Church in 1929.

DAVIES, Rachel (Rahel o Fon)
(1846-1915)

Baptist preacher and lecturer in Wales and America; a prominent supporter of **David LLOYD GEORGE**.

DAVIES, Rhys
(1903-78)

Novelist and short-story writer, author of

"The withered root" (1927) and "Black Venus" (1944). Much of his work is concerned with life in Welsh industrial communities.

DAVIES, Richard (1)
(c.1501-81)
Leading Protestant, exiled in Europe during the reign of **Mary TUDOR**. He returned to become bishop of St Asaph in 1558, and was Bishop of St David's from 1561. Under an Act of Parliament of 1563, he began the translation of the New Testament into Welsh, with assistance from **William SALES-BURY**.

DAVIES, Richard (2)
(1818-96)
Liberal politician, one of the first Nonconformist MPs (for Anglesey 1868-86), who made a historic stand against the long-established Tory dominance of Caernarfon.

DAVIES, Richard (3) (Mynyddog)
(1833-77)
Poet and musician, prominent member of the Eisteddfod movement. Works include the libretto of **Joseph PARRY**'s opera, "Blodwen".

DAVIES, Robert (Bardd Nantglyn; Robin Ddu o'r Glyn)
(1769-1835)
Poet, author of a grammatical treatise, "Ieithiadur nei Ramadeg Cymraeg" (1808); originator of the saying, "Beibl i bawb o bobl y byd" ("A Bible for everyone in the world").

DAVIES, Ryan
(1937-77)
Popular entertainer, well known for his singing and comic monologues, and for his partnership with Ronnie Williams. He performed in Welsh and English, appearing in television series such as "Fo a fe" as well as being a regular star of pantomime. He composed a number of popular songs.

DAVIES, Sarah Emily
(1830-1921)
Academic, English-born daughter of **John DAVIES (3)**. In 1873, having studied medicine and worked as a journalist, she founded Girton College, Cambridge, a landmark in the education of women. She was also prominent in the campaign for women's suffrage.

DAVIES, Sorobabel
(1806-77)
Baptist minister and schoolmaster, whose account of social conditions and educational practices in West Wales influenced the Education Commissioners of 1847. He emigrated to Australia, where he may have been the first person to preach in Welsh.

DAVIES, Stephen Owen
(1886-1972)
Labour MP for Merthyr Tydfil 1934-72. Originally a miner and union official, he was anti-Communist and anti-Nationalist, though in 1955 he introduced an unsuccessful Bill for a Welsh Parliament. Having criticised the party leadership over their response to the Aberfan disaster, he stood successfully as an Independent Labour candidate at the General Election of 1970.

DAVIES, Henry Walford
(1869-1941)
Composer, Professor of Music at the University College of Wales, Aberystwyth 1918-26 and director of the Council of Music in Wales. Knighted in 1922, he was Master of the King's Musick 1934-41.

DAVIES, William (1)
(c.1555-93)
Catholic priest and martyr; beatified in

1929. Together with **Robert PUW (1)**, he took refuge in caves on the North Wales coast, publishing Catholic pamphlets, but was captured and executed.

DAVIES, William (2)
(1814-91)
Palaeontologist employed by the British Museum. He studied fossils found in North Wales caves, and was the first recipient of the Murchison medal of the Geological Society (1873).

DAVIES, William (3) Cadwaladr
(1849-1905)
Journalist, husband of **Mary DAVIES**. Editor of "Cronicl Cymru" 1869-72, he later worked as assistant to Sir **Hugh OWEN (2)** at the University College of Wales, Aberystwyth. He played a major role in the fund-raising for the University College of North Wales, Bangor, and was its first registrar (1884).

DAVIES, William (4) Henry
(1871-1940)
Poet, author, and traveller, best known for his "Autobiography of a super-tramp" (1908) and the poem "Leisure". He lost a leg during his time in the USA, and started to write only after returning to Britain, with encouragement from Edward Thomas.

DAVIS, David (1) Daniel
(1777-1841)
Physician who attended at the birth of Queen Victoria (1819); later a professor at University College, London.

DAVIS, David (2)
(1821-84)
Industrialist, manager of his father's collieries and owner of quarries in Merioneth; a benefactor of the University of Wales and of the Wesleyan Reform movement.

DAVIS, William ("Golden Farmer")
(1627-90)
Highwayman, subject of popular legend, eventually executed for murder.

DAWKINS, William Boyd
(1837-1929)
Geologist and historian, knighted in 1919. He specialised in the study of caves inhabited by prehistoric man. His work on the Channel Tunnel project (1882) resulted in the discovery of the Kent coalfield.

DEE, John
(1527-1608)
Mathematician and astrologer, favoured by Queen Elizabeth I, who is said to have been the model for the character of Prospero in Shakespeare's "Tempest". He travelled widely, and dabbled with spiritualism.

DEINIOL
(6th-7th centuries; exact dates unknown)
Saint, descended from North Wales royal family, possibly the son of St **DUNAWD**. He founded the community at Bangor, and was the first bishop of Gwynedd.

DERFEL (formerly JONES), Robert **J**ones
(1824-1905)
Poet, author of the play, "Brad y llyfrau gleision" ("Treachery of the Blue Books") (1854). A socialist, he wrote political pamphlets in English and Welsh, some of which he published on his own press in Manchester.

DESPENSER, Hugh le
(1262-1326)
Norman lord, favourite of King **EDWARD II** of England, who by the King's patronage and marriage into the **CLARE*** family, came into possession of huge estates throughout Wales. In 1326, he was disgraced and executed.

DEVEREUX
See **DYFRIG**.

DEVEREUX, Dorothy
(c.1565-1619)
Daughter of **Walter DEVEREUX (2)**. She married firstly Sir Thomas Perrot (1583), and secondly (1595) Henry Percy, heir to the Earl of Northumberland. Through this second marriage, large **DEVEREUX*** estates passed into the Percy family.

DEVEREUX, Robert
(1567-1601)
2nd Earl of Essex, son of **Walter DEVEREUX (2)** and renowned favourite of Queen Elizabeth I; executed for treason after an unsuccessful "rebellion". He spent his formative years in Wales and the Marches.

DEVEREUX, Walter (1)
(c.1491-1559)
1st Viscount Hereford; founder of Carmarthen Grammar School. He served as a member of the Council of Wales (1517), Steward of the household of **Mary TUDOR** (1525), and Chamberlain of South Wales (1526), acquiring estates in West Wales confiscated from Sir **RHYS ap Gruffydd (3)** (1531).

DEVEREUX, Walter (2)
(1540-76)
2nd Viscount Hereford, 1st Earl of Essex; grandson of **Walter DEVEREUX (1)** and heir to the family's Welsh estates. He became a member of the Council of Wales in 1574, despite earlier disagreements with its President, Sir **Henry SIDNEY**.

DEWI SANT
See **DAVID**.

DIANA, Princess of Wales (née Diana SPENCER)
(1961-97)
Princess of Wales whose beauty and char-isma captured the imagination of the British public following her 1981 marriage to Charles Windsor. She gave birth to two sons, the Princes William (b.1982) and Henry ("Harry") (b.1984), earning further public approval for the seriousness with which she took her role as a parent. After her much-publicised separation from Charles in 1992 and their divorce in 1996, she devoted herself to humanitarian causes, continuing to visit Wales independently. Her death, as a result of a car crash, highlighted the difficulties faced by public figures in controlling the attentions of the press.

DILLWYN, Amy
(1845-1935)
Novelist and social benefactor, daughter of **Lewis DILLWYN (2)**. Following her father's death, she managed the Dillwyn Spelter Works at Swansea. Works include "The Rebecca rioter" (1880).

DILLWYN, Lewis (1) Weston
(1778-1855)
Controller of the Cambrian Pottery at Swansea 1802-17, during which period it absorbed the Nantgarw Potteries. A botanist, he was a Fellow of the Royal Society (1804) and co-founder of the Royal Institution of South Wales. He served as MP for Glamorgan 1832-7.

DILLWYN, Lewis (2) Llewelyn
(1814-92)
Industrialist and Radical politician, MP for Swansea 1855-92; younger son of **Lewis Weston DILLWYN (1)** by his marriage to Mary Llewelyn of Llangyfelach.

DILLWYN-LLEWELYN, John (1)
(1810-82)
Son of **Lewis Weston DILLWYN (1)** by his marriage to Mary Llewelyn of Llangyfelach. A botanist like his father, he became a Fellow of the Royal Society

(1836), as well as working with Wheatstone on the development of the electric telegraph and with Fox Talbot on improvements in photography.

DINELEY or DINGLEY, Thomas
(c.1650-95)
Traveller in the diplomatic service; author of the "Account of the official progress of the Duke of Beaufort through Wales" (1684)

DISRAELI (née EVANS), Mary Ann or Marianne
(1792-1872)
English wife of the Prime Minister, Benjamin Disraeli, who was many years her junior. She was strongly connected with Wales through her first marriage, to the MP, Wyndham Lewis, who died in 1838. The following year, she married Disraeli, and became his driving force.

DOGMAEL or DOGFAEL or DOGWEL
(6th century; exact dates unknown)
Saint, founder of a monastery in Pembrokeshire. *Gave his name to:* St Dogmael's (Llandudoch), Dyfed.

DOLBEN, John
(1625-86)
Clergyman, brother of **William DOLBEN**. He served in the King's army during the Civil War, and was later Dean of Westminster (1662), Bishop of Rochester (1666), and Archbishop of York (1683). He was associated with Lady Grace **WYNN (1)***.

DOLBEN, William
(1630-96)
Lawyer, secretary to the Earl of Manchester and later Recorder of London (1676) and a judge of the King's Bench (1678). He vied with his brother, **John DOLBEN**, for the attentions of Lady Grace **WYNN (1)***.

DON or DWNN, Henry
(14th-15th century; exact dates unknown)
Leading supporter of **OWAIN Glyndwr**. In 1406, he successfully stormed Kidwelly (Cydweli) Castle on Glyndwr's behalf. Following Glyndwr's disappearance, he obtained a royal pardon.

DOUGLAS-PENNANT, Edward Gordon **(originally DOUGLAS)**
(1800-86)
Scots-born heir to the Penrhyn estate; MP for Caernarfonshire 1841-66, created Baron Penrhyn in 1866.

DRISCOLL, James ("Peerless Jim")
(1880-1925)
Boxer, subject of the novel "Peerless Jim" (1984) by Alexander Cordell.

DUBRICIUS
See **DYFRIG**.

DUNAWD
(6th century; exact dates unknown)
Saint, abbot of Bangor Iscoed at the time of St Augustine's second meeting with Welsh church leaders in 602-3, according to Bede.

DWNN, Lewys (Lewys ap Rhys ab Owain)
(c.1550-1616)
Poet and genealogist, who served for a time as deputy to the heralds of Wales; a descendant of **Henry DON**.

DYFRIG or DUBRICIUS or DEVEREUX
(c.550-612)
Saint of Bardsey island, one of three patron saints of Llandaff (where he may have been the first to build a cathedral). A missionary, he lived on the Welsh borders and founded a monastery in Herefordshire. Details of his life are recorded by **GEOFFREY of Monmouth**.

DYMENT, Clifford
(1914-70)
English-born poet, author and film director, who worked for the BBC. His works include the poem, "Derbyshire born, Monmouth is my home" (1955), and an autobiography, "The railway game" (1962).

E

EDDOWES, Joshua
(1724-1811)
Printer and publisher of Welsh books at Shrewsbury, and also of "The Salopian Journal" (1794).

EDERN DAFOD AUR (Edern of the Golden Tongue)
(Dates unknown)
Author of a grammar or "dosbarth", the date of which is unknown, but which was recognised as an authority by 1525.

EDISBURY, John
(c.1608-77)
Lawyer, a Royalist supporter during the Civil War, and steward of Chirkland under **Thomas MYDDELTON (2)**. He purchased the Erthig estate in Denbighshire.

EDNYFED FYCHAN (Ednyfed ap Cynwrig)
(c.1190-1246)
Steward or "distain" of Gwynedd under **LLYWELYN Fawr** and **DAFYDD ap Llywelyn**. His wife, Gwenllian, was a daughter of **RHYS ap Gruffydd (1)**. He was succeeded in office by at least two of his sons, and twelve members of his family are known to have served as officials of the principality of Gwynedd at various times.

EDWARD I ("Longshanks")
(1239-1307)
King of England from 1272, responsible for the final submission of Wales to English rule. He defeated the Welsh Princes **LLYWELYN ap Gruffydd** and **DAFYDD ap Gruffydd**, and appropriated the title "Prince of Wales" for his own son, later **EDWARD II**. His ruthlessness made his name a hated one in Wales and Scotland.

EDWARD II (Edward of Caernarfon)
(1284-1327)
King of England, son of **EDWARD I** and Eleanor of Castile, born at Caernarfon Castle during the campaign of 1282-4; he became the first "English" Prince of Wales following the conquest, in 1301. He succeeded to the English throne in 1307, but was deposed and horribly murdered, probably on the orders of his wife, Isabella of France, and her lover, **Roger MORTIMER (3)**.

EDWARD III
(1312-77)
King of England from 1327, eldest son of King **EDWARD II** but never invested with the title Prince of Wales. In 1330, he ended the regency of his mother, Isabella of France, by exiling her and executing her lover, **Roger MORTIMER (3)**.

EDWARD V (Edward of York, Edward of the Sanctuary)
(1471-1483)
King of England, elder son of Edward IV. He was created Prince of Wales in 1477, and succeeded to the throne at the age of twelve. Deposed after a few months by his uncle, King Richard III, he ended his days a prisoner in the Tower of London, where he and his younger brother, Richard, died in mysterious circumstances ("the Princes in the Tower").

EDWARD VII (Prince Albert Edward; "Bertie")
(1841-1910)
Eldest son of Queen Victoria and the longest-serving Prince of Wales, holding the title for almost sixty years. His marriage to **ALEXANDRA of Denmark** in 1862

made him popular throughout Britain, but especially in Wales, where the well-known song "God Bless the Prince of Wales" was written in their honour for the Eisteddfod. Known as a playboy who kept mistresses and enjoyed pastimes such as cards and horse racing, he became a much-loved King.

EDWARD, DUKE OF WINDSOR (King Edward VIII; "David")
(1894-1972)
Prince of Wales and King of Britain, eldest son of King **GEORGE V**. He was invested at Caernarfon Castle in 1911, and became King in 1936. He showed sympathy for the plight of the miners during a visit to Wales in 1936, but his decision to marry a divorced woman, Wallis Simpson, forced him to abdicate. He was created Duke of Windsor, and spent the rest of his life in France.

EDWARD OF MIDDLEHAM
(1474-1484)
Prince of Wales from 1483 until his death a few months later; only legitimate child of King Richard III of England and his Queen, **Anne NEVILLE**.

EDWARD OF WESTMINSTER
(1453-71)
Prince of Wales, only child of King Henry VI of England. His mother, Margaret of Anjou, pursued his claim to the throne after his father's deposition. Following the defection of the Earl of Warwick to the Lancastrian cause, he was married to the Earl's younger daughter, **Anne NEVILLE**. He has the distinction of being the only "English" Prince of Wales to die in battle, at Tewkesbury.

EDWARD OF WOODSTOCK (The Black Prince)
(1330-76)
Prince, eldest son of King **EDWARD III** of England and father of **RICHARD II**.

Created Prince of Wales in 1343, he was the first also to hold the titles Earl of Chester and Duke of Cornwall. He died, worn out by military campaigning in France, before succeeding to the throne of England.

EDWARDS, Alfred George
(1848-1937)
Bishop of St Asaph (1889), and first Archbishop of Wales 1920-34. His published works include "Landmarks in the history of the Welsh Church" and "Memories".

EDWARDS, Charles
(c.1628-95)
Puritan clergyman, author of "Y ffydd ddifuant" (1667) and other theological works, including his autobiography, "An afflicted man's testimony concerning his troubles" (1691). He assisted **Thomas GOUGE** in setting up the Welsh Trust.

EDWARDS, Francis
(1852-1927)
Liberal MP for Radnorshire 1892-5, 1900-18, created a baronet in 1907. He translated much Welsh poetry into English, including that of **John HUGHES (3)**.

EDWARDS, Huw Thomas
(1892-1970)
Trade union leader, Chair of the Council for Wales and Monmouthshire 1948-58. At first an opponent of the campaign for a Welsh Parliament, he changed his view and resigned to join Plaid Cymru, also becoming President of Cymdeithas yr Iaith Gymraeg. In 1956 he bought the newspaper "Y Faner" to prevent it going out of business.

EDWARDS, Ifan ab Owen
(1895-1970)
Founder of Urdd Gobaith Cymru (the Welsh League of Youth) in 1922; son of Sir **Owen M EDWARDS**. He edited "Cymru'r plant", the children's paper launched by

his father, 1920-50, and was instrumental in the establishment of the first Welsh-medium primary school of modern times (1939). He made the first Welsh language film, "Y chwarelwr" (1935), and was knighted in 1947.

EDWARDS, John (1) (Sion y Potiau)
(c.1699-1776)
Poet, translator of "The Pilgrim's Progress" into Welsh.

EDWARDS, John (2)
(1770-1850)
Whig politician, MP for Montgomery 1833-41 (after losing a "rigged" election in 1832); created a baronet in 1838.

EDWARDS, John (3) Kelt
(1875-1934)
Painter, cartoonist and illustrator. His portraits of the famous included **David LLOYD GEORGE**. He designed the banner and badge of the "Comrades of the Great War".

EDWARDS, Joseph
(1814-82)
Sculptor, known for his allegorical works, busts of the famous, and headstones; designer of the Cymmrodorion Medal.

EDWARDS, Lewis
(1809-87)
Preacher, theologian and essayist, co-founder and principal of Bala Calvinistic Methodist College (1836), and founder of the periodical "Y traethodydd" (1845). Works include "Hanes Duwinyddiaeth", a history of theology; he also translated English hymns into Welsh.

EDWARDS, Ness
(1897-1968)
Anti-Nationalist Labour MP for Caerphilly,

Postmaster-General in the Attlee government of 1945-51.

EDWARDS, Owen Morgan
(1858-1920)
Academic, co-founder of Cymdeithas **DAFYDD ap Gwilym** at Oxford (1886); knighted in 1916. He was editor of "Cymru Fydd" (1890), "Cymru" (1891), and "Wales" (1894), and produced several popular and educational Welsh language publications, including the first children's magazine in Welsh, "Cymru'r plant" (1892). As Chief Inspector of Schools for Wales (1907), he encouraged the teaching of Welsh, and was the author of popular history books such as "Hanes Cymru" (1895). He served as MP for Merioneth 1899-1900.

EDWARDS, Sydenham Teak
(1768-1819)
Artist whose drawings of plants and animals appeared in "The Botanical Magazine", "Geographia Britannica", and "The Botanical Register".

EDWARDS, Thomas (1) (Twm o'r Nant; "The Cambrian Shakespeare")
(1739-1810)
Poet, follower of various professions, and an author of and actor in "interludes", including "Tri chryfion byd" (1789) and "Pedair colofn gwladwriaeth" (1786).

EDWARDS, Thomas (2) Charles
(1837-1900)
Methodist minister, son of **Lewis EDWARDS**; first Principal of the University College of Wales 1872-91 and Principal of Bala College 1891-1900.

EDWARDS, William (1)
(1719-89)
Methodist minister, architect of the controversial "New Bridge" at Pontypridd, built between 1746 and 1754. His other con-

structions included bridges at Usk, Pont-
ardawe, Betws and Aberafan.

EDWARDS, William (2)
(1851-1940)
Scholar and Inspector of Schools, author
of "A new proposal" (1929), an important
pamphlet on education.

EINION AP COLLWYN
(11th-12th century; exact dates unknown)
Legendary figure, credited with having
invited the Normans to invade Glamorgan
after a quarrel with **IESTYN ap Gwrgant**.

EINION OFFEIRIAD ("Einion the Priest")
(14th century; exact dates unknown)
Poet, probable author of the earliest known
Welsh grammar (c.1320).

EINION YRTH
(early 5th century; exact dates unknown)
Eldest son of **CUNEDDA**, credited with
the defeat of the Irish settlers, and claimed
as ancestor by **RHUN ap Maelgwn**.

ELEN (1) or HELEN LUYDDOG ("Helen of the Hosts")
(c.360-400)
Princess of North Wales, possibly the
daughter of Eudwy or Eudaf of Gwynedd,
who is reputed to have become the wife of
the Emperor **MAGNUS Maximus**. A fan-
tastic account of their meeting is given in the
Mabinogion. After her husband's death, she
is said to have returned to Britain with her
children, becoming a leader in the Christian
church. *Gave her name to:* Sarn Helen (a
stretch of Roman road).

ELEN (2)
(1207-53)
Princess, daughter of **LLYWELYN ap
Gruffydd** and **JOAN (1)**; sister of
DAFYDD ap Llywelyn. She married,
firstly, John "the Scot", Earl of Chester

(1222), an alliance which helped keep the
peace in North Wales until his death, and
secondly, Robert de Quincy (1237), the
younger of their two daughters becoming
the wife of **Humphrey de BOHUN (1)**.

ELFODD(W)
(c.730-809)
Bishop of Bangor and "archbishop" of
Gwynedd, referred to by his pupil,
NENNIUS; responsible for the adoption of
the Roman Easter by the Welsh Church.

ELIAS, John ("the Methodist Pope")
(1774-1841)
Calvinistic Methodist minister, the most
famous preacher of his day, and an opponent
of the Catholic Emancipation Act.

ELLI
(6th century; exact dates unknown)
Saint, adopted by St **CADOG** whom he
succeeded as abbot of Llancarfan. *Gave
his name to:* Llanelli, Dyfed.

ELLICE
See **ELLIS**.

ELLIOT, George
(1815-93)
English industrialist and philanthropist, MP
for Monmouth 1886-92, created a baronet in
1874. A director of the Powell Duffryn
Company, he had himself worked in coal-
mines as a child, and instituted many
reforms. He was also involved in funding the
Alexandra Dock at Newport (1875). *Gave
his name to:* Elliotstown, Rhymney valley.

ELLIS, Thomas (1) ("Tom")
(1859-99)
Liberal MP for Merioneth 1886-99, Chief
Whip 1894-5. In 1890, he put forward the
idea of a Welsh legislative assembly, which
was rejected by Gladstone. He took a special
interest in educational issues, and was also

an advocate of Disestablishment and land reform.

ELLIS, Thomas **(2)** Iorwerth
(1899-1970)
Academic, son of **Thomas ELLIS (1)**, author of a biography of his father; co-founder and secretary of Undeb Cymru Fydd, a Welsh-language pressure group (1941-67).

ELLIS-GRIFFITH, Ellis
(1860-1926)
Barrister, Liberal MP for Anglesey 1895-1918 and for Carmarthen 1923-4. Prominent in the passing of the Welsh Disestablishment Act, he was created a baronet in 1918.

ELSTAN GLODRYDD
(9th-10th century; exact dates unknown)
Legendary founder of one of the five "royal tribes" of Wales.

ELWYN-JONES, Frederick
(1909-89)
Lawyer and judge, Labour MP for English constituencies 1945-74 and Attorney-General 1964-70. Created a life peer in 1974 (Lord Elwyn-Jones of Llanelli and Newham), he was Lord Chancellor 1974-79.

EMLYN, Viscount
See **CAMPBELL, Frederick.**

EMRYS WLEDIG
See **AMBROSIUS AURELIANUS.**

ERBERY, William
(1604-54)
Prominent Puritan, a chaplain in the Parliamentarian army during the Civil War, having resigned his living as a clergyman following examination by the Court of High Commission in 1635. His theological works were collected as "The testimony of William Erbery" (1658).

EUDDOGWY or **OUDOCEUS**
(late 6th century; exact dates unknown)
Saint, possibly of Breton descent; said to be the nephew of **TEILO**, whom he succeeded as Bishop of Llandaff.

EVAN-THOMAS, Hugh
(1862-1928)
Admiral (1920), who played a leading role in the Battle of Jutland 1916 and was knighted in the same year; a descendant of the **EVANS (3)*** family.

EVANS, Beriah Gwynfe
(1848-1927)
Founder and editor of "Cyfaill yr Aelwyd" (1880), and editor of "Y genedl Gymreig" 1892-5; co-founder and secretary of Cymru Fydd (1895), the first secretary of the Society for the Utilisation of the Welsh Language (Cymdeithas yr Iaith Gymraeg) (1885), and an early member of Plaid Cymru. His talents as a playwright and author on historical subjects are notable, his play, "Glyndwr", becoming the first in Welsh to be performed, in 1880.

EVANS, Caradoc (David Evans)
(1878-1945)
Novelist, author and playwright in the English language, one of the founders of the "Anglo-Welsh" school of writers. His original and controversial works include three volumes of short stories, "My people" (1915), "Capel Sion" (1916), and "My neighbours" (1919). His second wife was the writer, Marguerite Helene.

EVANS, Christmas
(1766-1838)
Baptist minister and hymnist, the greatest preacher of his day. Based in Anglesey, he travelled throughout Wales raising funds for the building of chapels. His best-known hymns include "Dwy fflam ar ben Calfaria" and "Rhwn sy'n gyrru'r mellt i hedeg".

EVANS, David
See **EVANS, Caradoc**.

EVANS, David Treharne
(1849-1907)
Lord Mayor of London 1891. Head of the family firm of brewers, he had connections with several London guilds.

EVANS, Edgar
(1876-1912)
Explorer, member of Captain Scott's Antarctic expedition of 1910, who died on the return journey from the South Pole.

EVANS, Edward Ratcliffe Garth Russell
(1881-1957)
Admiral, who took part in expeditions to the Antarctic, succeeding Scott as commander in 1912-13; created Baron Mountevans in 1945.

EVANS, Ellis Humphrey (Hedd Wyn)
(1887-1917)
Merionethshire shepherd and poet who was awarded the bardic chair posthumously at the National Eisteddfod in 1917 for his 'awdl', "Yr arwr", having been killed in France at the Battle of Pilkem Ridge a short time before. He became the subject of an Oscar-nominated Welsh-language film in 1993.

EVANS, Evan (1) (Ieuan Fardd; Ieuan Brydydd Hir)
(1731-88)
Clergyman, scholar and poet, who devoted much of his life to working for the publication of Welsh literary and historical manuscripts. His "Specimens of the poetry of the antient Welsh bards" (1764) was the first such anthology.

EVANS, Evan (2) ("Squire y Hen Six")
(1809-86)
Industrialist, founder of the Dinas Main

colliery at Rhondda. The Six Bells colliery was named after a public house he had owned. *Gave his name to:* Evanstown, Glamorgan.

EVANS, Evan (3) Vincent
(1851-1934)
Journalist, lifelong friend of **David LLOYD GEORGE**. He held various official and honorary positions, such as Secretary of the Honourable Society of Cymmrodorion (1887), Secretary of the National Eisteddfod Association (1881), and Chairman of the Royal Commission on Ancient Monuments in England and Wales.

EVANS, Geraint Llewellyn
(1922-92)
Operatic baritone, knighted in 1969. He created roles in several works by Britten, and was also well known for his interpretation of Mozart, including the role of Figaro.

EVANS, Gwynfil (Arthur Gwynne; Barry Western)
(1898-1938)
Novelist, famous for his "Sexton Blake" series, though he did not invent the character. He himself created other popular characters such as Splash Page and Julius Jones.

EVANS, Harry
(1873-1914)
Composer and choir-master. He conducted Granville Bantock's choral symphony, "Vanity of vanities", which the composer dedicated to him.

EVANS, Henry Humphrey
See **LLOYD, Henry**.

EVANS, Horace
(1903-63)
Physician to King George VI 1949-52, to

Queen **MARY of Teck** 1949-53, and to Queen Elizabeth II 1952-63; created 1st baronet Evans of Merthyr Tydfil 1957.

EVANS, John (1)
(1723-95)
Cartographer whose maps of North Wales, engraved by Baugh, published in 1795 were the most reliable published before the Ordnance Survey edition.

EVANS, John (2) ("of Bala")
(1723-1817)
Methodist leader and itinerant preacher or "exhorter". He officiated at the first Calvinistic Methodist ordination in North Wales in 1811, and was the translator of some of Wesley's works into Welsh.

EVANS, John (3)
(1770-99)
Associate of **IOLO Morganwg**, with whose encouragement he led an expedition to find "Welsh Indians" in North America. He was used by the Spanish government to remove a French Canadian force from an outpost on the Missouri, and spent some time with the Maha and Mandan peoples.

EVANS, John (4) Gwenogvryn
(1852-1930)
Expert on, and publisher of, Welsh manuscripts. Whilst employed by the Historic Manuscripts Commission 1894-1910, he was instrumental in the purchase of the Peniarth manuscripts by Sir **John WILLIAMS (8)** (1905), a major factor in the creation of the National Library of Wales.

EVANS, Samuel (1) Thomas
(1858-1918)
Lawyer, Liberal MP for mid Glamorgan 1890-1910, and Solicitor General 1908-10. The last QC to be appointed by Queen Victoria (1901), he is known for his contribution to prize law.

EVANS, Samuel (2)
(1859-1935)
Educationist involved in the setting up of Witwatersrand University, South Africa. As private secretary to Sir Edgar Vincent, he worked in Egypt and later Johannesburg, where he became director of the Crown Mine.

EVANS, Theophilus
(1693-1767)
Clergyman, author of works on history and religion in English and Welsh, including "Drych y prif oesoedd" (1716), a Welsh classic dealing with the early history of Wales. An opponent of Methodism, he prevented the ordination of **William WILLIAMS (2)**.

EVANS, Thomas (Tomos Glyn Cothi; "Priestley Bach")
(1764-1833)
The first Unitarian minister in Wales. A poet, author and translator, he published an English-Welsh dictionary in 1809. He was imprisoned in 1803 as a result of his controversial political views.

EVANS-BEVAN, Evan.
See **BEVAN, Evan Evans**.

EVANS-JONES, Albert (Cynan)
(1895-1970)
Poet and playwright, three times winner of the Crown at the National Eisteddfod, also winner of the Chair, and Archdruid 1950-53. His best known work, "Mab y bwthyn" (1921), is on the subject of World War I.

EVEREST, George
(1790-1866)
Military engineer and surveyor, born at Gwernvale, Powys. *Gave his name to:* Mount Everest.

F

FARR, Tommy
(1914-86)
Boxer who became a folk hero after challenging Joe Louis for the World Heavyweight title in 1937.

FENTON, Ronald (Ronald Welch)
(1909-82)
Carnegie Medal-winning children's author, who took his pen-name from the regiment in which he served during World War II. His historical novels include "The gauntlet" (1951), and a series about the Carey family, stretching from the twelfth to the twentieth century.

FERRAR, Robert
(c.1500-1555)
Bishop of St David's from 1548 to 1554. Executed for heresy at Carmarthen during the reign of **Mary TUDOR**, he was one of only three Protestant martyrs in Wales.

FERRERS, Elizabeth (de)
(c.1250-1300)
Wife of **DAFYDD ap Gruffydd** and thus last Princess of Gwynedd and Wales; daughter of the Earl of Derby, and previously married briefly to John Marshall.

FITZALAN, Richard (1)
(c.1310-76)
10th Earl of Arundel who obtained extensive lands in Wales through the patronage of King **EDWARD III** of England.

FITZALAN, Richard (2)
(c.1348-97)
11th Earl of Arundel, son of **Richard FITZALAN (1)**. In 1389, the death of a Welsh nobleman in his custody caused civil unrest. He fell from favour with King

RICHARD II, and on his execution for treason, his lands in Wales were forfeit.

FITZGERALD, David
(c.1110-76)
Bishop of St David's 1148-76, son of **GERALD of Windsor** and **NEST (2)**; uncle of **GERALD of Wales**. In 1167, he obtained the release from prison of his half-brother, **Robert FITZSTEPHEN**, by interceding with **RHYS ap Gruffydd (1)**. He entertained King Henry II of England at St David's in 1171.

FITZHAMO or **FITZHAMON, Robert**
(c.1040-1107)
Norman lord, favourite of King William II of England, granted the earldom of Gloucester and the lordship of Glamorgan, which he proceeded to conquer, defeating the former ruler, **IESTYN ap Gwrgant**, at the Battle of Mynedd Bychan in 1093, with the aid of twelve Norman knights, including **STRADLING*** and **SULLY***. He married Sybil, daughter of **Roger (de) MONT-GOMERY**; their daughter, Mabel, married **ROBERT of Gloucester**.

FITZOSBERN, William
(c.1020-71)
Cousin of King William I of England, created Earl of Hereford in 1067. He built castles at Chepstow, Monmouth, Grosmont, Skenfrith and White Castle. Following his departure for France in 1170, his son's rebellion against the King interrupted in the Norman conquest of South Wales.

FITZSTEPHEN, Robert
(c.1120-83)
Norman lord, son of Stephen (Constable of Cilgerran Castle) by **NEST (2)**; benefactor

of Strata Florida abbey (1164). On succeeding his father, he attempted unsuccessfully to establish Norman supremacy in the district, supporting King Henry II against **OWAIN Gwynedd**. Following a period of imprisonment by **RHYS ap Gruffydd (1)** after the fall of Cardigan in 1165, he joined the expedition to conquer Ireland, and ruled Cork until his death.

FITZWARIN, Fulk (1)
(c.1190-1256)

Norman lord, at first an ally of **LLYWELYN Fawr**, but later his opponent and an ally of **MADOG ap Gruffydd**. A French prose work of around 1320, the "Romance of Foulques Fitz Warin", which seems to have been known in contemporary Wales, is based on the exploits of him and his son.

FITZWARIN, Fulk (2)
(c.1251-1315)

Grandson of **Fulk FITZWARIN (1)** and son-in-law of **GRUFFYDD ap Gwenwynwyn**; an opponent of **LLYWELYN ap Gruffydd**.

FOLEY, Thomas
(1757-1833)

Admiral, a commander at the Battles of the Nile and Copenhagen; knighted in 1815.

FOSTER, Thomas Campbell
(1813-82)

Journalist who covered the "Rebecca riots" for "The Times". His reports were instrumental in forcing the Government to take action against the movement.

FOTHERGILL, Richard
(1822-1903)

Industrialist, MP for Aberdare 1868-80. He became proprietor of Aberdare ironworks in succession to his uncle, Rowland Fothergill, and later owned the Plymouth and Penydarren works.

FRANCIS, David ("Dai")
(1911-80)

Communist miners' leader prominent during the industrial action of 1972 and 1974. In 1976 he stood unsuccessfully against the Prince of Wales for the post of Chancellor of the University of Wales.

FRANCIS, George Grant
(1814-82)

Historian, brother of **John Deffett FRANCIS**; founder of the Royal Institution of South Wales (1835) and the Cambrian Archaeological Association (1846). He contributed to the restoration of Swansea Grammar School and Oystermouth Castle.

FRANCIS, John Deffett
(1815-1901)

Artist, brother of **George Grant FRANCIS**. As a portrait painter, his subjects included Queen Victoria and Robert Peel. He left his collection of paintings to the city of Swansea. *Gave his name to:* Deffett Francis Art Gallery, Swansea.

FRANCKTON, Stephen de
(13th century; exact dates unknown)

Norman knight who unknowingly killed **LLYWELYN ap Gruffydd** at the Battle of Irfon Bridge in 1282.

FREDERICK LEWIS AUGUSTUS
(1707-51)

Prince of Wales from the accession to the throne of his father, King **GEORGE II**, in 1727, until his untimely death. Left behind in Hanover as a child, when his parents and grandparents came to England, he had a poor relationship with both his father and his mother, **CAROLINE of Anspach**, especially after his marriage to **AUGUSTA of Saxe-Gotha**.

FRONTINUS, Sextus Julius
(c.40-103)

Roman governor of Britain 75-78 AD,

responsible for the conquest of the Silures (the tribe resident in South Wales). He established the legionary fortress at Caerleon.

FROST, John
(1784-1877)
Monmouthshire politician and leading supporter of the Chartist movement. A one-time mayor of Newport, he organised a protest march, together with **William JONES (4)** and **Zephaniah WILLIAMS**, in 1839, which was forcibly put down by the authorities, effectively ending the movement in Wales. For this, he was convicted of treason and sentenced to death, but the sentence was commuted to transportation. He returned to Wales in 1856 with a full pardon.

G

GAM, Dafydd (Dafydd ap Llywelyn)
(c.1380-1415)

Brecon nobleman, ancestor of the **GAMES*** and **HERBERT (1)*** families. Unlike many of his countrymen, he was loyal to the English Crown during the period of **OWAIN Glyndwr**'s principate, and was captured by Glyndwr in 1412. He died serving King **HENRY V** at Agincourt.

GAM, Gwladus
(c.1400-54)

Daughter of **Dafydd GAM**, married first to Roger **VAUGHAN (1)*** of Bredwardine Castle (who died with her father at Agincourt), and second to Sir **WILIAM ap TOMOS** of Raglan. By her two marriages, she had six sons and seven daughters, her eldest son being **William HERBERT (1)**.

GAM, Morgan
See **MORGAN Gam**.

GAMAGE, Barbara
(1563-1621)

Famous beauty, heiress to the Coity estate. She was taken into the care of the **STRADLING*** family and married **Robert SIDNEY**, later Earl of Leicester.

GAMBOLD, John
(1711-71)

Bishop in the Moravian Brethren's Church 1753-68, son of **William GAMBOLD**. He published the Welsh translation of Zinzendorff's works and a Welsh Moravian hymn-book.

GAMBOLD, William
(1672-1728)

Clergyman, author of "Grammar of the Welsh language" (1727), the first English book to be printed in Wales.

GEE, Thomas
(1815-98)

Methodist minister and publisher, who exercised considerable political influence in Denbighshire. The cultural review and news-papers which he edited, such as "Baner ac amserau Cymru", had a circulation of 50,000 throughout Wales. His publishing company, Gwasg Gee, also produced an encyclopaedia, "Y Gwyddoniadur", in ten volumes (1854-78). A Liberal, he was President of the Welsh Land League (1886) and Chair of the Cymru Fydd League at Aberystwyth (1895).

GEOFFREY OF MONMOUTH
(c.1100-55)

Author of the Historia Regum Britanniae ("History of the Kings of Britain"), published in 1136. Probably born in Monmouth of Breton stock, he had a successful career in the Church, becoming Bishop of St Asaph in 1152, though he is not known to have visited the diocese.

GEORGE II (George Augustus)
(1683-1760)

Prince of Wales who was given the title in 1714, on the accession of his father, King George I. As a result of his parents' divorce, he had a poor relationship with his father, and years of quarrelling followed, with his wife, **CAROLINE of Anspach**, sometimes acting as an intermediary. He became King on his father's death in 1727.

GEORGE IV (The Prince Regent)
(1762-1830)

Prince of Wales from birth until the death of his father, King George III, in 1820, he effectively ruled the country during the period of his father's mental illness. Always surrounded by scandal, his popularity both as Regent and later as King rose and fell in cycles. His idea for a Welsh order of knighthood, the Order of St David, was abandoned by his successor, William IV.

GEORGE V
(1865-1936)

Second son of King **EDWARD VII** and **ALEXANDRA of Denmark**, who became Prince of Wales on his father's accession to the throne in 1901. In 1893, he had married **MARY of Teck**, his cousin, who proved an asset as his Queen. They reigned successfully throughout World War I and afterwards.

GERALD OF WALES (Giraldus Cambrensis)
(1146-1223)

Clergyman and author, son of William de Barri of Manorbier, and grandson of **NEST (2)**. In 1188, as an archdeacon, he toured Wales in the company of Baldwin, Archbishop of Canterbury, publishing his account of the journey in 1191. "The description of Wales" followed. He attempted unsuccessfully to obtain the office of Bishop of St David's, arguing for the independence of the Welsh Church.

GERALD OF WINDSOR (Gerald Fitzwalter)
(c.1080-1135)

Norman lord, Constable of Pembroke Castle. He married **NEST (2)**, the notorious beauty whose abduction in 1109 resulted in his relentless pursuit of **OWAIN ap Cadwgan**.

GERARD, Charles
(c.1615-94)

Royalist leader who campaigned successfully in Wales during the Civil War as a deputy to Prince Rupert. He continued to serve the royal family in exile, and after

the Restoration was created Earl of Macclesfield (1679). Suspected of collusion with the Duke of Monmouth, he was exiled again, but returned to become Lord President of the Council of the Welsh Marches in 1689.

GERVASE
See **IORWERTH**.

GIBSON, John
(1790-1866)

Sculptor who lived and worked in Rome from 1817. He returned to Britain to work on statues of prominent figures, including Queen Victoria, and some of his works were displayed at the Great Exhibition of 1862. He is best remembered for his coloured statue, "The tinted Venus".

GIFFARD, John
(1232-99)

Norman Marcher lord involved in the fighting which led to the death of **LLYWELYN ap Gruffydd** in 1282. As a reward for his support of King **EDWARD I**, he received the lordships of Iscennen and Cantref Bychan.

GILDAS
(c.495-570)

Monk, believed to be the author of "De excidio Brittaniae" ("The downfall of Britain"), an important if unreliable historical source; said to have been born in Strathclyde and brought up at Llanilltud Fawr (Llantwit Major).

GLADSTONE (née GLYNNE), Catherine
(1812-1900)

Owner of the Hawarden estate, which she inherited from her father, and where she founded an orphanage; wife of William Gladstone from 1839.

GLOUCESTER, Robert of
See **ROBERT OF GLOUCESTER**.

GLYNDWR, Owain
See **OWAIN GLYNDWR**.

GLYNNE, John ("the sergeant")
(1603-66)
MP for Caernarfonshire 1654-5 and 1660; baronet 1662. A supporter of Cromwell, he held various legal offices during the Commonwealth, but remained in favour after the Restoration. His purchase of the Hawarden estate (1654) was the foundation of the **GLYNNE (2)*** family.

GODWIN (née WEAVER), Judith
(c.1690-1746)
Correspondent of **Howell HARRIS**; married first to Samuel Jones and second to an Independent minister, Edward Godwin.

GOODMAN, Gabriel
(1528-1601)
Protestant Dean of Westminster 1561-1601, favoured by William Cecil; founder of Christ's Hospital, Ruthin (1590), and a grammar school (1595) which he supported with church funds. He was also involved in the translation of the "Bishop's Bible" of 1568 into Welsh.

GORE, Hugh (Bishop Gore)
(1613-91)
Bishop of Waterford and Lismore (Ireland) 1666-89; founder of Swansea Grammar School (1682). *Gave his name to:* Bishop Gore School, Swansea.

GORONWY-ROBERTS (formerly ROBERTS), Goronwy Owen
(1913-81)
Labour MP for Caernarfon 1945-74, a strong supporter of Welsh home rule and founder of the Gwerin movement (1935). In 1964, he was appointed Minister of State in the newly-created Welsh Office, but ultimately lost his Parliamentary seat to Plaid Cymru and was created a life peer.

GOUGE, Thomas
(c.1605-81)
Puritan preacher based in London, founder of the "Welsh Trust" providing free schooling. It lapsed with his death, but some schools survived, and the influence of the movement continued to be felt.

GOUGH or GOCH, Matthew
(1386-1450)
Professional soldier, related to the **HANMER*** family and thus by marriage to **OWAIN Glyndwr**. He distinguished himself during the latter part of the Hundred Years War, becoming known to his French opponents as 'Matego', and was killed during the rebellion of Jack Cade.

GOWER, Erasmus
(1742-1814)
Naval officer who served under Cornwallis during the Napoleonic Wars; knighted in 1792, and created a full admiral in 1809.

GOWER, Henry
(c.1278-1347)
Bishop of St Davids from 1328, responsible for the building of the cathedral, and also of parts of St Mary's Church, Swansea, and Swansea Castle.

GRANVILLE-WEST, Baron
See **WEST, Granville**.

GRENFELL, David Rhys
(1881-1968)
Labour MP for Gower 1922-59. Originally a miners' agent, he served as Minister for Mines during World War II, and campaigned for the creation of the Welsh Office. He was "Father of the House" of Commons 1953-9.

GREVILLE, Charles
(1749-1809)
Younger son of the Earl of Warwick; founder of Milford Haven under an act of 1790 allowing the development of his father's Pembrokeshire lands. The town's early occupants included Quaker immigrants from Massachusetts, and a shipbuilding business was established there. Nelson visited in 1802.

GREY, Reginald (1)
(c.1250-1308)
1st Lord Grey of Wilton, Justice of Chester and north-east Wales 1281-99, presented by King **EDWARD I** of England with the North Wales estates of the late Gwenllian de **LACY***, daughter of **LLYWELYN Fawr**, including Ruthin Castle. He played a leading part in suppressing the rebellion of 1294-95, led by **MADOG ap Llywelyn**.

GREY, Reginald (2) ("of Ruthin")
(c.1362-1440)
Norman lord whose dispute over land with his neighbour, **OWAIN Glyndwr**, was a cause of rebellion; later captured and ransomed by Glyndwr.

GRIFFITH (née ELLIS), Alice
(1730-1801)
Daughter of Rhys Ellis of the literary family of Tyddyn Mawr in Caernarfonshire, and wife of the Moravian, William Griffith, from 1753 to 1782. Their one son and eight daughters who were also involved in the Moravian Church, and their home was a meeting-place for the sect.

GRIFFITH, Ellis
See **ELLIS-GRIFFITH, Ellis**.

GRIFFITH, Hugh
(1912-1980)
Character actor who won an Academy Award for his supporting role in the 1959 film, "Ben Hur".

GRIFFITH, James Milo
(1843-97)
Sculptor, best known for his statue of **Hugh OWEN (2)** at Caernarfon (1888). Other works were placed in Bristol Cathedral and Margam Castle. He designed the shield presented to the Prince and Princess of Wales on their jubilee in 1885, and also worked in the USA.

GRIFFITH, John (1) (Y Gohebydd)
(1821-77)
Shopkeeper and Liberal journalist, grandson of **John ROBERTS (2)**; co-founder of the Society of Cymmrodorion (1873). He supported causes such as the University College of Wales, the Eisteddfod, and the secret ballot.

GRIFFITH, John (2) Owen (Ioan Arfon)
(1828-81)
Poet, whose grocery store in Caernarfon became an important meeting place for local literary society; also a geologist, the author of books in Welsh on the subject.

GRIFFITH, Llewelyn Wyn
(1890-1977)
Novelist, broadcaster, poet and translator. He won the Croix de Guerre in World War I, and recorded his wartime experiences in "Up to Mametz" (1931).

GRIFFITH, Moses
(1747-1819)
Artist who accompanied **Thomas PENNANT** on his tours of Wales and Scotland, illustrating the text of Pennant's books with drawings and water-colours; also a portrait painter. Works are held by the National Library and National Museum of Wales, and the Victoria & Albert Museum.

GRIFFITH, Pirs or Perys
(1568-1628)
North Wales nobleman, heir to the Penrhyn

estate, who turned to piracy and forfeited most of his property.

GRIFFITH, Samuel Walker
(1845-1920)
Barrister and judge who lived in Australia from his early childhood. He became Chief Justice and three times Prime Minister of Queensland, and helped draft the Australian constitution (1900).

GRIFFITH (née WYNNE), Sidney ("Madam Griffith")
(c.1720-52)
Wife of William Griffith, of the GRIFFITH (1)* family of Cefn Amwlch. His treatment of her caused her to turn for help and inspiration to the Methodists, Daniel ROWLAND and especially Howell HARRIS; her close friendship with Harris caused some scandal. She was a financial benefactor of the movement, and claimed to possess powers of prophecy.

GRIFFITH, Thomas Taylor
(1795-1876)
Surgeon who attended Queen Victoria before her accession to the throne, and gave financial support to health and education services in Wrexham. He was the keeper of the genealogical and antiquarian collections of his great-grandfather, John Griffith of Cae Cyriog (d. 1698).

GRIFFITH, William (1)
(c.1445-1506)
Chamberlain of North Wales 1483-90, a descendant of GWILYM ap Griffith. His first wife, Joan Troutbeck, was related to the Stanleys, connecting him with the Earl of Derby; his second, Elizabeth GREY*, was related by marriage to Queen Elizabeth Woodville.

GRIFFITH, William (2)
(c.1480-1531)
Chamberlain of North Wales 1508-31; son

of William GRIFFITH (1). A close associate of Charles Brandon, Duke of Suffolk, he served with distinction in the French campaign of 1513, and was knighted at Tournai. He married, first, Jane STRADLING*, and second, Jane PULESTON*.

GRIFFITH, William (3)
(1853-1918)
Mining engineer who worked in Wales, Australia, and South Africa. His expedition to Central Africa with Cecil Rhodes is described in "Anturiaethau Cymro yn Affrica" (1894-5).

GRIFFITHS (née THOMAS), Ann
(1776-1805)
Christian mystic, wife of Thomas Griffiths. Their home at Dolwar Fach became a centre for Methodists. A poet and prolific hymnist, her letters provide a valuable record of her experiences. Her collected works were published in 1805-6 by the efforts of Thomas CHARLES.

GRIFFITHS, James ("Jim")
(1890-1975)
Labour MP for Llanelli 1936-70, the first Secretary of State for Wales (1964-66). He had been President of the South Wales Miners' Federation in 1934, and held Government office as Minister of National Insurance 1945-50 and Secretary of State for the Colonies 1950-1, as well as Chairman of the Labour Party 1948-9.

GRIFFITHS, John
(1837-1918)
Artist, Principal of the College of Arts at Bombay in the 1860s, responsible for the decoration of that city's public buildings and the preservation of much ancient Indian art.

GRIFFITHS, Richard
(1756-1826)
Mine-owner, first to exploit the resources

of the Rhondda valley (1790), where he built a tramroad to connect the mine with the canal via a bridge across the Taff.

GRIFFITHS, Thomas (1)
(1645-1725)
Baptist minister, leader of a group of emigrants who settled Welsh Tract, Delaware, in 1703.

GRIFFITHS, Thomas (2) ("Tom")
(1867-1955)
Labour MP for Pontypool 1918-35, formerly a steelworker and trade union leader.

GRIFFITHS, William
(1788-1861)
Calvinistic Methodist minister, known as the "Apostle of Gower" for taking Methodism to its English-speaking population.

GRINDELL-MATTHEWS, Harry
(1880-1941)
Scientist, inventor of the "aerophone" (1910) and the mysterious "Death Ray", which was never demonstrated. He sent the first press message by radio telephone from the Westgate Hotel, Newport, to the "Western Mail" (1911).

GROVE, William Robert
(1811-96)
Scientist and lawyer; Professor of Experimental Philosophy at the London Institution 1840-7, Vice-President of the Royal Institution 1844, awarded the Royal Society's medal in 1847. Created a QC in 1853 and knighted in 1872, he served as a judge 1871-87 and a member of the Privy Council from 1887.

GRUFFUDD
See GRUFFYDD.

GRUFFYDD AB YR YNAD COCH ("son of the red judge")
(late 13th century; exact dates unknown)
Poet, known for an elegy on LLYWELYN ap Gruffydd which is unique in form and style.

GRUFFYDD AP CYNAN
(c.1054-1137)
Ruler of Gwynedd from 1081; grandson of Iago, a previous prince of Gwynedd. Born in Ireland (his mother being Rhagnell or Rhagnhildr, a Scandinavian princess from Dublin), he married ANGHARAD (2), and campaigned for years to regain his grandfather's territory with the aid of allies including RHYS ap Tewdwr. At the Battle of Mynydd Carn (1081), they resoundingly defeated their rivals, but later he was betrayed to ROBERT of Rhuddlan, and spent twelve years as a prisoner in Chester, escaping in 1094 to continue to fight the Normans. The peace made with King Henry I of England in 1114 gave him greater security for the rest of his reign.

GRUFFYDD AP GWENWYNWYN
(c.1215-1286)
Prince, son of GWENWYNWYN of Powys. At first accepting the overlordship of LLYWELYN ap Gruffydd, he later became the greatest threat to the supremacy of Gwynedd from within Wales, and, influenced by his wife, Hawise LESTRANGE, plotted unsuccessfully with DAFYDD ap Gruffydd to overthrow Llywelyn in 1274. As a result, he forfeited the cantref of Arwystli; his dispute with Llywelyn over its ownership was indirectly responsible for the rebellion of 1282.

GRUFFYDD AP LLYWELYN (1)
(c.1007-63)
Son of LLYWELYN ap Seisyll and a grandson of MAREDUDD ab Owain. Ruler of Gwynedd from 1039, he united Wales and was recognised as its "king" from 1055. His successful raids on English territory, notably the city of Hereford, expanded Welsh possessions, and he held

court at Rhuddlan, formerly a Saxon settlement. Following his marriage to the daughter of his ally, Aelfgar, Earl of Mercia, he was seen as a real threat to England, and was eventually defeated by Harold Godwinson and assassinated by his own men.

GRUFFYDD AP LLYWELYN (2)
(1196-1244)
Son of **LLYWELYN Fawr**, by his liaison with **TANGWYSTL Goch**. As a boy, he spent some time as a hostage in King John's custody. His marriage to **SENENA** produced four sons, the most able of whom, **LLYWELYN ap Gruffydd**, was to become Prince of Wales. During his lifetime, however, Gruffydd's jealousy of his legitimate half-brother, **DAFYDD ap Llywelyn**, led to his imprisonment in the Tower of London, and he was killed in an escape attempt.

GRUFFYDD AP MADOG
See **GRUFFYDD MAELOR**.

GRUFFYDD AP MAREDUDD (AP DAFYDD)
(c.1330-82)
Prolific poet of the "Gogynfeirdd" school, composer of elegies to the family of Penmynydd, including Syr **HYWEL ap Gruffydd (2)**, and of religious and love poems. He used the "awdl" form, and helped introduce "englynion".

GRUFFYDD AP NICOLAS
(c.1400-56)
Powerful official of the lordship of Dynefwr (Dynevor). After the disgrace of his patron, the Duke of Gloucester, he was imprisoned, but later regained office, and supported the Lancastrian cause. He judged the Carmarthen eisteddfod in about 1452, and repaired Carreg Cennen Castle in 1454-5.

GRUFFYDD AP RHYDDERCH
(c.1020-55)
Ruler of Dehaubarth, who successfully

resisted the invasion of **GRUFFYDD ap Llywelyn (1)** for some years, and made incursions into England with Danish assistance.

GRUFFYDD AP RHYS (1)
(1093-1137)
Prince, son of **RHYS ap Tewdwr**. Following his father's death in 1093, he spent some years in exile in Ireland, returning to attack the Normans in west Wales in 1115, with little success. He regained only Cantref Mawr; his wife **GWENLLIAN (1)** died in battle against the Normans, but four sons carried on the re-conquest of Deheubarth.

GRUFFYDD AP RHYS (2)
(c.1160-1201)
Prince, eldest son of **RHYS ap Gruffydd (1)** and a grandson of **MADOG ap Maredudd**. He married Matilda de **BRAOSE***. Following his father's death in 1197, he failed to maintain control of Deheubarth, quarrelling with his brothers **MAELGWN ap Rhys** and **RHYS Gryg**. Captured and imprisoned by **GWENWYNWYN** in 1197, he was released in order to mediate, unsuccessfully, with the Normans.

GRUFFYDD HIRAETHOG
(c.1500-64)
Humanist poet and teacher, compiler of a Welsh dictionary and a collection of Welsh proverbs, and an associate of **William SALESBURY**. As Deputy Herald for Wales, he traced the histories of prominent Welsh families.

GRUFFYDD LLWYD ("Syr")
See **LLWYD, Gruffydd**.

GRUFFYDD MAELOR (1) (Gruffydd ap Madog)
(1140-1191)
Prince of Powys, son of **MADOG ap Maredudd**. He inherited Bromfield and Yale

(Maelor and Ial) as a share of his father's lands in 1160, along with his brothers, Owain Fychan and **OWAIN Brogyntyn**, and married Angharad, daughter of **OWAIN Gwynedd**.

GRUFFYDD MAELOR (2) (Gruffydd ap Madog)
(c.1210-69)
Prince of Powys, son of **MADOG ap Gruf-fydd**. At first a supporter of **LLYWELYN ap Gruffydd**, he was driven out of Powys by him in 1257, but later joined him and was an arbiter in the resolution of his dispute with **DAFYDD ap Gruffydd** in 1267.

GRUFFYDD, Elis ("the soldier of Calais")
(c.1490-1552)
Author of a "Chronicle of the history of the world" beginning from the Creation, includ-ing a full description of his own career; also a copyist and translator. He spent years in the service of the Wingfield family, and was present at the Field of the Cloth of Gold (1521).

GRUFFYDD, William John
(1881-1954)
Poet and critic, Professor of Welsh at University College, Cardiff, 1918-46, and editor of "Y llenor" 1922-5. He served as Liberal MP for the University of Wales 1943-50, winning the seat against **Saunders LEWIS**, but had Nationalist sympathies.

GUEST (née BERTIE), Charlotte
(1812-95)
Translator of the Mabinogion (her own name for the collection of Welsh folk tales) into English (1838). The daughter of the Earl of Lindsey, she came to Wales in 1833 as a result of her marriage to Sir **John Josiah GUEST**. She later married Charles Schreiber, MP, and became notable as the originator of the Schreiber collection of ceramics, which she bequeathed to the

Victoria & Albert Museum. She wrote books about fans and playing cards, which she also collected. Her journal was published by her son in 1911.

GUEST, John Josiah
(1785-1852)
Iron-master of Dowlais, first husband of Lady **Charlotte GUEST**. A progressive and compassionate employer, he involved her in his work, founding schools, a church and a working men's library at Dowlais church. He was the first chairman of the Taff Vale railway, served as Liberal MP for Honiton 1825-31 and first MP for the Merthyr constituency 1832-52, and was created a baronet in 1838.

GUNDLEIUS
See **GWYNLLYW**.

GUTO'R GLYN
(c.1435-93)
Bard and satirist, author of many "cywyddau"; supporter of the Yorkist cause in the Wars of the Roses. His patrons included the **NANNAU*** and **GRIFFITH (4)*** families.

GUTUN OWAIN (Gruffydd ap Huw ab Owain)
(c.1430-98)
Poet and historian, a pupil of **DAFYDD ap Edmwnd**, also a copyist of important Welsh manuscripts, a genealogist and calendar-maker. He recorded the history of Basingwerk Abbey, and laid down rules of grammar and prosody.

GWALCHMAI AP MEILYR
(c.1120-80)
Poet, son of **MEILYR Brydydd**. He wrote in praise of **OWAIN Gwynedd** and his sons, his best-known work being the "Gor-hoffedd", a "vaunting poem" on various themes including Owain's military cam-paigns.

GWENFREWI
See **WINIFRED**.

GWENLLIAN (1)
(c.1097-1136)
Princess of Deheubarth, daughter of **GRUFFYDD ap Cynan** and wife of **GRUFFYDD ap Rhys (1)**. In 1136, whilst her husband was away in North Wales seeking assistance against the Normans, she joined the rebellion in the South, and led an army against Cydweli (Kidwelly). She and her two sons, Morgan and Maelgwn, were defeated by **MAURICE de Londres**, and Gwenllian herself was killed. The site of the battle became known as "Maes Gwenllian".

GWENLLIAN (2)
(1282-1337)
Only known child of **LLYWELYN ap Gruffydd**, by his wife **Eleanor de MONTFORT**. Following her father's death in 1282, she was captured and sent by King **EDWARD I** to a convent at Sempringham in Lincolnshire for the rest of her life.

GWENT, Richard
(c.1490-1543)
Archdeacon of London and Brecon, chaplain to King **HENRY VIII**; a lawyer and agent of Thomas Cromwell. He represented Queen **KATHERINE of Aragon** at an ecclesiastical court of 1529.

GWENWYNWYN
(c.1150-1216)
Prince of Powys and great rival of **LLYWELYN Fawr**. Son of **OWAIN Cyfeiliog** and grandson of **OWAIN Gwynedd**, he succeeded his father in Arwystli in 1197. His unsuccessful attempt to establish himself as the scourge of the Normans and leader of Wales ended with submission to King John in 1208. Eventually he was dispossessed and exiled by Llywelyn.

GWGON AP MEURIG
(c.830-71)
King of Ceredigion, brother of **ANGHARAD (1)**. Following his drowning, his brother-in-law, **RHODRI Mawr**, annexed the state of Seisyllwg.

GWILYM AP GRIFFITH
(c.1370-1431)
Founder of the family of **GRIFFITH (4)***. He married Morfydd, daughter of Goronwy ap Tudur, and was thereby related to **OWAIN Glyndwr**, whom he half-heartedly supported, defecting to the English King by 1407 and thus obtaining the forfeited lands of his wife's uncles in 1410. His second marriage, to Joan, daughter of Sir William Stanley, was another important and profitable alliance.

GWLADUS DDU
(1198-1251)
Illegitimate daughter of **LLYWELYN Fawr**, half-sister to **DAFYDD ap Llywelyn**; married first (1215-28) to **Reginald de BRAOSE**, and second (1230-46) to **Ralph MORTIMER**. Through her the Yorkist kings of England claimed descent from Llywelyn.

GWRTHEYRN or VORTIGERN
(5th century; exact dates unknown)
British leader who opposed the Romans, and invited the Saxon leaders Hengist and Horsa to Britain, possibly marrying the daughter of Hengist; other sources say he was the son-in-law of **MAGNUS Maximus**. Much of the information we have about him comes from **NENNIUS**. *Gave his name to:* Gwerthrynion or Caer Wrtheyrn (possible site of his court).

GWYN or WHITE, Richard (St)
(c.1557-84)
Catholic schoolmaster executed for treason at Wrexham, after several years of impris-

onment and torture for his opposition to Queen Elizabeth I. Canonised in 1970, he is regarded as the first Roman Catholic martyr in Wales.

GWYN or JONES, Robert
(c.1550-94)
Catholic priest trained at Douai, who carried out a successful mission to Wales. He influenced **Robert PUW (1)** to set up a secret printing press, providing material in Welsh for publication, including "Y drych Cristionogowl" (1586).

GWYNEDD, Owain
See **OWAIN GWYNEDD**.

GWYNLLYW or GUNDLEIUS or GUNDLYU or WOOLO
(5th-6th century; exact dates unknown)
Saint, prince of Glywysing in South Wales, descended from **CUNEDDA**. He became a hermit, along with his wife Gwladys (daughter of **BRYCHAN**), reputedly at the instigation of their son, St **CADOG**.

GWYNNE, Arthur
See **EVANS, Gwynfil**.

GWYNNE, Marmaduke
(c.1694-1769)
Mid-Wales gentleman converted to Methodism by **Howell HARRIS** and closely associated with the Wesley brothers.

GWYNNE or WYN, Owen
(c.1560-1633)
Clergyman, a younger son of Griffith **WYNN (2)*** of Berth-ddu. He was Master of St John's College, Cambridge 1612-33, during which period the life of the college was greatly influenced by his cousin and former pupil, Archbishop **John WILLIAMS (2)**.

GWYNNE, Rowland
(1660-1726)
Whig MP for Radnorshire 1678-85 and for Brecknock 1689-90, 1698, and 1700-1. Knighted in 1680, he was a member of the royal household of William and Mary, but fell into disfavour under Queen Anne.

GWYNNE, Sackville
(c.1751-94)
Harpist and patron of harpists, responsible for the tradition of the harp at his family estate of Glanbran which lasted into the 19th century.

GWYNNE, Sarah
See **WESLEY, Sarah**.

GWYNNE-VAUGHAN, David Thomas
(1871-1915)
Botanist, Professor of Botany at Belfast 1911-15 and Reading 1915. An expert on ferns, he led botanic expeditions in South America and the Far East. His wife, Dame Helen Gwynne-Vaughan, was also a well-known botanist.

H

HALL (née WADDINGTON), Augusta
See **LLANOVER, Lady**.

HALL, Benjamin (1)
(1778-1817)
Industrialist who married the daughter of Richard **CRAWSHAY***, becoming a partner in the Rhymney ironworks and owner of Hensol Castle and the Abercarn estate. He served as MP for Totnes 1806-12, Westbury 1812-14, and Glamorgan 1814-17.

HALL, Benjamin (2)
(1802-67)
MP for Monmouth 1832-7, son of **Benjamin HALL (1)**; instrumental in the passing of the Truck Act 1831. He was created a baronet in 1838 and Baron Llanover in 1859, after being appointed Commissioner for Works in 1855. *Gave his name to:* "Big Ben".

HANBURY, John
(1664-1734)
Industrialist of a Worcestershire family, who inherited the ironworks at Pontypool in 1704 and introduced tinplating and the "rolling mill". He served as Whig MP for Gloucester 1701-15 and Monmouthshire 1720-34.

HANMER, David
(c.1350-88)
Justice of the King's Bench, knighted in 1387; father-in-law of **OWAIN Glyndwr**.

HANMER, John (1)
(1575-1629)
Bishop of St Asaph (1624) and chaplain to King James I, a descendant of the **HANMER*** family of Flintshire.

HANMER, John (2)
(1809-81)
Liberal MP for constituencies in England and Wales 1841-72; also a poet, and the author of a family history. He was created 1st Baron Hanmer in 1872.

HANMER, Margaret (Marred ferch Dafydd)
(c.1370-1420)
Daughter of Sir **David HANMER** and wife of **OWAIN Glyndwr** (c.1383). After several years of happy family life, during which six sons and several daughters were born to them, she and most of her children were taken hostage by the future King **HENRY V**.

HANMER, Thomas
(1677-1746)
4th Baronet Hanmer, Tory MP for various constituencies in Wales and England 1701-27, and an ambassador to the court of King Louis XIV of France. He was Speaker of the House of Commons in 1714, when the monarchy passed from the House of Stuart to that of Hanover.

HARDIE, James Keir
(1856-1915)
First Labour MP, elected for Merthyr Tydfil in 1900. Though himself Scottish, he earned great respect in Wales, holding the seat until his death.

HARLECH, Baron
See **ORMSBY-GORE, David**.

HARLEY, Robert
(1579-1656)
Knight (1603), who served as MP for Radnor 1604-11 and was a member of the

Council of the Marches. A prominent Presbyterian, his home at Brampton Bryan became a haven for Puritan leaders such as **Walter CRADOC**, and was defended during the Civil War by his wife, Brilliana.

HARRIES
See also **HARRIS**.

HARRIS, Frederick William
(1833-1917)
English Quaker industrialist, founder of the Deep Navigation colliery near Pontypridd. *Gave his name to:* Treharris, Glamorgan.

HARRIS, Howell
(1714-73)
Leader of the Methodist revival in Wales. A stirring preacher and hymnist, he worked closely with the Wesley brothers and was nicknamed "Utgorn y Diwygiad" ("Trumpet of the Revival"). His diaries and correspondence have been published. In 1743, he founded the Association of Welsh Methodists. After many years in partnership with **Daniel ROWLAND**, he left the movement in 1750, while under the influence of "Madam" **Sidney GRIFFITH**, and founded a community or "Family" of followers at Trefecca, establishing an agricultural society and a preachers' training college.

HARRIS, John
(1680-1738)
Bishop of Llandaff 1729-38, responsible for the building of the "Italian temple" attached to the cathedral.

HARRIS, Joseph (1)
(1704-64)
Brother of **Howell HARRIS**, with whom he corresponded regularly. He was Assay-Master at the Royal Mint 1748-64, and the author of works on navigational science.

HARRIS, Joseph (2) (Gomer)
(1773-1825)
Baptist minister, author of several theological works, hymnist and publisher of hymnbooks. The weekly, "Seren Gomer" (1814-15), was the first in Welsh. It was succeeded in 1818 by a fortnightly periodical of the same name, which ultimately became the official organ of the Welsh Baptist Union. One of his works, "Cofiant Ieuan Ddu", commemorates the life of his son, John Ryland Davies.

HARRIS, Thomas
(1705-82)
Brother of **Howell HARRIS**, with whom he corresponded. He spent much of his life in London, but was Sheriff of Brecknock in 1768, and bought the estates of Trefecca and Tregunter, rebuilding the mansion at the latter.

HARRY, George Owen
(c.1553-1614)
Clergyman, historian and genealogist, author of a genealogy of King James I of England (1604), intended to show the rightfulness of his claim to the throne.

HARRY, Miles
(1700-76)
Baptist minister, the greatest of his time. He founded several churches and the Trosnant Baptist Academy, and was of help to **Howell HARRIS** when the latter was on trial for causing a riot at Pontypool during his early career.

HARTSHORN, Vernon
(1872-1931)
Miners' leader who played a prominent role in the strikes of 1912 and 1920, and was a member of **David LLOYD GEORGE**'s Commission of Industrial Unrest in 1917. He served as Labour MP for Ogmore 1918-31, becoming Postmaster General in 1924

and Lord Privy Seal in 1929, and was part-author of the Simon Commission's report on India (1927).

HATTON (née KEMBLE), Julia Ann (Ann of Swansea)
(1764-1838)
Poet and novelist, sister of **Sarah SID-DONS**. A disability prevented her from following the Kemble family theatrical tradition. In 1792, she married William Hatton and lived with him in the USA and later in Swansea, where she ran a bathing-house.

HAWYS or HAWISE GADARN ("the hardy")
(c.1291-1353)
Heiress to the lands of her grandfather, **GRUFFYDD ap Gwenwynwyn**, after the death of her brother in 1309. She was made a ward of the Crown and married John **CHARLTON***, who thus became lord of Powys.

HEDD WYN
See **EVANS, E**llis Humphrey.

HEMANS (née BROWNE), Felicia
Dorothea
(1793-1835)
Poet, highly regarded in her day, whose parents settled in Wales when she was very young. She married a sea captain, and remained in Wales until 1827. She is best remembered for her poem, "Casabianca" (beginning "The boy stood on the burning deck"), though she also wrote books and plays, one of which was performed in London by Kemble.

HENRY V (Henry of Monmouth)
(1387-1422)
King of England, son of Henry IV by **Mary de BOHUN**, the only Welsh-born Prince of Wales since **EDWARD II**. He took the title in 1399 when his father usurped the throne from **RICHARD II**. His own military skills resulted in the death of "Hotspur" and ended the reign of **OWAIN Glyndwr**. He became one of England's most celebrated kings after his miraculous victory at Agincourt (1415), and married **KATHERINE of Valois**, daughter of the French King.

HENRY VII
See **TUDOR, Henry**.

HENRY VIII
(1491-1547)
One of England's most memorable Kings, mainly because of his role in the Reformation. The second son of **Henry TUDOR**, he was made Prince of Wales after the death of his brother **Arthur TUDOR**, and married Arthur's widow, **KATHERINE of Aragon**, after his accession to the throne in 1509. Her failure to produce a male heir led to divorce, followed by religious and political upheaval. The Act of Union of 1536, linking Wales with England as one nation, was enacted by the English Parliament during his reign, revealing an awareness of his own ancestry.

HENRY STUART
See **STUART, Henry**.

HERBERT, Edward (1)
(1513-93)
MP for Montgomeryshire 1553-88, son of **William HERBERT (2)**. He fought in Mid Wales against the army of Mary Stuart (1557). He was created Lord of Cherbury in 1553, and in 1587 purchased the lordship of Powis, later serving as squire to Queen Elizabeth I, under the patronage of the Earl of Leicester.

HERBERT, Edward (2)
(1583-1648)
1st Baron **HERBERT (1)*** of Cherbury (1629); a diplomat under James I/VI, also a poet and philosopher. His posthumously-

published autobiography, one of the first in the English language, describes his experiences travelling in Europe between 1608 and 1624, including a period as British ambassador in Paris.

HERBERT, Edward (3)
(c.1591-1657)
Lawyer, son of **Edward HERBERT (1)**. Knighted in 1640, he was a Royalist supporter, serving as Solicitor General and later Attorney General, in which capacity he was responsible for the arrest of the "Five Members". Exiled with Prince Rupert in 1648, he later held a post in King **CHARLES II**'s unofficial Court.

HERBERT, Edward (4)
(c.1633-78)
Politician, who succeeded to the barony of Cherbury in 1655, but was involved in Booth's rebellion of 1659. After the Restoration, he served in official posts until 1677, when he opposed the court candidate in the Montgomeryshire election.

HERBERT, Edward (5)
(1645-98)
Son of **Edward HERBERT (3)**; successor of **George JEFFREYS** as Chief Justice of the King's Bench (1685). He fell from favour with King James II of England, but followed the King into exile and was "Earl of Portland" and Lord Chancellor in his unofficial Court until 1692.

HERBERT, George
(1593-1633)
Clergyman, poet and author, younger brother of **Edward HERBERT (2)**. Public Orator at Cambridge University 1620-7, he also served as MP for Montgomery 1624-5. His collected poems were published as "The temple" in 1633, and his chief prose work, "A priest to the temple", in 1652.

HERBERT, Henry (1)
(c.1534-1601)
2nd Earl of Pembroke, son of **William HERBERT (2)**, whose property (including Cardiff Castle, which he restored) and offices he inherited. He married Catherine, sister of Lady Jane Grey, but divorced her after the accession of **Mary TUDOR** and married **Mary SIDNEY**, whose father he succeeded as President of the Council of Wales in 1586. Under Elizabeth I, he was involved in the trial of Mary Stuart.

HERBERT, Henry (2)
(1595-1673)
Courtier and diplomat, younger brother of **Edward HERBERT (2)**. He was Master of the King's Revels under James I/VI, **CHARLES I**, and, after supporting the Royalist cause during the Civil War, **CHARLES II**.

HERBERT, Henry (3)
(c.1640-91)
Brother of **Edward HERBERT (4)**, whom he joined in supporting Booth's rebellion. He later served with the Duke of Monmouth, whose claim to the throne he supported. His Protestant credentials led to his becoming Cofferer of the Household of King William III. He was also the first colonel of the Royal Welch Fusiliers.

HERBERT, Henry (4) Arthur
(c.1703-72)
Protestant 4th Earl of Powis (1748), descended from **William HERBERT (1)**; created a general in 1772, after assisting in putting down the second Jacobite rebellion. He married Barbara Herbert, niece of the 3rd Marquess of Powis, had mining interests in Wales, and was an associate of **Lewis MORRIS (1)**.

HERBERT, John ("of Neath")
(1550-1617)
Lawyer and diplomat under Queen Eliza-

beth I and King James I of England; a descendant of **William HERBERT (1)** and brother of **William HERBERT (3)**. Knighted in 1602, he was MP for various constituencies in England and Wales between 1586 and 1614, and was a member of the Council of Wales.

HERBERT, Mary
See **SIDNEY, Mary**.

HERBERT, Philip
(1584-1650)

4th Earl of Pembroke, younger son of **Henry HERBERT (1)**, who named him after King Philip II of Spain (consort of **Mary TUDOR**). A favourite of James I/VI, who made him Earl of Montgomery (1605) and a member of the Council of Wales, he defected to Parliament during the Civil War. His interests included a glass works at Milford Haven.

HERBERT, Richard
(1468-1539)

Knight of Montgomery, nephew of Sir **RHYS ap Thomas** and also of **William HERBERT (1)**. A follower of **Charles SOMERSET**, Earl of Worcester, he became his agent in Mid Wales, settling at Montgomery. In 1536, he supported the Act of Union, whilst petitioning King **HENRY VIII** for equal rights for Welshmen.

HERBERT, Thomas
(c.1597-1642)

Sailor, younger brother of **Edward HERBERT (2)**. He took part in **Robert MANSEL**'s expedition to Algiers (1620), and commanded the ship in which the future King **CHARLES I** travelled to Spain in 1623.

HERBERT, William (1) ("Black William")
(c.1425-69)

Merchant and soldier, grandson of **Dafydd GAM**, whose successes on behalf of the Yorkist faction in Wales during the Wars of the Roses resulted in his elevation to the titles Lord Herbert of Raglan (1461) and Earl of Pembroke (1468). (The famous Welsh song, "Rhyfelgyrch Gwyr Harlech", refers to this campaign.) As such, he was given custody of the young **Henry TUDOR**, whom he planned to marry to his own daughter, and held the office of Chief Justice and Chamberlain of Wales, but fell out with his rival, the Earl of Warwick. He was executed after the Lancastrian victory at Banbury.

HERBERT, William (2)
(c.1501-70)

1st Earl of Pembroke (of the second creation 1551), grandson of **William HERBERT (1)** through an illegitimate son. He profited by being brother-in-law of Queen Catherine Parr, and was knighted in 1543 and given lands and offices in South Wales, becoming President of the Council of Wales and the Marches 1550-3 and 1555-8. A Privy Councillor under King Edward VI, he was fortunate to retain the favour of **Mary TUDOR** after supporting her rival, Lady Jane Grey, and prospered further under Elizabeth I.

HERBERT, William (3)
(c.1550-93)

Direct descendant of **William HERBERT (1)**, married to Florentia **MORGAN (1)*** of Llantarnam. Knighted in 1578, he was Sheriff of Glamorgan in the same year and of Monmouthshire in 1580, Deputy Constable of Conway Castle in 1579, and MP for Monmouthshire in 1584, 1586, and 1593. Having been given charge of lands forfeit to the Crown in Ireland, he became a benefactor of the local population.

HERBERT, William (4)
(1573-1656)

MP for Montgomeryshire 1597-1629, son

of **Edward HERBERT (1)**; created 1st Baron Powis in 1629. A Roman Catholic, he obtained the patronage of the Earl of Pembroke, was a member of the Council of Wales, and held Powis Castle for King **CHARLES I** until 1644.

HERBERT, William (5)
(1580-1630)
3rd Earl of Pembroke, son of **Henry HERBERT (1)**. He was a favourite of James I, but a critic of Buckingham, and served as Lord Chamberlain (1615) and a member of the Council of Wales. He developed his South Wales estates, and was a patron of Shakespeare and other theatrical figures. **Rhys PRICHARD** referred to him as "colofn y deyrnas" ("pillar of the kingdom").

HERBERT, William (6)
(c.1617-96)
1st Earl of Powis, grandson of **William HERBERT (4)**. A Roman Catholic, he was implicated in the "Popish Plot" and imprisoned 1678-85, but was favoured by King James II. He took charge of the Prince of Wales, **James Francis Edward STUART**, whom he and his wife smuggled to France in 1688. He was created Marquess of Powis in 1687, and was later made Duke of Powis and a Knight of the Garter in exile.

HERBERT, William (7)
(c.1665-1745)
Viscount Montgomery, son of **William HERBERT (6)**; a supporter of King James II. In 1689, he was imprisoned on a charge of treason; on his release, he built Powis House. Following the Jacobite rebellion of 1715, he was again imprisoned and released, and restored to the title of Marquess of Powis.

HERBERT, Winifred
(c.1680-1749)
Daughter of **William HERBERT (6)** and

wife of William Maxwell, 5th Earl of Nithsdale, famous for the daring rescue of her husband from the Tower of London where he was imprisoned for his part in the Jacobite rebellion of 1715.

HEYLIN or HEILYN, Rowland
(c.1562-1631)
Puritan merchant who co-financed the publication of Welsh books, including the re-printing of the Welsh Bible in 1630, with **Thomas MYDDELTON (1)**.

HILL, Anthony
(1784-1862)
Industrialist, named by his father, Richard Hill, after **Anthony BACON**. He inherited responsibility for the Plymouth ironworks, which he continued to work by water-power. He remained as director after the death of his brother, **Richard HILL**, experimenting with new methods, and also founded a school and church at Pentre-bach.

HILL, Richard
(1774-1844)
Industrialist, brother of **Anthony HILL**. While working at the Plymouth ironworks, he was involved in legal battles with officials of the Glamorganshire Canal. He inherited the works from his father, in partnership with his two brothers.

HILLS-JOHNES, James
(1833-1919)
Soldier, awarded the Victoria Cross during the Indian Mutiny 1857-8, and created a general in 1893; Treasurer of the University College of Wales 1898-1919.

HIRAETHOG, Gwilym
See **REES, William**.

HODGES, Frank
(1887-1947)
South Wales miners' leader, of English

origin, active in the Central Labour College movement. He was secretary of the Miners' Federation of Great Britain (1918), and of the International Miners' Federation (1924).

HOGGAN, Frances Elizabeth
(1843-1927)
First British woman to obtain a degree in medicine from a university on the Continent, which she achieved at Zurich in 1870. She later practised in London as a specialist in women's and children's diseases.

HOLBACHE, David
(c.1377-1423)
Lawyer, founder of Oswestry Grammar School (c.1420), and MP for Shrewsbury 1406-17. He sought Crown compensation for damages done him by **OWAIN Glyndwr**, and was instrumental in obtaining the pardon of **ADAM of Usk** in 1411.

HOLLAND, Hugh
(1569-1633)
Poet, of the Denbigh branch of the **HOLLAND*** family. His poems, in English and Latin, included commendatory verses accompanying the works of contemporaries such as Shakespeare and Jonson.

HOLLAND, William
(1711-61)
Original member of the Moravian congregation in London (1746). He did missionary work abroad and in Wales, keeping a journal of his travels in 1746-7, but later defected to the Wesleyans.

HOMFRAY, Francis
(1726-98)
English industrialist who founded the Penydarren ironworks in 1784 to set up two of his sons, and devised an innovative iron floor for furnaces.

HOMFRAY, Jeremiah
(1759-1833)
Industrialist, son of **Francis HOMFRAY**. He founded the Ebbw Vale ironworks in 1789, continuing to share responsibility for the Penydarren works with his brother, **Samuel HOMFRAY**, and was knighted in 1810. He was later associated with the works at Abernant and Hirwaun, but was bankrupted in 1813.

HOMFRAY, Samuel
(c.1760-1822)
Industrialist, son of **Francis HOMFRAY**. He took over the management of the Penydarren ironworks in 1789, and discovered the method of making "finers metal". He also promoted the use of the Glamorgan canal and a tramway from Penydarren to Abercynon, on which, in 1804, **Richard TREVITHICK** successfully ran a locomotive. After marrying into the **MORGAN (1)*** family of Tredegar Park, he established the Tredegar works.

HOOSON, Isaac Daniel
(1880-1948)
Poet, a lawyer by profession. His poems, including "Wil", "Y siamplar", "Barti Ddu" and "Guto Benfelyn", are popular with children and often recited.

HOPCYN, Wil
(1700-41)
Poet associated with the village of Llangynwyd in Glamorgan. Supposedly the lover of **Ann MADDOCKS**, the "Maid of Cefn Ydfa", he was reputed to be the author of the popular song, "Bugeilio'r gwenith gwyn".

HOPKINS, Gerard Manley
(1844-89)
English-born Jesuit priest and poet, whose style and originality owe much to his Welsh origins. He learned the Welsh language, and used its rhythms and traditional metres. His

work became well known only after his death, through the efforts of his friend Robert Bridges.

HORNER, Arthur
(1894-1968)
Miners' leader, at first a deputy to **A J COOK**. A founder member of the Welsh and British Communist Party, he stood unsuccessfully for Parliament and became President of the South Wales Miners' Federation in 1936 and of the National Union of Mineworkers in 1946.

HOWELL, James
(c.1594-1666)
Diplomat and Historiographer Royal, MP for Richmond 1627, imprisoned during the Civil War; best known as the author of "Familiar epistles" (the first volume of genuine correspondence to be published in English). Other works include an multilingual dictionary and a collection of Welsh proverbs.

HOWELL, Thomas
(16th century; exact dates unknown)
Founder by his will of 1540 of the "Thomas Howell Charity", entrusted to the Drapers Company for the benefit of his unmarried female relatives. *Gave his name to:* Howell's Schools at Denbigh and Llandaff (1859).

HOYLE, William Evans
(1855-1926)
First director of the National Museum of Wales (1909-24).

HUET, Thomas
(c.1530-91)
Clergyman and scholar who assisted **William SALESBURY** in translating the New Testament and Book of Common Prayer.

HUGH D'AVRANCHES ("Hugh the Fat")
(c.1040-1101)
Norman Earl of Chester, who at the time of the Domesday Book controlled vast areas of North Wales and the Marches, being one of the three most powerful Marcher lords.

HUGHES, Anne Harriet (Gwyneth Vaughan)
(1852-1910)
Poet and novelist in the Welsh language, the editor of women's pages in various English and Welsh periodicals. Her books, such as "O gorlannau y defaid" (1905) and "Plant y gorthrwm" (1908), describe contemporary events.

HUGHES, Charles Evans
(1862-1948)
American politician, son of a Welsh immigrant. He narrowly lost the 1916 Presidential election to Woodrow Wilson, and was later Chief Justice of the US Supreme Court.

HUGHES, Elizabeth Phillips (Merch Myrddin)
(1851-1925)
Scholar and teacher, first Principal of the Cambridge Training College for Women Teachers 1885-99; a campaigner for women's education and the only woman on the committee which drafted the charter of the University of Wales.

HUGHES, Henry Maldwyn
(1875-1940)
Wesleyan minister, last to serve as President of the Wesleyan Conference before its amalgamation with the Methodists; also the first principal of Wesley House, Cambridge (1921), and author of numerous theological works.

HUGHES, Hugh (1)
(1778-1855)
Wesleyan minister, the first Welsh minister to be elected to the "Legal Hundred" (1834); author, translator, and the founder of numerous chapels.

HUGHES, Hugh (2)
(1790-1863)
Artist, son-in-law and collaborator of **David CHARLES**. He toured Wales in 1819-21, publishing a journal of his travels, and is best known for a subsequent illustrated work, "The beauties of Cambria" (1823).

HUGHES, Hugh (3) (Cadfan Gwynedd, Hughes Cadfan)
(1824-98)
One of the first Welsh settlers in Patagonia (1865), who became governor of the colony in 1875.

HUGHES, Hugh (4) Price
(1847-1902)
Wesleyan minister, founder of the "Methodist Times" (1885) and in charge of the West London Mission. A socialist, he helped turn public opinion against Parnell.

HUGHES, Isaac (Craigfryn)
(1852-1928)
Poet and novelist, a coal-miner by trade, blind for the last few years of his life; an expert on folklore. Works include "Y ferch o Cefn Ydfa" (1881) (the story of **Ann MADDOCKS**) and "Y ferch o'r Scer" (1892).

HUGHES, James (Iago Trichnig)
(1779-1844)
Calvinistic Methodist minister and poet, best known for his Biblical commentary, "Esboniad ar y Beibl" (completed after his death), which became popularly known as "Esboniad Siams Huws".

HUGHES, Jane (Deborah Maldwyn)
(c.1811-80)
Hymnist, daughter of **John HUGHES (1)**; author of fifteen collections of hymns published 1846-89. She travelled through the country, living off the sale of her work.

HUGHES, John (1)
(1775-1854)
Calvinistic Methodist minister, author and hymnist. His wife, Ruth Evans, was maid to **Ann GRIFFITHS**, whose work he preserved and of whom he published a memoir in 1846.

HUGHES, John (2)
(1814-89)
Industrialist, founder of the New Russia Company (1869) for the expansion of the iron and steel industries in that country. The town which grew up around his works became a haven for Welsh immigrants. *Gave his name to:* Yuzovka (Hughesovka), later renamed Stalino.

HUGHES, John (3) (Ceiriog)
(1832-87)
Poet, collector and publisher of Welsh rhymes and airs. An associate of the singer, Idris Fychan, and of **R J DERFEL**, he published many songs, including "Dafydd y garreg wen", "Nant y mynydd", and "Alun Mabon".

HUGHES, John (4)
(1873-1932)
Composer, best known for the hymn-tune, "Cwm Rhondda".

HUGHES, Megan Watts
(1842-1907)
Singer, who performed with **Joseph PARRY** and Jenny Lind. As a composer, she is best known for the hymn-tune "Wilton Square" and the song "Y gwcw ar y fedwen". She invented a musical device called 'Voice Figures', and also founded a boys' home in London.

HUGHES, Owen (Yr Arian Mawr)
(c.1640-1708)
Lawyer, at first associated with the **BULKELEY*** family. He amassed great wealth

and became very influential, serving as MP for Beaumaris 1698-1700.

HUGHES, Richard (1)
(1794-1871)
Printer, of Wrexham; founder of the publishing firm Hughes and Son (with his son Charles), known for the production of Welsh books and music, including the work of **John HUGHES (3)**, a relation.

HUGHES, Richard (2) Arthur Warren
(1900-76)
English-born poet and novelist, whose works include the uncompleted multivolume saga, "The human predicament". His most successful work was "A high wind in Jamaica" (1929). He lived for some time at Laugharne Castle, with his wife, the painter Frances Bazley.

HUGHES, Stephen
(1622-88)
Clergyman, Nonconformist leader, and publisher of religious books in Welsh, starting in 1658 with the work of **Rhys PRICHARD**. He assisted **Thomas GOUGE** and **Charles EDWARDS** in the provision of charity schools.

HUGHES, Thomas **Rowland**
(1903-49)
Poet, playwright and novelist, whose works, such as "O law i law" (1943) and "Chwalfa" (1946), are set against the background of the North Wales slate quarries. He won the Chair at two National Eisteddfodau (1937, 1940) with his poems "Y ffin" and "Pererinion", but was crippled by multiple sclerosis.

HUGHES, William (1)
(c.1535-1600)
Bishop of St Asaph 1573-1600, a patron of **William MORGAN (1)** and a supporter of the Welsh language.

HUGHES, William (2) Bulkeley
(1797-1882)
Barrister, MP for Caernarfon as both a Tory (1837-59) and a Liberal (1865-82). Owner of the Plas Coch estate at Llanidan in Anglesey, he was instrumental in the development of the town of Llandudno.

HUGHES, William (3) Meloch
(1860-1926)
A settler in Patagonia, who arrived in the Welsh colony there in 1881 and remained for forty years. The record of his experiences was published as "Ar lannau'n Camwy" (1927).

HUGHES, William (4) Morris
(1864-1952)
Labour politician, who lived in Australia from 1884. He was Prime Minister of Australia 1915-23, and later founded the United Australian Party.

HUMPHREYS, Hugh
(1817-96)
Printer who set up at Caernarfon in 1837, publishing penny and sixpenny books, including **Thomas PENNANT**'s "Tours in Wales", and some periodicals. He built the Paternoster Buildings in Castle Square, Caernarfon, to house his business.

HUMPHREYS, Humphrey
(1648-1712)
Bishop of Bangor 1689-70 and Hereford 1701-12; an associate of **Edward LHUYD**, who praised his historical scholarship. He worked hard for the diocese of Bangor as Dean and later as Bishop, and supported the work of the SPCK in Wales.

HUMPHREYS (-DEVONPORT), Salusbury Pryce
(1778-1845)
Rear-admiral, who gained notoriety for his seizure of the American ship "Chesapeake"

in 1807, which provoked an international incident.

HUWS, Rhys Jones
(1862-1917)
Independent minister and poet, leader of the school of "New Poets" and controversial winner of the chair at the Merioneth eisteddfod of 1894; one of the originators of children's eisteddfodau.

HYWEL AB EDWIN
(c.1000-44)
Descendant of **HYWEL Dda**, who ruled Deheubarth jointly with his brother Maredudd 1033-5, and later on his own until deposed by **GRUFFYDD ap Llywelyn (1)**.

HYWEL AB OWAIN (GWYNEDD)
(c.1120-1170)
Illegitimate son of **OWAIN Gwynedd** by Pyfog, an Irishwoman. A celebrated poet and soldier, he conquered Ceredigion, defeating the Normans, but later lost the territory to **CADELL ap Gruffydd**. He was killed in battle at Pentraeth, against his half-brothers (sons of **CRISTIN**), immediately after his father's death.

HYWEL AP CADELL
See **HYWEL DDA**.

HYWEL AP GORONWY
(14th century; exact dates unknown)
One of the murderers of **Henry de SHALDEFORD**, attorney to **EDWARD of Woodstock**, in 1345, along with his brother, **TUDUR ap Goronwy**.

HYWEL AP GRUFFYDD (1) (AP IORWERTH) (Hywel y Pedolau, "Hywel of the Horseshoes")
(c.1290-1340)
Knight, a favourite of King **EDWARD II**. He gained his nickname by his great physical strength (he was reputed to be able to bend horseshoes with his bare hands). Following Edward's fall from power, he was imprisoned, but later served as MP for Anglesey.

HYWEL AP GRUFFYDD (2) (Hywel y Fwyall, "Hywel of the Axe")
(c.1310-81)
Soldier who served with distinction under **EDWARD of Woodstock**, in the battles both of Crecy (where he was knighted on the field) and Poitiers. His famous axe was given honorary status in the royal presence, and he himself became Constable of Criccieth Castle in about 1360.

HYWEL AP MAREDUDD
(12th century; exact dates unknown)
Chieftain of western Brycheiniog, whose invasion of Gower in 1136 led to full-scale rebellion against the Normans throughout South Wales.

HYWEL DDA ("Hywel the Good"; Hywel ap Cadell)
(c.890-950)
King, son of **CADELL ap Rhodri**, from whom he inherited Seisyllwg, at first jointly with his brother, Clydog. Later, by his marriage to Elen, he added to it Dyfed, creating the kingdom of Deheubarth. He was the only Welsh ruler to issue his own coinage, and in 928 made a pilgrimage to Rome, where he was declared "King of Wales", nevertheless continuing to pay homage to the Saxon ruler of England, Athelstan. In 930 he called an assembly at Whitland, where certain standard codes of conduct were laid down in an effort to unite the various regions under his rule, hence his reputation as the instigator of Wales' legal system.

HYWELL Y FWYALL
See **HYWEL AP GRUFFYDD (2)**.

I

IAGO AB IDWAL (FOEL)
(c.930-79)

Son of **IDWAL Foel**, expelled from Gwynedd by **HYWEL Dda** on his father's death in 942. Following Hywel's own death in 950, he returned, but civil war with his brother Ieuaf ensued, culminating in the succession of Hywel ap Ieuaf to the throne of Gwynedd.

IDWAL FOEL ("Idwal the Bald")
(c.890-942)

Son of **ANARAWD ap Rhodri** and his successor as King of Gwynedd from 916. He died in an unsuccessful revolt against his Saxon overlords.

IESTYN AP GWRGANT
(c.1060-93)

Last independent prince of Glamorgan, which he ruled from 1081; founder of the fifth royal tribe of Wales, from which most important Glamorgan families claimed descent. He may have brought about the Norman invasion of the county during an internal power struggle with **EINION ap Collwyn**.

IEUAN AP RHYDDERCH AP IEUAN LLWYD
(c.1430-70)

Gentleman-poet of Cardiganshire, known for a poem linking ancient Welsh prophecies with the Wars of the Roses; possibly also translator of the 'Te Deum' into Welsh.

IEUAN BRYDYDD HIR; IEUAN FARDD
See **EVANS, Evan (1)**.

IFOR AP LLYWELYN ("Ifor Hael": "Ifor the Generous")
(c.1315-80)

Chief patron of **DAFYDD ap Gwilym**, who gave him his nickname; ancestor of the **MORGAN (1)*** family. His association with patronage and philanthropy resulted in an eighteenth-century benevolent society, Yr Iforiaid, being named after him.

IFOR AP CADIFOR or IFOR AP MEURIG ("Ifor Bach": "Little Ifor")
(12th century; exact dates unknown)

Lord of Senghenydd, subject to Earl William of Gloucester. In 1158, to obtain justice in a territorial dispute, he daringly kidnapped the Earl and his family from Cardiff Castle. The episode became a popular literary theme.

ILLTUD
(c.470-530)

Saint and philosopher, one of the founders of Christianity in Wales. Of Breton origin, he lived as a hermit in Gower and the Usk valley, and is supposedly buried in the Brecon Beacons. His nickname, "Illtud Farchog" (Illtud the Knight), suggests his original occupation as a soldier. *Gave his name to:* Llanilltud Fawr (Llantwit Major).

INNES, James Dickson
(1887-1914)

Artist in water-colours and oils, mainly of landscapes in an original style inspired by Continental travel.

IOLO GOCH
(c.1320-98)

Poet of noble birth. His description of the home life of **OWAIN Glyndwr** at Sycharth is famous, but he wrote works in praise of other princes and nobles, including King

EDWARD III of England and **Roger MORTIMER (4)**. Other poems include a description of a tour through Wales in about 1387.

IOLO MORGANWG (Edward Williams)
(1747-1826)
Scholar, poet, and hymnist; a charlatan and forger who invented Welsh "traditions" including the Gorsedd of Bards, which he introduced to the National Eisteddfod in 1819. His major work, "Cyfrinach beirdd ynys Prydain", was written while in prison for debt.

IORWERTH or GERVASE
(12th-13th centuries; exact dates unknown)
Bishop of St David's 1215-29, previously Abbot of Talley. As a native Welshman, his appointment as Bishop immediately after the signing of Magna Carta was significant.

IORWERTH AP MADOG
(c.1240-68)
Lawyer, believed to be the final redactor of the "Venedotian Code".

IORWERTH DRWYNDWN ("Iorwerth the Flat-Nosed")
(c.1130-74)
Prince, son of **OWAIN Gwynedd** by his first wife, Gwladus; son-in-law of **MADOG ap Maredudd**. He lost his inheritance of Arfon to his half-brother, **DAFYDD ab Owain**, in 1174.

ISFAEL
(6th century; exact dates unknown)
Saint, nephew of **TEILO**, possibly the successor of St **DAVID** as Bishop of Menevia.

ISLWYN
See **THOMAS, William (3)**.

J

JAMES OF ST GEORGE
(13th century; exact dates unknown)
Military architect, designer of castles built by King **EDWARD I** of England to dominate Wales after its conquest.

JAMES, Arthur Lloyd
(1884-1943)
Scholar, Professor of Phonetics at London University from 1933; adviser on correct pronunciation to the BBC.

JAMES, Daniel (Gwyrosydd)
(1847-1920)
Poet, an iron-worker by trade, best known for the words of the hymn "Calon Lan".

JAMES, Evan (Ieuan ab Iago)
(1809-78)
Poet from Pontypridd, a weaver by trade, who wrote the words of the Welsh national anthem, "Hen Wlad fy Nhadau", the tune being composed by his son, **James JAMES**. It came into popular use following its inclusion in the Llangollen Eisteddfod of 1858.

JAMES, Ivor
(c.1840-1909)
First Registrar of the University of Wales (1895-1906), a supporter of the campaign for a University College in South Wales; author on Welsh language and history.

JAMES, James (Iago ap Ieuan)
(1833-1902)
Harpist and composer, son of **Evan JAMES**. A tavern-keeper by trade, he wrote the music to the Welsh national anthem, matching his father's words.

JAMES, John (Ioan Meirion)
(1815-51)
Author in English and Welsh, editor of "Y Cymro" in London 1850-51; a member of the Commission of Enquiry into education in Wales which produced the controversial "Blue Books" report in 1847.

JAMES, Robert (Jeduthyn)
(1825-79)
Singer and composer of church music, brother-in-law of **Joseph PARRY**; best known for the hymn tune, "Aberafan".

JAMES, Thomas
(c.1593-1635)
Explorer, an associate of **Thomas BUTTON**. He was employed by Bristol merchants as navigator in an expedition to find the north-west passage. The crew survived an Arctic winter and returned home.

JEFFREYS, George ("Judge Jeffreys")
(1645-89)
Lawyer, who gained his reputation for harshness as a judge during the reign of King James II. Knighted in 1677, he was made a judge in 1678, a baronet in 1681, Lord Chief Justice in 1683 and Lord Chancellor in 1685. In the latter year he was created 1st Baron Jeffreys of Wem (the title died out with his son). His career was dominated by bitter professional rivalry with Sir **William WILLIAMS (1)**. He fell from office when the King was deposed in 1688, and died a prisoner in the Tower of London.

JENKINS, David
(1848-1913)
Composer, Professor of Music at the University College of Wales, Aberystwyth, 1910-13. Works include "Yr ystorm" and "The

psalm of life" (which was performed at Crystal Palace in 1895), as well as the popular hymn-tune, "Penlan".

JENKINS, John (Ifor Ceri)
(1770-1829)

Clergyman, vicar of Kerry, Montgomeryshire, 1807-29. He founded the provincial eisteddfodau which began at Carmarthen in 1819, and was a collector of Welsh airs, which were later published by **Maria Jane WILLIAMS**.

JENKINS, Leoline
(1625-85)

Lawyer and diplomat; benefactor of educational institutions, including Cowbridge School where he was educated. He was rewarded for his Royalist service in the Civil War by King **CHARLES II**, becoming a judge and a Fellow of Jesus College, Oxford in 1660. As Principal (1661-73), he built and endowed the college library.

JENKINS, Thomas (1)
(1774-1843)

Radical poet, one of the leading figures in the movement which brought about the "Rebecca Riots".

JENKINS, Thomas (2) John Price
(1864-1922)

International rugby player, who founded the London Welsh Football Club while working as a physician in London.

JENKINS, Walter
(c.1600-61)

One of the first Welsh Quakers, imprisoned for his beliefs in 1660. His home at Pant in Monmouthshire became a Quaker meeting house.

JESSE or JESSEY, Henry
(1601-63)

English clergyman, associate of **Walter**

CRADOC; co-founder of the first Welsh Independent church at Llanfaches (1639).

JOAN (1) or JOANNA
(c.1195-1237)

Wife of **LLYWELYN Fawr**; mother of **DAFYDD ap Llywelyn** and **ELEN (2)**. As an illegitimate daughter of King John (later legitimised by order of her half-brother, King Henry III of England), she played an important diplomatic role in Anglo-Welsh relations. Her imprisonment by her husband from 1230 to 1232, supposedly for an affair with **William de BRAOSE (2)**, ended in reconciliation; on her death, he founded the Franciscan friary at Llanfaes in her memory.

JOAN (2) ("The Fair Maid of Kent")
(1328-85)

Countess of Kent in her own right, Princess of Wales by her marriage to **EDWARD of Woodstock**, and mother of King **RICHARD II**; she was directly descended from both **LLYWELYN Fawr** and King **EDWARD I**.

JOHN AP JOHN
(c.1625-97)

Independent minister, converted to Quakerism by Fox in 1653; founder of Quaker meeting-places throughout Wales.

JOHN OF WALES (Johannes Wallensis)
(c.1230-83)

Franciscan friar, author of works in Latin, mostly on theology. He was involved in Archbishop **PECHAM**'s diplomatic mission to **LLYWELYN ap Gruffydd**.

JOHN, Augustus
(1878-1961)

Painter, mostly of portraits, famous for his unconventional lifestyle; brother of **Gwen JOHN**. He travelled widely, was a close associate of **Dylan THOMAS**, and wrote an autobiography in two volumes. His best-known works include studies of Shaw, Thomas Hardy, and the cellist, Madame Suggia.

JOHN, Edward Thomas
(1857-1931)
Industrialist, Liberal MP for East Denbighshire 1910-18, tireless campaigner for Welsh self-government. He began his career at Middlesbrough, and managed the Dinsdale iron-works. Opposing conscription during World War I, he joined the Labour Party, but was always a political outsider.

JOHN, Gwen
(1876-1939)
Painter, sister of **Augustus JOHN**, who considered her talent greater than his own; mistress of the sculptor Rodin.

JOHN, William Goscombe
(1860-1952)
Sculptor. As a boy, he assisted his father, the craftsman Thomas John, in the decoration of Cardiff Castle, and later became well known for his portrait heads of famous people.

JOHNS, Thomas
See **JONES, Thomas (1)**.

JONES, Alfred Lewis
(1845-1909)
Shipping magnate, knighted in 1901. He founded the British Cotton Growing Association, and assisted the Chamberlain government in developing trade with the West Indies, also sponsoring the study of tropical medicine.

JONES, Alice Gray (Ceridwen Peris)
(1852-1943)
Journalist, poet and author, an early feminist; editor of the women's magazine, "Y Gymraes", 1896-1919.

JONES, Alun Jeremiah (Alun Cilie)
(1897-1975)
Poet, son of **Jeremiah JONES**; youngest and possibly most accomplished member of the extraordinary family who lived at Y Cilie, a Cardiganshire farm. His works include "cywyddau" and "englynion" on the subject of rural life.

JONES, Arthur (Arthur Machen)
(1863-1947)
Journalist, actor, author and translator. Works such as "The hill of dreams" (1907) and "The great return" (1915) reflect his interest in Arthurian legend, ancient religion, and the supernatural.

JONES, Daniel (1)
(1811-61)
Mormon convert, present at the death of Joseph Smith. He returned to Wales from the USA as a missionary, and in the period 1845-56 made many converts, some of whom travelled with him to Salt Lake City, Utah.

JONES, Daniel (2) Jenkin
(1912-93)
Composer, a childhood friend of **Dylan THOMAS**, many of whose poems he set to music. Other works include three symphonies, eight string quartets, and a set of tone poems, "Scenes from the Mabinogion" (1946).

JONES, David (1)
(1796-1841)
Missionary in Madagascar from 1818. He helped translate the Bible into Malagasy, and worked with David Johns to establish the orthography of the language.

JONES, David (2) Watkin (Dafydd Morgannwg)
(1832-1905)
Poet, best known for the textbook, "Yr

ysgol farddol" (1869) and grammar, "Yr ysgol Gymreig". He also wrote "Hanes Morgannwg" (1874), a history of Glamorgan.

JONES, David **(3) Brynmor**
(1852-1921)
Lawyer, brother of John **Viriamu JONES (10)** and **Leif JONES**; Liberal MP for Swansea 1895-1914. Knighted in 1906, he became a member of the Privy Council in 1912. He was co-author of "The Welsh people" (1900).

JONES, David (4) Michael
(1895-1974)
English-born poet, essayist and painter, of the "Anglo-Welsh" literary school. His experiences in World War I are recorded in his best-known poem, "In parenthesis" (1937). As an artist, he was closely associated with Eric Gill.

JONES, David (5) James **(Gwenallt)**
(1899-1968)
Poet, twice winner of the Chair at the National Eisteddfod (1926 and 1931). His experiences as a conscientious objector during World War I are described in the novel, "Plasau'r Brenin" (1934). A founder member of Yr Academi Gymreig (the Welsh Academy), he was the first editor of its occasional publication, "Taliesin", 1961-5.

JONES, Edward (1)
(c.1560-86)
An associate of **Thomas SALUSBURY**, involved with him in the Babington Plot of 1586. He was executed for treason, and his estate of Plas Cadwgan in Denbighshire was forfeit.

JONES, Edward (2) (Bardd y Brenin)
(1752-1824)
Harpist, honorary bard to the Prince of Wales from 1790 to 1820, and resident for part of this time at St James's Palace. He continued in this role after the Prince became King **GEORGE IV**, publishing three important collections of Welsh music, and was present at the Gorsedd held on Primrose Hill in 1792.

JONES, Elizabeth Mary **(Moelona)**
(1878-1953)
Novelist and translator, best known for "Teulu bach Nantoer" (1913). She wrote for adults and children, and in stories such as "Alys Morgan" (1911), reveals herself as a supporter of women's rights.

JONES, Elwyn
See also **ELWYN-JONES, Frederick**.

JONES, Elwyn
(1923-82)
Playwright and author, associated with successful television drama, such as "Softly, softly". He also wrote documentaries, including "The Ripper file" (1975) and "Death trials" (1981).

JONES, Ernest
(1879-1958)
Psychoanalyst, an associate of Freud (whose biography he wrote (1953-7)); founder of the British Psycho-analytical Society (1913). He was also interested in politics, becoming an early member of Plaid Cymru. His first wife was the composer, **Morfydd Llwyn OWEN**.

JONES, Evan (Ieuan Gwynedd)
(1820-52)
Independent minister, Radical journalist and poet; editor of " Y Gymrac" and "Adolygydd", periodicals subsidised by **Lady LLANOVER**.

JONES, Gareth Richard Vaughan
(1905-35)
Foreign affairs secretary to **David LLOYD**

GEORGE 1930-33. He later worked for the "Western Mail", and was murdered while travelling in Mongolia.

JONES, Griffith
See **JONES, John (1)**.

JONES, Griffith (1) (Llanddowror)
(1683-1761)
Preacher who began as a schoolmaster at Laugharne under the auspices of the SPCK, and in 1731 established the first of a network of circulating schools which resulted in the spread of literacy throughout Wales. He married the sister of his greatest benefactor, Sir **John PHILIPPS**, also winning support for his movement from **Howell HARRIS** and financial assistance from Madam **Bridget BEVAN**.

JONES, Griffith (2) Hugh (Gutyn Arfon)
(1849-1919)
Composer, conductor and music teacher; best known for the hymn-tune, "Llef".

JONES, Griffith (3) Rhys (Caradog)
(1834-97)
Founder and conductor of "Cor Caradog" and other choirs in Aberdare and Treorchy. He conducted a massed choir at Crystal Palace in 1872, which later sang for the Prince and Princess of Wales.

JONES, Henry
(1852-1922)
Philosopher and academic, a professor at various Welsh and Scottish universities 1884-1922. An educational reformer, he was instrumental in the passing of the Intermediate Education Act 1889, and helped devise recruitment propaganda in World War I.

JONES, Hugh Robert
(1894-1930)
Founder of Byddin Ymreolaeth Cymru (the "Home Rule Army") (1921), which developed into the Welsh Nationalist Party, of which he was the first Secretary. A quarryman before World War I, he later worked for the Co-operative Society and founded the periodical "Y ddraig goch".

JONES, Jack
(1884-1970)
Novelist and playwright who served in World War I, followed many professions and stood as a Liberal candidate for Parliament before becoming well-known for books such as "Rhondda roundabout" (1934) and "Off to Philadelphia in the morning" (based on the life of **Joseph PARRY**) (1947). Other works include three volumes of autobiography and a biography of **David LLOYD GEORGE**.

JONES, Jenkin
(c.1700-42)
Arminian minister, author and translator; founder of the first Arminian chapel in Wales (1733).

JONES, Jeremiah
(1855-1902)
Poet, founder of a dynasty of poets known as "Bois y Cilie" at his farm in Cardiganshire. Six of his seven sons and several grandchildren inherited his literary talent.

JONES, John (1) (St) or Griffith
(1559-98)
Franciscan friar and Catholic martyr, arrested on his return to England from Rome in 1594 and eventually executed; canonised in 1970.

JONES, John (2) (Maesygarnedd; "the regicide")
(c.1590-1660)
Colonel of Horse in the Parliamentarian army during the Civil War, MP for Merioneth and Denbighshire; one of two

Welshmen who signed the death warrant of King **CHARLES I**. A leading Puritan, he married Oliver Cromwell's sister in 1656. He served as Commissioner for Ireland during the Protectorate, but was executed following the Restoration.

JONES, John (3) Rice
(1759-1824)
First Attorney-General of the Territory of Indiana, having emigrated from Wales in 1784; instrumental in the admission of Indiana, Illinois and Missouri as states of the Union.

JONES, John (4) Richard
(1765-1822)
Baptist minister and author, founder of the "Scottish Baptists" sect; composer of the hymn-tune, "Ramoth".

JONES, John (5) (Jac Glan-y-gors)
(1766-1821)
Poet and political pamphleteer in the Welsh language. He took various jobs, and was a leader of the London Welsh community. His character, "Dic Sion Dafydd", represents the type of Welshman who denies his national identity.

JONES, John (6) (Tegid)
(1792-1852)
Clergyman, translator and poet. He adapted the orthography devised for the Welsh language by **William OWEN PUGHE** and obtained the patronage of **Lady LLAN-OVER**. His views, as expressed in "A defence of the reformed system of Welsh orthography", were initially controversial, but his orthography was accepted by the Society of Cymmrodorion.

JONES, John (7) (Talysarn)
(1796-1857)
Calvinist preacher, generally regarded as one of the greatest in the history of Wales.

JONES, John (8) (Talhaiarn)
(1810-69)
Poet and architect who lived in England and France but wrote in Welsh, collaborating with John Owen on the popular song, "Mae Robin yn swil". Other works include English lyrics such as "Watching the wheat".

JONES, John (9) (Shoni Sguborfawr)
(c.1811-60)
One of the leaders of the Rebecca Riots. Known as a drunkard and criminal, he was paid to take part in the riots at Pontyberem, and was transported to Australia for life in 1844, but conditionally pardoned in 1858.

JONES, John (10) Viriamu
(1856-1901)
Scientist, brother of David **Brynmor JONES (3)** and **Leif JONES**. He was the first principal of University College, Cardiff (1883) and the first vice-chancellor of the University of Wales (1895-6). He became a Fellow of the Royal Society in 1894.

JONES, John (11) Puleston
(1862-1925)
Blind Calvinistic Methodist minister and author, co-founder of Cymdeithas **DAFYDD ap Gwilym** at Oxford in 1886; deviser of a Welsh version of the Braille system. Rejected for his pacifist views during World War I, he regained respect after the war, and campaigned on behalf of the Coalition Government.

JONES, John (12) Edward
(1905-70)
Secretary and organiser of Plaid Cymru 1930-62. He joined the party as a student at the University College of Bangor, and orchestrated the campaign of 1935-6 against the bombing school at Llyn. Besides his political activities, he wrote books on travel and gardening, and became a television personality. He was killed in a car accident during the 1970 election campaign.

JONES, John (13) Robert
(1911-70)
Professor of Philosophy at University College, Swansea, 1952-70, author of "Ac onide" (1970), a collection of essays about the position of Wales in the twentieth century. He conceived the term "cydymdreiddiad tir ac iaith" to summarise the essence of Welsh nationality.

JONES, Josiah Towyn
(1858-1925)
Congregational minister, Liberal MP for East Carmarthenshire and later Llanelli 1912-22. Despite his opposition to conscription in World War I, he took Government office in 1917 as a Whip and Junior Lord of the Treasury.

JONES, Leifchild Stratten
(1862-1939)
Liberal MP for various English constituencies 1905-18, 1923-4 and 1929-31, created Baron Rhayader in 1932; brother of **David Brynmor JONES (3)** and John **Viriamu JONES (10)**.

JONES, Lewis (1) ("the church-building parson")
(1793-1866)
Clergyman responsible for building eighteen churches and schools, to all of which he appointed Welsh clergymen.

JONES, Lewis (2)
(1836-1904)
Author, co-editor of "Pwnsh Cymraeg", who joined the Welsh Colony movement and travelled to Patagonia in 1862. The colonists, misled by his glowing description of the country, rejected him, and he worked in Buenos Aires 1865-7, returning to serve as governor and publish two Welsh language newspapers in the colony.

JONES, Lewis (3)
(1897-1939)
Communist miners' leader, involved in the General Strike of 1926 and the hunger marches of the 1930s; author of the novels "Cwmardy" (1937) and "We live" (1939), which portrayed life in mining communities.

JONES, Lowry
(1623-94)
Niece and ward of **John JONES (2)**. She married, firstly, in 1639, Ellis **WYNNE (5)*** of Glyn, and secondly, after his death in 1653, Edward Prys (grandson of **Edmwnd PRYS**). Their son, Edmund Price, inherited Maesygarnedd.

JONES, Mary
(1784-1872)
Daughter of a weaver in a rural area of Merionethshire, who became famous at the age of sixteen for walking twenty-five miles in her bare feet to buy a Welsh Bible with her life savings. She was an inspiration to **Thomas CHARLES** in his work for the British and Foreign Bible Society, and her story continues to be used as an example.

JONES, Michael Daniel
(1822-98)
Independent minister, scholar, and politician, Principal of Bala Independent College 1853-92. In 1865, inspired by a visit to the USA, he was responsible for the Welsh settlement in Patagonia in Argentina, known as "Y Wladfa". His purpose was to unite Welsh emigrants in a community where their native language and culture could be preserved. He was forced to sell his home to finance the venture, but is today regarded as a founder of the Nationalist movement.

JONES, Owen (1) (Owain Myfyr)
(1741-1814)
Co-founder of the Gwyneddigion society (1770), while working in London as a

skinner. In collaboration with **William OWEN PUGHE**, he edited the work of **DAFYDD ap Gwilym** for the society in 1789, and funded other publications.

JONES, Owen (2)
(1809-74)
Architect, son of **Owen JONES (1)**. As Superintendent of Works for the Great Exhibition of 1851, he was responsible for the decoration of the Crystal Palace, and was also the designer of St James's Hall.

JONES, Philip
(1618-74)
Colonel in the Parliamentarian army during the Civil War, second in command at the Battle of St Fagans (1648) and afterwards governor of Cardiff Castle, where he entertained Cromwell in 1649. He was made a peer, purchased Fonmon Castle, and became a member of Cromwell's Council of State and a Commissioner under the Propagation (of the Gospel) Act of 1650, but survived the Restoration.

JONES, Pryce
See **PRYCE-JONES, Pryce**.

JONES or JOHNES, Richard (1)
(c.1540-1602)
Printer of Welsh and English books in London from 1564.

JONES, Richard (2)
(c.1787-1855)
Printer and publisher, founder of the "Gomerian Press". His presses at Dolgellau, Pontypool, Merthyr Tydfil, Machynlleth and Llanfyllin produced several periodicals, Bibles, and an English-Welsh dictionary (1815).

JONES, Robert
See also **ARMSTRONG-JONES, Robert; DERFEL, R(obert) J(ones); GWYN, Robert**.

JONES, Robert (1)
(1560-1615)
Jesuit priest, founder of the Welsh Jesuit College at Llanrothal. As Vice-Prefect of the Jesuit Mission in England and Wales in 1609-13, he sent many pupils from the Welsh Borders to train as priests at Valladolid and Douai.

JONES, Robert (2)
(c.1706-42)
Great-grandson of **Philip JONES**. At his home, Fonmon Castle, he often entertained the Wesley brothers.

JONES, Robert (3) Ambrose (Emrys ap Iwan)
(1851-1906)
Calvinistic Methodist minister, author and literary critic, whose published sermons are Welsh classics. He was an outspoken opponent of the "English fever" which led his denomination to establish English-language chapels in an attempt to attract immigrants, and a supporter of Home Rule, which he called "ymreolaeth".

JONES, Robert (4)
(1857-1933)
Orthopaedic surgeon, first President of the International Society of Orthopaedic Surgery and founder of an orthopaedic hospital at Baschurch, Salop (1904). He was responsible for advances in military surgery during World War I, and was created a baronet in 1926.

JONES, Robert (5) Thomas
(1874-1940)
Secretary of the North Wales Quarrymen's Union, instrumental in obtaining the "Quarrymen's Charter". He served as Labour MP for Caernarfonshire 1922-3 and was a supporter of home rule for Wales and of the Welsh language.

JONES, Simon Bartholomew
(1894-1966)
Minister and poet, a younger son of **Jeremiah JONES** of Y Cilie. He was a conscientious objector during World War I, and later won both the Crown (1933) and Chair (1936) at the National Eisteddfod.

JONES or **JOHNS, Thomas (1) (Twm Sion Cati)**
(c.1530-1609)
Gentleman of Carmarthenshire, a poet and genealogist and the subject of much folklore. His nickname came from his mother, Catherine or Cati, who was descended illegitimately from the **WYNN (1)*** family. He has been called "the Welsh Robin Hood", but his identification with contemporary highwaymen is unsubstantiated.

JONES, Thomas (2)
(1614-92)
Shropshire-born judge, later resident at Carreghwfa Hill, Montgomery. He was knighted in 1671, and held various offices before his impeachment in 1680 for apparent support of the future King James II. He later opposed James's actions as King, and was dismissed from office in 1686.

JONES, Thomas (3)
(c.1648-1713)
Printer and publisher, based in London and Shrewsbury, who produced works in Welsh including a Welsh-English dictionary (1688), a translation of the "Pilgrim's Progress", and the first Welsh almanac.

JONES, Thomas (4)
(c.1680-1731)
Lawyer, first Treasurer and Secretary of the "Society of Antient Britons", founded in London. He was knighted on the accession of King George I in 1715.

JONES, Thomas (5)
(1752-1820)
Clergyman, author and translator, involved with **Thomas CHARLES** in the setting up of the British and Foreign Bible Society. His best-known work, "The Welsh looking-glass" (1812), criticises the Calvinistic Methodists for leaving the Established Church.

JONES, Thomas (6)
(1756-1820)
Calvinistic Methodist minister, one of the first to be ordained; also a poet, author, hymnist and translator, whose works include an English-Welsh dictionary (1800), an autobiography, and the hymns, "Mi wn fod fy Mhrynwr yn fyw" and "O arwain fy enaid i'r dyfroedd". He was a close friend of, and great influence on, **Thomas CHARLES**.

JONES, Thomas (7) (T.J.)
(1870-1955)
Scholar, civil servant and author, founder of Coleg Harlech (1927). He helped set up the Welsh National Memorial Association to combat tuberculosis in 1910, while Secretary to the National Health Insurance Commissioners. He founded the monthly, "Welsh outlook" (1914), and played a leading role in the establishment of the Arts Council. As Deputy Secretary to the Cabinet 1916-30, he was close to **David LLOYD GEORGE**, opposing the aims of Plaid Cymru.

JONES, Thomas (8) Artemus
(1871-1943)
Journalist and lawyer, involved in a famous libel case against the publishers Hutton & Co in 1908. He served as a county court judge 1930-42, was knighted in 1931, and helped achieve recognition of the Welsh language in court.

JONES, Thomas (9) Gwynn (Tir-na-n'Og)
(1871-1949)
Journalist, poet, novelist, biographer, play-

wright and translator, Professor of Welsh Literature at the University College of Wales, Aberystwyth, 1919-37. His poem, "Ymadawiad Arthur" won the Chair at the National Eisteddfod of 1902, signalling a revival in Welsh literature. Much of his work draws on Celtic legend.

JONES, William (1)
(1566-1640)
Judge, legal adviser to Sir **John WYNN** and MP for Beaumaris and Caernarfonshire. He was knighted in 1617, and was Lord Chief Justice of the King's Bench in Ireland until 1620. On his return, he rebuilt the family home at Castellmarch.

JONES, William (2)
(c.1675-1749)
Mathematician who obtained the patronage of the **BULKELEY*** family, and later of the Earl of Macclesfield. An associate of Newton and Halley, he became a Fellow of the Royal Society in 1712, and later its Vice-President.

JONES, William (3) Ellis (Cawrdaf)
(1795-1848)
Poet and artist, who travelled widely in Britain and Europe. His prose work, "Y bardd, neu'r meuddwy Cymreig" (1830), has been called "the first Welsh novel".

JONES, William (4)
(19th century; exact dates unknown).
One of the three leaders of the Chartist rally in Newport 1839 (along with **John FROST** and **Zephaniah WILLIAMS**); they were transported to Australia for their activities.

JUSTINIAN or STINAN
(6th century; exact dates unknown)
Saint associated with Ramsey Island. *Gave his name to:* Porth Stinan and Llanstinan, Dyfed.

K

KATHERINE OF ARAGON
(1485-1536)
Spanish princess, Princess of Wales by her marriage to **Arthur TUDOR**; later the first queen of King **HENRY VIII** and mother of **Mary TUDOR**. The nearest she ever came to Wales was Ludlow Castle. After their divorce, Henry attempted to placate her with the title "Dowager Princess of Wales".

KATHERINE OF VALOIS
(1401- 37)
Princess of France, Queen of England by her marriage of 1420 to King **HENRY V**. Their son, King Henry VI, was born a few months before his father's death in 1422, following which she lived in seclusion, entering into a secret marriage with the courtier, **Owen TUDOR**, in about 1428; their four or five children included **Edmund TUDOR** and **Jasper TUDOR**.

KATHERYN OF BERAIN (Katheryn Tudor; "Mam Gymru": "Mother of Wales")
(c.1534-91)
Noblewoman, nicknamed both for her philanthropy and her family connections. She was married four times, to John **SALUSBURY (1)***, **Richard CLOUGH**, Maurice **WYNN (1)*** (father of Sir **John WYNN**), and Edward **THELWALL***.

KAY-SHUTTLEWORTH, James
(1804-77)
English physician and educationist, responsible for the Commission on Education in Wales which produced the infamous report known as the "Blue Books" in 1837.

KEMBLE, John (St)
(c.1599-1679)
Catholic priest and martyr, executed as a result of the activities of **John ARNOLD**, in the wake of the "Popish Plot". He was canonised in 1970.

KEMSLEY, Viscount
See **BERRY, James (2)**.

KENYON, Lloyd
(1732-1802)
Lawyer and politician; Attorney-General 1782-84, Master of the Rolls 1784-88, and Lord Chief Justice of the King's Bench 1788. He was created Baron Kenyon of Gredington, Flintshire, in 1788.

KEYNE or CAIN
(5th-6th centuries; exact dates unknown)
Saint, daughter of **BRYCHAN**. The girls' names, Gaynor and Ceinwen, are derived from hers. *Gave her name to:* Llangeinor and Llangeinwen; also Keynsham, Somerset.

KILVERT, Francis
(1840-79)
English clergyman, curate of Clyro, near Brecon, and later vicar of Bredwardine. His diary of the years 1870-79 is famous for its vivid picture of contemporary village life.

KITCHIN, Anthony
(1477-1563)
Bishop of Llandaff 1545-63, who succeeded in retaining his position through the changes of religious opinion of the reigns of Edward VI, **Mary TUDOR** and Elizabeth I.

KNOVILL, Bogo de
(late 13th century; exact dates unknown)
First Justiciar of West Wales, appointed by King **EDWARD I** of England in 1280.

KYFFIN, Morris
(c.1555-98)
Soldier, poet and author. His translation of Bishop Jewel's "Apologia" for the Anglican faith was published as "Deffyniad Ffydd Eglwys Loegr" (1594).

KYFFIN, Richard
(c.1450-1502)
Lawyer and clergyman, supporter of **Henry TUDOR**.

L

"LADIES OF LLANGOLLEN"
See **BUTLER, Eleanor** and **PONSONBY, Sarah**.

LAUGHARNE, Rowland
(c.1610-76)
Successful Parliamentarian leader during the Civil War, who joined in the Royalist rebellion of 1648 and was defeated at the Battle of St Fagans.

LAWGOCH, Owain
See **OWAIN LAWGOCH**.

LAWRENCE, Thomas Edward ("Lawrence of Arabia")
(1888-1935)
Welsh-born soldier and scholar, of Anglo-Irish parentage. He gained notoriety for his activities in North Africa and the Middle East during World War I, but is also known for his books, especially "The seven pillars of wisdom" (1927).

LEE or LEGH, Rowland
(c.1490-1543)
Bishop of Lichfield appointed by King **HENRY VIII** of England to administer justice in Wales as President of the Welsh Council 1534-43. He conducted a heavy-handed campaign against crime in the border areas.

LELAND, John
(c.1506-52)
Royal antiquary of King **HENRY VIII** who journeyed through Wales in the period 1536-9, reporting on geographical and social conditions and leaving a valuable historical record.

LEONOWENS, Anna Harriette
(1834-1914)
Teacher, born in Caernarfon, famous for her stay in Siam where she tutored the children of King Mongkut. Her memoirs (1870) became the basis of a successful film, "Anna and the King of Siam", and a musical play, "The King and I".

LESTRANGE, Hawise
(c.1230-80)
Norman wife of **GRUFFYDD ap Gwenwynwyn**, an active participant in his plot to assassinate **LLYWELYN ap Gruffydd** in 1274, with the support of her family; sister of **Roger LESTRANGE**.

LESTRANGE, Roger
(c.1230-1311)
Norman knight, brother of **Hawise LESTRANGE**. He was involved in **EDWARD I**'s Welsh campaign of 1282, and reported the death of **LLYWELYN ap Gruffydd**.

LEWES, Watkin
(1740-1821)
Lawyer, knighted in 1773; prominent in London civic life as Lord Mayor 1780 and MP for the City of London 1780-96.

LEWIS AP IEUAN (Lewis Byford)
(c.1360-1410)
Bishop of Bangor 1404-8, a leading supporter of **OWAIN Glyndwr**.

LEWIS GLYN COTHI (Llywelyn y Glyn)
(c.1420-90)
Poet, at one time outlawed for his support of the **TUDOR*** family; probably the main author of the "White Book of Hergest" (now lost).

LEWIS OF CAERLEON
(c.1450-1500)
Scholar, skilled in mathematics, medicine and theology; royal physician under **Henry TUDOR**. [Sometimes confused with Bishop Lewis Charlton, who lived a century earlier.]

LEWIS, David (1)
(c.1520-84)
Lawyer and MP for Monmouthshire under Queen Elizabeth I; first Principal of Jesus College, Oxford, 1571-72.

LEWIS, David (St) (2) (Charles Baker)
(1617-79)
Jesuit priest, implicated in the "Popish Plot" of 1678. At the instigation of **John ARNOLD**, he was tried and executed. He was canonised in 1970.

LEWIS, Eiluned
(1900-79)
Journalist, poet and novelist, assistant editor of the "Sunday Times" 1931-36; best known for the 1934 novel, "Dew on the grass".

LEWIS, Francis
(1713-1802)
Merchant who emigrated to America and was one of the signatories of the American Declaration of Independence.

LEWIS, George Cornewall
(1806-63)
English-born baronet, son of **Thomas Frankland LEWIS (1)**; Liberal MP for Herefordshire 1847-52 and for Radnor Boroughs 1855-63, Chancellor of the Exchequer 1855-58 and Home Secretary 1859-61.

LEWIS, John Herbert
(1858-1933)
Liberal MP for various constituencies 1892-1922. He became minister of Education in 1916, and was knighted in 1922.

LEWIS, Lewis (Lewsyn yr Heliwr, Lewis the Huntsman; Lewsyn Shanco Lewis)
(c.1793-1850)
Leader of the miners' protest march in 1831 which gave rise to the "Merthyr Riots", during which some demonstrators were killed by troops from the Highland regiment. He was arrested and condemned to death, along with **Dic PENDERYN**, but the sentence was commuted to transportation.

LEWIS, Owen or OWEN, Lewis
(1533-95)
Catholic priest, founder of the English College in Rome (1578).

LEWIS, Richard
See **PENDERYN, Dic.**

LEWIS, John Saunders
(1893-1985)
Catholic writer and academic, co-founder of Plaid Cymru (1925) and later its President. His experiences in World War I, combined with contemporary events in Ireland, led him towards nationalism. Works include plays in English and Welsh, and an appreciation of **William WILLIAMS (2)**. In 1936, along with **Lewis VALENTINE**, and **David J WILLIAMS (5)**, he started a fire at an air base in Penrhos, for which he was arrested and imprisoned, losing his lecturing post at the University College of Swansea. In the 1960s, he advocated militant action to ensure the future of the Welsh language, resulting in the activities of Cymdeithas yr Iaith Gymraeg. In 1970, he was nominated for the Nobel Prize for Literature.

LEWIS, Thomas (1) Frankland
(1780-1855)
Politician, a member of the **LEWIS (1)*** family; MP for Beaumaris, Radnorshire, and an Irish constituency between 1812 and 1834, and for Radnor 1847-55. He was succeeded as Chairman of the Poor Law

Commission by his son, **George Corn-ewall LEWIS**, and was created a baronet in 1846.

LEWIS, Thomas (2)
(1881-1945)
Cardiologist, a pioneer of the electrocardiogram and a specialist in clinical science; founder and first chairman of the Medical Research Society (1930). He spent his entire career at University College Hospital, London, and was knighted in 1921.

LEWIS, William Thomas
(1837-1914)
Industrialist who dominated the Coalowners' Association and controlled Cardiff docks. In 1875, he chaired the committee appointed to administer the Sliding Scale for the determination of miners' wages, which continued in operation until 1898. He was created Baron Merthyr of Senghenydd in 1911.

LHUYD, Edward
(1660-1709)
Scientist and researcher, assistant keeper of the Ashmolean Museum on its foundation in 1683 and a pioneer in the studies of palaeontology and philology. He travelled throughout Wales for five years, accumulating data for a historical geography of the country, "Archaeologica Britannica" (1707), one of the first works to study the origins of Welsh and its relationship with other Celtic languages. Only one volume was published during his lifetime.

LIFRIS OF LLANCARFAN
(11th-12th century; exact dates unknown)
Teacher at a "clas" or monastic school at Llancarfan, the author of a life of St **CADOG**.

LLANOVER, Baron
See **HALL, Benjamin (2)**.

LLANOVER, Lady (formerly Augusta HALL) (Gwenynen Gwent)
(1802-96)
Heiress to the Llanover estate, wife of Sir **Benjamin HALL (2)**. Under the influence of **Thomas PRICE (1)**, she learned Welsh, becoming an important patron of the arts in Wales, and "designed" what is now regarded as traditional Welsh costume. The first Welsh language periodical aimed at women, "Y Gymraes" (1850), was founded under her patronage. Other interests included cookery (on which she published a book) and folk music; she encouraged the production and use of the traditional Welsh triple harp.

LLAWDDOG or LLEUDDAD
(6th-7th centuries; exact dates unknown)
Saint, son of a king of Bryn Buga (Usk). *Gave his name to:* Llanllawddog, Dyfed, and Llauddad, Llyn.

LLEWELLYN
See **LLYWELYN**.

LLEWELLYN, Dillwyn
See **DILLWYN-LLEWELLYN, John**.

LLEWELLYN, Richard (Richard Llewellyn Lloyd)
(1907-83)
Author of novels in English with a Welsh theme, the best-known of which, "How green was my valley" (1939), immortalised the way of life of the South Wales mining communities.

LLOYD, Thomas Alwyn
(1881-1960)
Architect and town planner. He designed new villages, municipal housing, school and hospital buildings, etc, throughout Wales and England.

LLOYD, Charles (1)
(1602-61)
Leading military engineer under King

CHARLES I, knighted 1644; a member of the **LLOYD (1)*** family of Leighton.

LLOYD, Charles (2) ("the banker")
(1748-1828)
Co-founder of Taylor's and Lloyd's, Birmingham's first bank; a descendant of the **LLOYD (2)*** family. The Lloyd interest was later transferred to London, and remains one of Britain's five major banks.

LLOYD, Evan
(1800-79)
Publisher, founder of the firm of "John and Evan Lloyd", with his brother John (c.1799-1860). Between 1833 and 1840, they published various periodicals at Mold, including the Radical journal, "Cronicl yr oes".

LLOYD, Henry (Henry Humphrey Evans)
(c.1720-83)
Military draughtsman and engineer, a Jacobite sympathiser who attempted unsuccessfully to raise support in Wales for the rebellion of 1745; also the author of two major works on military history.

LLOYD, John (1) (St)
(c.1630-79)
Catholic priest captured in a family home following the "Popish Plot" of 1678, and executed; canonised in 1970.

LLOYD, John (2) ("the philosopher")
(1749-1815)
Lawyer and politician, owner of the estates of Wigfair and Hafodunos and of a huge library; correspondent of Herschel, **Thomas PENNANT**, **Hester THRALE**, and others.

LLOYD, John (3) Edward
(1861-1947)
Wales' greatest historian, author of "A history of Wales from the earliest times to the Edwardian conquest" (1911), "Owen Glendower" (1931.), and other works of his-

torical scholarship; knighted 1934. He also edited the first edition of the Welsh Dictionary of Biography (1950).

LLOYD, Ludovic
(c.1550-1610)
Poet and courtier, favoured by Queen Elizabeth I and Sergeant-at-Arms under King James I/VI.

LLOYD, Marmaduke
(c.1585-1651)
Royalist lawyer and judge, founder of the **LLOYD (4)*** family; knighted in 1622.

LLOYD, Richard (1)
(1606-76)
Royalist lawyer, Attorney General for North Wales 1641-3. He was knighted in 1643, and became Governor of Holt Castle 1644-47, surrendering to **Thomas MYTTON**. He went into exile until the Restoration, serving as MP for Cardiff and Radnorshire 1660-76.

LLOYD, Richard (2)
(1834-1917)
Minister of the Church of the Disciples of Christ (the "Campbellites") at Criccieth; uncle of **David LLOYD GEORGE**, whom he brought up.

LLOYD, Richard Llewellyn
See **LLEWELLYN, Richard**.

LLOYD, Robert (Llwyd o'r Bryn)
(1888-1961)
Author, originator of the phrase, "Y pethe" ("The things"), which expresses the complex make-up of Welsh culture.

LLOYD (née BOWEN), Sarah
(1727-1807)
First "matron" of the Trefecca family. **Howell HARRIS** opposed her marriage.

LLOYD, Thomas
(1640-94)
Quaker, who emigrated to America to escape persecution and served as deputy governor of Pennsylvania 1684-93.

LLOYD, Vaughan
(1736-1817)
Artillery commander, involved in the Battle of Minden (1759); later a general and commander of the Woolwich Arsenal.

LLOYD, William (1)
(1627-1717)
Bishop of St Asaph 1680-92, one of the "Seven Bishops" who petitioned King James II.

LLOYD, William (2)
(1637-1710)
Bishop of Llandaff 1675-9. Though not one of the "Seven Bishops", he shared their views and after the revolution of 1688, became leader of the "Nonjurors".

LLOYD GEORGE, David ("The Welsh Wizard")
(1863-1945)
Liberal politician, MP for Caernarfon 1890-1945 and Prime Minister 1916-22. As Chancellor of the Exchequer 1908-15, he introduced old age pensions. A national hero at the close of World War I, his popularity declined in the years of economic depression that followed, his party ceasing to dominate the Coalition Government elected in 1918. Once in power, he abandoned his early support for Welsh self-government. The Council of Action for Peace and Reconstruction of 1935 was his last major initiative. He retained a following in Wales, and was created Earl Lloyd-George of Dwyfor in the year of his death. After the death of his first wife, Margaret, he married his secretary, Frances Stevenson, in 1943.

LLOYD GEORGE, Gwilym
(1894-1967)
Liberal MP for Pembrokeshire 1929-50, first Welshman to hold the post of Minister of Welsh Affairs (1954-7); son of **David LLOYD GEORGE**. He was created Viscount Tenby of Bulford in 1957.

LLOYD GEORGE, Megan
(1902-66)
Liberal MP for Anglesey 1929-51, the first woman MP in Wales; daughter of **David LLOYD GEORGE**. She later joined the Labour Party, becoming MP for Carmarthen from 1957 until her death.

LLOYD-JONES, David Martyn
(1899-1981)
Presbyterian minister and author, originally a physician; best known for his long association with Westminster Chapel, London.

LLOYD PRICE, Richard John
See **PRICE, Richard John Lloyd**

LLWYD, Dafydd ("of Mathavarn")
(c.1395-1486)
Prolific poet, whose works include the only known life of St **TYDECHO**. He was a supporter of **Henry TUDOR**, whose victory at Bosworth he supposedly prophesied.

LLWYD, Gruffydd (Gruffydd ap Rhys ap Gruffydd ap Ednyfed)
(1260-1335)
Knight, advisor to King **EDWARD II**. Though descended from **EDNYFED Fychan**, he was loyal to the English Crown from his entry into the service of **EDWARD I** in 1283, and held several official posts, carrying out a valuable diplomatic role in Wales and raising troops for military campaigns abroad. In 1321, he assisted the King in putting down the rebellion of **Roger MORTIMER (2)** and captured Chirk.

LLWYD, Humphrey
(1527-68)
Physician and topographer whose maps of England and Wales (the first separately published maps of Wales) were published after his death by Ortelius, largely by the influence of his friend, **Richard CLOUGH**.

LLWYD, Morgan
(1619-59)
Itinerant Puritan preacher, converted by **Walter CRADOC**; Parliamentarian supporter, member of the "Fifth Monarchist" sect, and author of "Llyfr y tri aderyn" (1653).

LLYWARCH AP BRAN
(12th century; exact dates unknown)
Steward and brother-in-law to **OWAIN Gwynedd** (his wife was sister of **CRISTIN**); founder of one of the "fifteen noble tribes of Gwynedd".

LLYWARCH AP LLYWELYN (Prydydd y Moch, "Poet of the Pigs")
(c.1150-1220)
Court poet of Gwynedd in the time of **LLYWELYN Fawr**. His "Canu mawr" and "Canu fach" (the "long poem" and "short poem") are both addressed to Llywelyn.

LLYWARCH HEN
(6th century; exact dates unknown)
Legendary prince, cousin of **URIEN Rheged** and an ancestor of the princes of Gwynedd.

LLYWELYN AP GRUFFYDD
See **LLYWELYN BREN**.

LLYWELYN AP GRUFFYDD (Llywelyn y Llyw Olaf, Llywelyn the Last)
(c.1230-1282)
Prince of Gwynedd who successfully dispossessed his three brothers (the sons of **GRUFFYDD ap Llywelyn (2)**) in the cause of a united Wales, and at one point controlled most of the country, using the title "Prince of Wales" originated by his uncle, **DAFYDD ap Llywelyn**. He formed an alliance with Simon de Montfort (whose daughter he married) during the reign of King Henry III of England, and held out for some years against King **EDWARD I**'s incursions. He was eventually killed in a skirmish at Irfon Bridge after giving support to a rebellion instigated by his brother, **DAFYDD ap Gruffydd**. With his death, the independence of Gwynedd was effectively lost.

LLYWELYN AP IORWERTH
See **LLYWELYN Fawr**.

LLYWELYN AP SEISYLL
(c.990-1023)
Ruler of Gwynedd from his defeat of Aeddan ap Blegyrwyd in 1018 until his own murder.

LLYWELYN BREN (Llywelyn ap Gruffydd)
(c.1265-1317)
South Wales nobleman who revolted against Pain de **TURBERVILLE (1)***, the Norman Lord of Morgannwg, in 1316, winning support as a result of famine in the Glamorgan area and unsuccessfully besieging Caerphilly Castle. Defeated by the army of **EDWARD II** under **Humphrey de BOHUN (3)**, he himself was executed, but many of his supporters escaped punishment. [Sometimes confusingly called Llywelyn ap Rhys.]

LLYWELYN FAWR (Llywelyn the Great)
(1173-1240)
Prince of Gwynedd and effective ruler of Wales, though he never took the title Prince of Wales. Son of **IORWERTH Drwyndwn**, he joined his cousins, Gruffydd and Maredudd ap Cynan, to repossess the lands

held by his uncles, **RHODRI ab Owain** and **DAFYDD ab Owain**, later inheriting Gruffydd's own lands and becoming sole ruler of Gwynedd by 1201. He maintained peace with England throughout most of his reign, marrying in 1201 **JOAN (1)**, daughter of King John; she acted as an intermediary in times of strife. He subdued his rivals within Wales, notably **GWENWYNWYN** of Powys, so as to unite the country under one dominant ruler, recognised as overlord by the other princes. Having rejected the Welsh tradition of dividing a man's lands equally between all his sons, he was succeeded by **DAFYDD ap Llywelyn**, his son by Joan, despite the protests of his elder, illegitimate, son, **GRUFFYDD ap Llywelyn (2)**.

LLYWELYN SION (Llywelyn of Llangewydd)
(c.1540-1615)
Poet and copyist of manuscripts, such as the "Long book of Shrewsbury" and "Long book of Llanharan". He was instrumental in preserving the work of many minor poets.

LLYWELYN Y GLYN
See **LEWIS Glyn Cothi**.

LONDRES, Maurice de
See **MAURICE de Londres**.

LOYD, Lewis
(1767-1858)
Founder of the banking firm of Jones, Loyd & Co (later incorporated into the London and Westminster Bank).

LYNN-THOMAS, John
(1861-1939)
First consulting surgeon in Wales, specialising in the thyroid. He served at the Welsh Hospital in South Africa, founded the Prince of Wales Hospital, Cardiff, and was knighted in 1919.

M

MABON
See **ABRAHAM, William**.

MACCLESFIELD, Earl of
See **GERARD, Charles**.

MACHEN, Arthur
See **JONES, Arthur**.

MACKWORTH, Humphrey
(1657-1727)
Shropshire barrister; knighted in 1683. He married Mary **EVANS (3)*** of the Gnoll, Neath, heiress to her family's coal-mining interests, which he developed, constructing the first tramroad in Wales and building furnaces for smelting. He co-founded the Society for the Promotion of Christian Knowledge (SPCK) in 1699 and was Tory MP for Cardiganshire 1701-5. The financial scandal surrounding the Company of Mine Adventurers, formed in 1704, affected his career.

MADDOCKS (née THOMAS), Ann ("The Maid of Cefn Ydfa")
(1704-27)
Heiress, of Llangynwyd, Glamorgan. The legend that she was forced to marry Anthony Maddocks in 1725, whilst really in love with the poet **Wil HOPCYN**, and died of a broken heart, has no basis in the known facts.

MADOC
See also **AIDAN**.

MADOC or MADOG
(12th century; exact dates unknown)
Legendary Welsh prince reputed to have discovered America in 1170. One of the many sons of **OWAIN Gwynedd**, forced to leave Wales by the civil war which broke out after his father's death, he is reputed to have sailed from Gwynedd and arrived in Alabama, becoming the forefather of a tribe of white Indians.

MADOCKS, William Alexander
(1773-1828)
Industrialist and Radical politician, MP for Boston 1802-18 and Chippenham 1820-6, who spent much of his fortune on improving conditions in his native North Wales. Tremadoc, which he built, and Porthmadog are named after him.

MADOG AP GRUFFYDD
(c.1170-1236)
Prince of northern Powys (named Powys Fadog in his honour) and founder of Valle Crucis abbey (1201), son of **GRUFFYDD Maelor (1)** and grandson of **OWAIN Gwynedd**. He allied himself with **LLYWELYN Fawr**, except for the period 1211-15.

MADOG AP GWALLTER
(late 13th century; exact dates unknown)
Franciscan friar and poet, best known for "Geni Crist", sometimes described as the first Welsh Christmas carol.

MADOG AP LLYWELYN
(c.1260-1300)
Descendant of **OWAIN Gwynedd** who led the great rebellion of 1294-5 in North Wales, assuming the title Prince of Wales. Having supported the English Crown, he had fought a legal action against **LLYWELYN ap Gruffydd** to regain his father's estate, but after Llywelyn's death he assumed the role of national leader because of his royal blood. After his defeat at Mais Meidog in 1295, his fate is unknown.

MADOG AP MAREDUDD

(c.1110-1160)

Prince of Powys 1132-60, a grandson of **BLEDDYN ap Cynfyn**. He enjoyed some military successes against his Norman neighbours, maintaining the independence of Powys and achieving unity, but joined the English King Henry II in attacking **OWAIN Gwynedd**, whose dominance he resented.

MAELGWN AP RHYS

(c.1170-1231)

Lord of Ceredigion, son of **RHYS ap Gruffydd (1)**. In 1199 he gave up Cardigan Castle to win the favour of King John, an act for which he was reviled. He lost most of his lands to **LLYWELYN Fawr** in 1207, but later became his ally. From 1216 he ruled Deheubarth jointly with his brother, **RHYS Gryg**, and two nephews.

MAELGWN GWYNEDD (Maelgwn Hir, "the Tall")

(c.490-549)

Prince who gave his name to the principality of Gwynedd, extending and consolidating its power. A pupil of St **ILLTUD** and contemporary of **GILDAS**, he is criticised by the latter for crimes including the murder of his wife; yet he was a benefactor of the Church, donating land on which St **CYBI** and St **DEINIOL** built their foundations. **NENNIUS** describes his death from plague.

MAGNUS MAXIMUS (Macsen Wledig)

(c.335-388)

Spanish Celt who was declared Emperor of Rome by his troops in Britain, and held on to the title for five years, until defeated and killed by Theodosius I. According to legend, as described in the "Mabinogion", he took as his wife **ELEN (1)**, daughter of a Caernarfon chieftain. He is believed to have been responsible for the withdrawal of Roman troops from Wales, which was left self-governing. Many Welsh royal families subsequently claimed descent from him.

MAINWARING, William Henry

(1884-1971)

Militant miners' leader, co-author of the "Miners' next step" document (1912) and a tutor in economics at the Central Labour College; Labour MP for Rhondda East 1933-59.

MALDWYN, Deborah

See **HUGHES, Jane**.

MALO

See **MECHELL**.

MANSEL

See **MANSELL**.

MANSEL, Bussy

(1623-99)

Gentleman of Briton Ferry in Glamorgan, a relation of the **MANSEL*** family of Margam, who married the widow of Sir **Edward STRADLING (3)**. He served as MP for Glamorgan 1679-98.

MANSEL, Rice

(c.1490-1559)

Knight who obtained the buildings of Margam Abbey following the dissolution of the monastery in 1536, and founded the Margam branch of the **MANSEL*** family.

MANSEL, Robert

(1573-1656)

Admiral, knighted for his service at Cadiz. Besides being Vice-Admiral of England 1618-20, he was MP for various constituencies between 1601 and 1628, including Carmarthen and Glamorgan. In 1620, he led an expedition against Algerian pirates. His interests included the manufacture of glass, and he set up several works in England and Wales.

MANSEL, Thomas

(1667-1723)

Fifth baronet **MANSEL***, MP for Cardiff

1689-98 and Glamorgan 1699-1711. He belonged to the circle of Swift and **Robert HARLEY**; **Edward LHUYD** dedicated his work to him. He was created Baron Mansel of Margam in 1712, also serving as Controller of the Household to Queen Anne.

MAP, Walter
(c.1140-1209)
Clergyman, possibly Welsh, an associate of **GERALD of Wales**. His book, "De nugis curialium", is a miscellany of fact and fiction, much of the material having a Welsh connection.

MAREDUDD AB OWAIN
(c.935-99)
Grandson of **HYWEL Dda**. He inherited Deheubarth from his father, Owain ap Hywel, in about 986, having already conquered and lost Gwynedd. His attempted conquest of Powys was unsuccessful, but he held off attempted invasions by the English and the Danes, as well as other Welsh rulers.

MAREDUDD AP RHYS GRYG
(c.1230-71)
Prince of Deheubarth, younger son of **RHYS Gryg**. On his father's death, he inherited lands including Llandovery and Dryslwyn castle, but quarrelled with his brother, Rhys Mechyll. At first an ally and supporter of **LLYWELYN ap Gruffydd**, he withdrew his support in 1259 and was imprisoned by Llywelyn at Criccieth until he agreed to pay homage to him in 1261.

MARQUAND, Hilary Adair
(1901-72)
Professor of Industrial Relations at Cardiff University College, whose industrial and economic surveys of South Wales in 1932 highlighted the depressed conditions in the area. In 1945, he became Labour MP for Cardiff East, and immediately joined the Government as Secretary for Overseas Trade 1945-7.

MARSH, John
(1747-95)
Publisher, son of **Richard MARSH** and his successor as owner of a printing press at Wrexham. His publications included "Tracts of Powys" (1795) by **Philip YORKE**.

MARSH, Richard
(c.1710-92)
Bookseller and publisher, owner of a press at Wrexham from around 1755, producing mainly cheap booklets and ballads.

MARSHAL, Gilbert
(c.1205-41)
4th Earl of Pembroke, younger brother and successor of **William MARSHAL (2)** and **Richard MARSHAL**. He was also granted Carmarthen and Cardigan by King Henry III of England.

MARSHAL, Richard
(c.1200-34)
Earl of Pembroke in succession to his brother, **William MARSHAL (2)**; one of the leaders of the English barons in their resistance to King Henry III, he fought alongside **LLYWELYN Fawr** in 1233-4, capturing Usk and other South Wales strongholds.

MARSHAL, William (1)
(c.1146-1219)
First **MARSHAL*** Earl of Pembroke, by his marriage to Isabel, Countess of Strigoil and Pembroke, daughter of **Richard de CLARE**. He fell from favour with King John in 1207, but was restored in 1211 and fought successfully against **LLYWELYN Fawr**, marrying John's daughter and becoming regent of England after his death. Under the Peace of Worcester in 1218, he gave up the custody of the royal castles to Llywelyn.

MARSHAL, William (2)
(c.1190-1231)
Earl of Pembroke, first of the five sons of **William MARSHAL (1)** to bear the title. An enemy of **LLYWELYN Fawr**, he recaptured some of his father's lost territories in 1223.

MARY I
See **TUDOR, Mary**.

MARY OF TECK (May of Teck)
(1867-1953)
Princess of Wales and queen of King **GEORGE V**. The daughter of the Duke of Wurttemberg, she was engaged in 1891 to Prince Albert, eldest son of the future King **EDWARD VII**, but he died after a few months. In 1895, she married his younger brother, becoming Princess of Wales on the death of Queen Victoria in 1901 and Queen in 1910. Her five children included **EDWARD, Duke of Windsor**, and King George VI.

MATHEW
See **MATHEWS**.

MATHEWS, Abraham
(1832-99)
Congregational minister, one of the first Welsh settlers in Patagonia in 1865, author of an unbiased history of the colony entitled "Hanes y wladfa Gymreig" (1894).

MATHEWS, Thomas
(1676-1751)
Vice-admiral, descended from the **MATHEW*** family of Llandaff; commander-in-chief at the battle of Toulon (1744) and MP for Glamorgan 1745-7.

MAURICE de Londres.
(12th century; exact dates unknown)
Norman lord of Cydweli (Kidwelly),

involved in suppressing the rebellion of 1136.

MAURICE, William
(c.1600-80)
Antiquary, a collector of manuscripts, most of which were destroyed in a fire at Wynnstay (home of the **WILLIAMS-WYNN** family) in 1858. He also acquired manuscripts on behalf of his friend, **Robert VAUGHAN (1)**.

MECHELL or MALO
(c.590-640)
Saint, born and brought up in Llancarfan, Glamorgan; later Alet in Brittany. *Gave his name to:* Llanfechell, Anglesey; St Malo, Brittany.

MEILYR BRYDYDD
(c.1100-37)
Court poet of **GRUFFYDD ap Cynan**; first of the "Gogynfeirdd" or "early poets", and founder of a poetic dynasty. *Gave his name to:* Trefeilyr, Anglesey.

MELANGELL or MONACELLA
(c.550-590)
Irish princess, patron saint of small animals; founder of a convent in Montgomeryshire.*Gave her name to:* Pennant Melangell.

MELCHETT, Baron
See **MOND, Alfred**.

MERFYN FRYCH ("the freckled")
(c.790-844)
A descendant of **CUNEDDA**, ruler of Gwynedd from about 825. His marriage to **NEST (1)** resulted in his son, **RHODRI Mawr**, inheriting Powys and becoming ruler of most of Wales.

MERLIN
See **MYRDDIN**.

MERRICK, Rice (Rhys Meurig)
(c.1520-87)
Historian and genealogist, author of "A book of Glamorganshire antiquities" (1578). He collaborated with Sir **Edward STRADLING (2)**.

MERTHYR of Senghenydd, Baron
See **LEWIS, William** Thomas

MEYRICK, Gelly or **Gilly**
(c.1556-1601)
Soldier, son of **Rowland MEYRICK** and a follower of **Robert DEVEREUX**, Earl of Essex, who knighted him in 1596 at Cadiz. He owned Wigmore Castle, which was obtained for him by Essex, but was executed after the latter's rebellion against Queen Elizabeth I.

MEYRICK, John
(c.1590-1659)
Soldier, a nephew of Sir **Gelly MEYRICK**; knighted in 1614. He served under the 3rd Earl of Essex and Gustavus Adolphus. As MP for Newcastle-under-Lyme, he supported Parliament during the Civil War. His descendants owned the estate of Bush in Pembrokeshire until 1837.

MEYRICK, Rowland
(1505-66)
Protestant Bishop of Bangor 1559-66, favoured by King James I; founder of the Pembrokeshire branch of the **MEYRICK*** family, through his marriage to Catherine Barrett of Gellisant.

MIDLETON, MIDDLETON
See **MYDDELTON**.

MILES, John
(1621-83)
Baptist leader, founder of the first Baptist church at Ilston in Glamorgan. In 1663, he emigrated to America to avoid religious persecution, founding the settlement of Swanzey in Massachusetts.

MILLAND, Ray (Reginald Truscott-Jones)
(1908-86)
Film actor born in Neath. He won the Academy Award for Best Actor for his performance in "The lost weekend" (1946), but his later career was mediocre.

MITTON, Thomas
See **MYTTON, Thomas**.

MONACELLA
See **MELANGELL**.

MOND, Alfred Moritz
(1868-1930)
Founder of the Mond nickel works at Clydach (1902), the largest in the world at the time. He was Liberal MP for Swansea 1910-23 and Carmarthen 1924-8 before entering the House of Lords as 1st Baron Melchett, and was Minister of Health 1922. From his interests came ICI (1926), of which he was the first chairman.

MONTFORT, Eleanor de
(1252-1282)
Princess of Gwynedd, wife of **LLYWELYN ap Gruffydd** and daughter of Simon de Montfort, Earl of Leicester. Her marriage was contracted after the death of her father ended his alliance with Llywelyn, which had brought no benefit to Wales. King **EDWARD I** of England, her first cousin, kidnapped her in 1275, and used her as a hostage to force concessions from Llywelyn before allowing their wedding to take place in 1278. She died giving birth to a daughter, **GWENLLIAN (2)**.

MONTGOMERY, Arnulf (de)
(c.1060-1110)
Son of **Roger de MONTGOMERY**, heir to

his territory of Dyfed. In 1102, he forfeited the lordship of Pembroke by joining the rebellion of his brother, **ROBERT of Belleme**.

MONTGOMERY, Roger (de)
(c.1030-94)
Norman lord, created Earl of Shrewsbury in 1070. He built a castle at Trefaldwyn, and renamed the town after himself. *Gave his name to:* Montgomery, Montgomeryshire.

MORGAN AP MAREDUDD
(13th century; exact dates unknown)
Disinherited prince of south-east Wales, who rebelled against King **EDWARD I** of England in 1294, at the same time as **MADOG ap Llywelyn** in the North, and successfully drove out **Gilbert de CLARE (3)**. After the failure of the rebellion, he was pardoned and given an official post.

MORGAN FYCHAN
(c.1220-88)
Lord of Avan Wallia (Nedd-Afan), son of **MORGAN Gam**; founder of the de Avene family, with its seat at Baglan, and ancestor of the **EVANS (3)*** and **WILLIAMS (1)*** families.

MORGAN GAM
(c.1190-1241)
Lord of Avan Wallia (Nedd-Afan), descended from **IFOR ap Cadifor**. He succeeded to the lordship in 1213, and supported **LLYWELYN Fawr**, opposing the **CLARE*** lords of Glamorgan but marrying his daughter into the **TURBERVILLE (1)*** family.

MORGAN HEN AB OWAIN
(c.900-75)
King of Morgannwg from about 930, the kingdom at that time including Gwent. He was on good terms with the Saxons.

MORGAN MWYNFAWR (Morgan ab Athrwys; "the benefactor")
(7th or 8th century; exact dates unknown)
King of South Wales, who ruled an area roughly equivalent to Glamorgan. *Gave his name to:* Morgannwg (Glamorgan).

MORGAN, Charles (1)
(c.1575-1643)
Soldier, nephew of Sir **Thomas MORGAN (1)**; knighted in 1603. He served in Flanders and Cadiz under **Robert DEVEREUX**, Earl of Essex, and later fought on behalf of the Protestants in the Netherlands and Denmark, taking part in the Siege of Breda (1637).

MORGAN, Charles (2) Godfrey
(1831-1913)
2nd Baron and 1st Viscount Tredegar (1905). He served in the Crimean War, taking part in the Charge of the Light Brigade, and was Conservative MP for Brecknock 1858-75.

MORGAN, George Osborne
(1826-97)
Barrister, Liberal MP for Denbighshire 1868-97 and chairman of the Welsh Parliamentary party 1894-7, Queen's Counsel in 1869, created a baronet in 1892. Himself an Anglican, he was nevertheless a vocal campaigner for Disestablishment, and worked with **Hugh OWEN (2)** for the establishment of the University of Wales.

MORGAN, Godfrey
See **MORGAN, Charles (2)**.

MORGAN, Griffith (Guto Nyth Bran)
(1700-37)
Glamorgan athlete, subject of popular legend, who reputedly died suddenly after winning a twelve-mile race.

MORGAN, Gwenllian (Miss Philip Morgan)
(1852-1939)
The first woman to serve as a borough councillor (and later mayor) in Wales; also an amateur historian, she studied the life of the poet **Henry VAUGHAN**.

MORGAN, Henry
(c.1635-88)
Buccaneer who made his fortune in the West Indies, serving the Jamaican government as a privateer against the Spaniards. He was famous for his capture of Panama in 1671, but was temporarily imprisoned in England following the disgrace of his employer, Sir Thomas Modyford. In 1674, having gained the favour of King **CHARLES II**, he was knighted and made Deputy Governor of Jamaica, where he established the estates of Lanrumney and Pencarn.

MORGAN, John (1) (Y Marchog Tcw)
(c.1420-92)
Supporter of **Henry TUDOR**, knighted by him and made constable of Newport.

MORGAN or YO(U)NG, John (2)
(c.1450-1504)
Bishop of St David's 1496-1504, responsible for the building of the episcopal throne in the cathedral there; a strong supporter of **Henry TUDOR**.

MORGAN, John (3) ("of Matchin")
(1688-1733)
Clergyman, poet and translator, active in London Welsh society from 1713, when he became curate of Matchin(g) in Essex. His prose work, "Myfyrdodau bucheddol ar y pedwar peth diweddaf" (1714) became a minor classic.

MORGAN, John (4)
(1929-88)
Journalist and broadcaster, who wrote and reported on Welsh issues. He was a founder director of HTV, Independent Television for Wales and the West of England.

MORGAN, Morien Bedford
(1912-78)
Aeronautics engineer, knighted 1969. Based at the Aero Flight research establishment in 1935-48, he was later Controller of Aircraft and Controller of Guided Weapons at the Ministry of Aviation. He was Director of the Royal Aircraft Establishment, Farnborough, 1969-72 and Master of Downing College, Cambridge, 1972-8.

MORGAN, Richard Humphreys
(1850-99)
Calvinistic Methodist minister and author, adapter of Pitman's shorthand method for the Welsh language (1878).

MORGAN, Robert
(1608-73)
Bishop of Bangor 1666-73, involved in the restoration of the cathedral, in which he installed an organ; an opponent of Puritanism.

MORGAN, Thomas (1) (The Warrior)
(c.1542-95)
Soldier who fought in the Netherlands for the Protestant cause, and was knighted in 1587. He later served as Governor of Flushing and Bergen-op-Zoom.

MORGAN, Thomas (2)
(c.1543-1611)
Secretary to Mary, Queen of Scots, involved in the Ridolfi and Throgmorton Plots, and instigator of the Babington Plot of 1586 (while imprisoned in the Bastille by King Henry III of France). He continued to support the Stuarts, but in 1605 was imprisoned on a conspiracy charge; his subsequent fate is unknown.

MORGAN, Thomas (3) ("the Dwarf")
(1604-79)
Soldier, veteran of the Thirty Years' War, commander-in-chief of the Parliament forces in south-east Wales during the Civil War. He was involved in the capture of Raglan Castle in 1646, and was knighted by Richard Cromwell in 1658. After the Restoration, he was created a baronet (1661) and served as Governor of Jersey (1665-79).

MORGAN, Thomas (4) ("the general")
(1702-69)
MP for Brecon 1723-4, Monmouthshire 1734-47, and Brecknock 1747-69; also Judge Advocate-General 1741-68; head of the Rhiwpera branch of the **MORGAN (1)*** family.

MORGAN, William (1)
(1545-1604)
Protestant Bishop of Llandaff 1595-1601 and St Asaph 1601-4. A brilliant Hebrew scholar, sponsored by the **WYNN (1)*** family, he was encouraged by John Whitgift, Archbishop of Canterbury, in his task of translating the Bible into Welsh (1588), an achievement which had major significance for the survival and development of the Welsh language.

MORGAN, William (2) ("the judge")
(c.1600-49)
Lawyer, King's Attorney for South Wales 1639-49 and MP for Brecknock 1640-9. His daughter, Blanche, married her first cousin, William Morgan, in 1661; the estate thus passed to the Tredegar branch of the **MORGAN (1)*** family.

MORGAN, William (3) ("Y Bardd")
(1819-78)
Poet, initiator of the "cymanfa ganu" movement (1859).

MORGANEU
(c.950-999)
Bishop of St David's, killed in the last Viking raid on Wales.

MORGANWG
See **IOLO Morganwg**.

MORRIS
See also **MORYS**.

MORRIS, David
(1630- 1703)
Roman Catholic priest, involved in the "Popish Plot" of 1680, during which he gave false evidence against the Jesuits before the Privy Council.

MORRIS, John (1)
(1706-40)
Sailor, youngest brother of **Lewis MORRIS (1)**, killed in action in Spain, during the attack on Cartagena.

MORRIS, John (2)
(1745-1819)
Industrialist, son of **Robert MORRIS**. He built the village of Morriston in about 1770, with the help of the architect **William EDWARDS (1)**. He was created a baronet in 1806, and in the following year was the driving force behind the opening of the Mumbles railway, the first passenger railway in the world. *Gave his name to:* Morriston (district of West Glamorgan).

MORRIS, Lewis (1) (Llewelyn Ddu o Fôn)
(1701-65)
Eldest of the four Morris brothers of Anglesey ("Morrisiaid Môn"). A surveyor, he published the "Plans of the Harbours, Bays and Roads in St George's and the Bristol Channel" (1748), based on work done for the Navy Office. In 1746 he became a Crown official and collector of

tolls in Cardiganshire, and suffered financially. He was a successful poet, remembered especially for his "penillion", and attempted a revision of the "Dictionarium" of **John DAVIES (2)** and a dictionary of Welsh place names.

MORRIS, Lewis (2)
(1833-1907)
Popular poet of the "Anglo-Welsh" school, descendant of **Lewis MORRIS (1)**. He campaigned for the University of Wales, and was knighted in 1895, but failed to win the post of Poet Laureate because Queen Victoria disapproved of his associations with the circle of Oscar Wilde. His best-known poem, "Gwen" (1880), is set in the Tywi valley.

MORRIS, Richard
(1703-79)
Folklorist, younger brother of **Lewis MORRIS (1)**. He worked in London as a clerk and court interpreter, and by 1757 was Chief Clerk to the Comptroller of the Navy. A collector and editor of Welsh manuscripts, he founded the Cymmrodorion Society for the London Welsh in 1751.

MORRIS, Robert
(c.1700-68)
Industrialist, owner of the copper works at Landore in Swansea, and founder of a community near the present-day Morriston, which was named after his son, **John MORRIS (2)**.

MORRIS, William (1)
(1705-63)
Botanist, brother of **John MORRIS (1)**, **Lewis MORRIS (1)**, and **Richard MORRIS**. A customs officer by profession, he differed from his brothers by remaining in Anglesey, and left behind an important collection of letters.

MORRIS, William (2)
(c.1800-75)
Educationist, assistant to the Education Commissioners of 1846-7; a prime mover in the setting up of Calvinistic Methodist Sunday schools, and editor of a periodical, "Yr Athraw", for their use.

MORRIS-JONES, John
(1864-1929)
Professor of Welsh at the University College of North Wales, Bangor, 1895-1929, knighted in 1918. His works, "Welsh orthography" (1893) and "Welsh grammar" (1913), added to the status of the language. He was an accomplished poet, co-founder of Cymdeithas **DAFYDD ap Gwilym** at Oxford (1886) and founder and editor of the literary journal, "Y beirniad" (1911-19).

MORTIMER, Edmund (de)
(c.1376-1409)
Youngest brother of **Roger MORTIMER (5)**, captured in 1402 by the forces of **OWAIN Glyndwr**. King Henry IV, aware of his superior claim to the English throne, failed to ransom him, and he allied himself with Glyndwr, marrying one of his daughters, Catherine. By his own family links with Henry Percy ("Hotspur"), he encouraged the latter to join the alliance, and in 1405 the three embarked on the "Tri-partite Indenture", a plan to overthrow the English King, but his untimely death, following Hotspur's defeat, put an end to Glyndwr's hopes.

MORTIMER, Ralph (de)
(c.1200-1246)
Norman lord, 5th Baron Wigmore. He became the second husband of **GWLADUS Ddu** in 1230, thus allying himself with her father, **LLYWELYN Fawr**.

MORTIMER, Roger (de) (1)
(1231-82)
6th Baron Wigmore 1246-82, son of **Ralph**

(de) MORTIMER and **GWLADUS Ddu**; the enemy and later ally of **LLYWELYN ap Gruffydd**, an alliance eventually used by his sons to lure Llywelyn to his death. By his marriage to Matilda **(de) BRAOSE***, he greatly extended the family's Welsh territories.

MORTIMER, Roger (de) (2)
(c.1256-1326)
Lord of Chirk, son of **Roger MORTIMER (1)**. He took Chirk, originally the property of Llywelyn Fychan, in 1282. As Justice of Wales 1308-15, under King **EDWARD II**, he opposed the **DESPENSER*** family, but was defeated at Shrewsbury in 1322, and died a prisoner in the Tower of London.

MORTIMER, Roger (de) (3)
(1287-1330)
Norman lord of Wigmore, grandson of **Roger (de) MORTIMER (1)**; Earl of March from 1328. He formed an alliance with his uncle, **Roger (de) MORTIMER (2)**, to oppose the powerful **DESPENSER*** family. The lover of Isabella of France, Queen of King **EDWARD II** of England, he played a part in Edward's murder, became Justice of Wales 1326-30, and effectively ruled England during the minority of King **EDWARD III** (believed by popular rumour to be his son), until convicted of treason and executed.

MORTIMER, Roger (de) (4)
(c.1327-60)
Grandson of **Roger (de) MORTIMER (3)**, whose lands he recovered. He acquired the lordships of Radnor and Ceri, and was knighted by **EDWARD of Woodstock** in 1346 and created 2nd Earl of March in 1355.

MORTIMER, Roger (de) (5)
(1374-98)
4th Earl of March and 4th Earl of Ulster,

descended on his mother's side from King **EDWARD III**. The childless King **RICHARD II** made him his heir. By the time of his death at the Battle of Kells, he held sixteen Welsh lordships, including Denbigh, Usk and Caerleon.

MORUS
See **MORRIS, MORYS**.

MORYS, Hugh (Eos Ceiriog)
(1622-1709)
Prolific poet in Welsh and English, connected with the **MYDDELTON*** family. A Royalist supporter during the Civil War, his work reflected the political climate. Many of his poems were set to music, and he developed new verse-forms making use of the traditional 'cynghanedd'.

MOSTYN, Roger (1)
(1560-1642)
Lawyer, MP for Flintshire 1621-2; knighted 1606. He married into the **WYNN (1)*** familyr, becoming involved in the dispute between his father-in-law, Sir **John WYNN** and Bishop **William MORGAN (1)**.

MOSTYN, Roger (2)
(1624-90)
Soldier, a Royalist supporter in the Civil War, a colonel at the age of twenty, and later governor of Flint. He was created a baronet on the Restoration of the monarchy in 1660, and acquired lead and coal mines in Flintshire.

MOSTYN, Savage
(c.1705-1757)
Admiral, of the **MOSTYN (2)*** family. He held the positions of Vice-Admiral of the Blue, Comptroller of the Navy, Lord of the Admiralty, and Constable of Flint Castle.

MOSTYN, Thomas
(c.1651-1700)

2nd baronet **MOSTYN (1)***, MP for Caernarfonshire 1673-81; a patron of the arts and an associate of Bishop **William LLOYD (1)**.

MUTTON, Peter or Piers
(1565-1637)

Lawyer, who served as a judge and HM Attorney in Wales and the Marches; MP for Denbighshire 1604 and Caernarfonshire 1624, knighted in 1622. A letter to his mother in Welsh is one of the earliest surviving in the language.

MYDDELTON, Hugh
(1560-1631)

Goldsmith, son of **Richard MYDDELTON (1)**. Like his elder brother **Thomas MYDDELTON (1)**, he prospered in London, and initiated the "New River" project (1609-13) for bringing fresh water to the city. He was MP for Denbigh 1603-28, and was created a baronet in 1622. Much of his income came from lead-mines in Cardiganshire.

MYDDELTON, Richard (1)
(c.1508-75)

Governor of Denbigh Castle and MP for Denbigh, founder of the **MYDDELTON*** dynasty through his nine sons.

MYDDELTON, Richard (2)
(1654-1716)

Fourth baronet **MYDDELTON***, elected thirteen times as MP for Denbighshire 1685-1716.

MYDDELTON, Thomas (1)
(1550-1631)

Merchant, son of **Richard MYDDELTON (1)**. It was in London that he made his fortune, becoming a shareholder in the East India and Virginia Companies, a knight (1603), and later Lord Mayor. He helped **Rowland HEYLIN** finance the re-printing of the Bible in 1630, and served as MP for Merioneth. In 1595 he bought Chirk Castle and the lordship of Chirk.

MYDDELTON, Thomas (2)
(1586-1667)

MP for Weymouth 1624 and Denbighshire 1625, son and heir of **Thomas MYDDELTON (1)**. He was knighted in 1617, and in 1633 added Ruthin Castle to the family's assets. A Parliamentary commander during the Civil War, he was later instrumental in the Restoration of **CHARLES II**.

MYDDELTON, William (Gwilym Ganoldref)
(c.1556-1603)

Poet and sea captain, son of **Richard MYDDELTON (1)**. He served the **HERBERT (2)*** family until around 1580, and died overseas. His Welsh translation of the Psalms was published posthumously by **Thomas SALUSBURY**, and his manual on poetry (1593) is a landmark in Welsh literary history. Other works included a bardic handbook, "Bardhoniaeth" (1593-4). According to **Thomas PENNANT**, he was one of the first men to smoke tobacco in public.

MYRDDIN or MERLIN
(6th century; exact dates unknown)

Legendary prophet and magician associated with King **ARTHUR**. His life is recorded by **GEOFFREY of Monmouth** in the "Vita Merlini", but he was probably Geoffrey's own invention, possibly an amalgamation of characters from folk tradition.

MYTTON or MITTON, Thomas
(1608-56)

Colonel in the Parliamentary forces commanded by **Thomas MYDDELTON (2)** during the Civil War. He succeeded Myddelton as commander as a result of the "Self-denying Ordinance" of 1645.

N

NASH, John
(1752-1835)
Architect, who designed parts of St David's Cathedral, but is chiefly known for his work on Regent Street, Regent's Park and the Marble Arch in London and the rebuilding of Brighton Pavilion for King **GEORGE IV**.

NASH, Richard ("Beau" Nash)
(1674-1761)
Lawyer and architect, born in Swansea, known as "the King of Bath", where he lived by gaming and enforced his own rules of conduct on public life.

NASH-WILLIAMS, Victor Erle
(1897-1955)
Archaeologist, a specialist in the Roman period; Keeper of Archaeology at the National Museum of Wales.

NENNIUS
(8th century; exact dates unknown)
Historian based in South Wales; his "Historia Brittonum" is one of the main sources of information about the Dark Ages in Britain, much of it of doubtful veracity.

NEST (1)
(9th century; exact dates unknown)
Princess of Powys, daughter of Cadell ap Brochwel, sister of **CYNGEN** and wife of **MERFYN Frych**.

NEST (2) ("The Helen of Wales")
(c.1080-1115)
Daughter of **RHYS ap Tewdwr** and sister of **GRUFFYDD ap Rhys (1)**; heiress to the lordship of Carew (Caerau). Following her father's death, she was given in marriage by her guardian, King Henry I of England (who had already fathered her illegitimate son) to **GERALD of Windsor**. A famous beauty, she gained notoriety by eloping in 1109 with **OWAIN ap Cadwgan** during a raid on the castle of Cenarth Bychan (possibly Cilgerran). Following her husband's death, she had liaisons with other men, notably Stephen, the Constable of Caernarfon Castle (hence some of her children bore the name Fitzstephen).

NEUFMARCHE or NEWMARCH, Bernard de
(c.1050-1125)
Norman lord of Brycheiniog (Brecon) from about 1093. He began his conquest of the territory after participating in the rebellion against King William II of England in 1088, and was helped by infighting among the native princes. He delegated the custody of strategic areas to lesser lords.

NEVILLE, Anne
(1456-85)
Daughter of Richard Neville, Earl of Warwick (Warwick the Kingmaker). Following her father's quarrel with the Yorkist faction during the Wars of the Roses, she was married to **EDWARD of Westminster**, thus becoming Princess of Wales. After his death, she became the wife and later Queen of her childhood friend, King Richard III of England.

NEWMARCH, Bernard of
See **NEUFMARCHE, Bernard of**.

NICHOL, William
(c.1500-58)
One of the three Protestant martyrs executed in Wales during the reign of **Mary TUDOR**.

NICHOLAS, Jemima
(1750-1832)
Working-class woman of Fishguard whose courageous conduct during the attempted French invasion of 1797 won her the title of "the Pembrokeshire heroine".

NICHOLAS, Thomas Evan (Niclas y Glais)
(1878-1971)
Congregational minister (later a practising dentist), poet and Welsh editor of the Labour newspaper, the "Merthyr Pioneer"; a founder-member of the British Communist Party. During World War II, he was imprisoned for his political activities, and produced a volume of "Prison sonnets".

NICHOLLS, Erith Gwyn
(1875-1939)
English-born rugby player, captain of the Welsh international team, and author of "The modern rugby game and how to play it" (1916). He is commemorated by the gates of Cardiff Arms Park, erected in 1949.

NITHSDALE, Countess of
See **HERBERT, Winifred**.

NON or NONNA
(late 5th century; exact dates unknown)
Saint, reputedly the mother of St **DAVID** by Sant or Sanctus, King of Ceredigion. *Gave her name to:* places in Wales, Brittany, and the West Country.

NOTT, William
(1782-1845)
Soldier, knighted for his role as commander of the force which defeated the Afghans at Ghuznee in 1842.

NOVELLO (formerly DAVIES), Ivor
(1893-1951)
Actor-manager and musician, composer of operettas such as "King's Rhapsody", "The Dancing Years", and "Perchance to Dream"; son of **Clara Novello DAVIES**, whose stage name he adopted. His fame began with the World War I popular song, "Keep the home fires burning". After the War, he appeared in silent films in Britain and America, then embarked on a career as a playwright. During the World War II, he was imprisoned for an offence against the rationing regulations, but made a successful comeback.

O

OFFA
(c.730-96)

King of Mercia 757-796. He built an earthwork or "dyke" marking the boundary of Wales, in the years 784-795, during a period of peace between the Welsh and Saxons. *Gave his name to:* Offa's Dyke.

OGMORE, Baron
See **REES-WILLIAMS, David**.

OLIVERS, Thomas
(1725-99)

Methodist leader and author of religious tracts, best known for his hymns, "Come, immortal King of glory" and "The God of Abram praise". He was an associate of John Wesley, whose printing press in London he supervised from 1775 to 1789.

ORMSBY-GORE, William **David**
(1918-85)

5th Baron Harlech, British ambassador to the USA 1961-5, also associated with the television station HTV.

OSBWRN WYDDEL (Osborn the Irishman)
(late 13th century; exact dates unknown)

Ancestor of several landed families of Merioneth, such as **WYNNE (1)*** and **VAUGHAN (5)***. He was himself supposedly descended from **GERALD of Windsor**.

OUDOCEUS
See **EUDDOGWY**.

OWAIN AP CADWGAN
(c.1080-1116)

Prince of Powys, son of **CADWGAN ap Bleddyn**. In 1109, he abducted his cousin, **NEST (2)**, as a result of which Ceredigion was invaded by the Normans, Owain was forced to flee to Ireland, and his father's lands were lost. He returned and eventually won back part of Powys. While campaigning against **GRUFFYDD ap Rhys (1)**, he was killed by supporters of **GERALD of Windsor**.

OWAIN AP GRUFFYDD
See also **OWAIN CYFEILIOG; OWAIN GLYNDWR; OWAIN GOCH; OWAIN GWYNEDD**.

OWAIN BROGYNTYN
(c.1140-88)

Lord of Dinmael and Edeyrnion; son of **MADOG ap Maredudd**, brother of **GRUFFYDD Maelor (1)** and Owain Fychan. Despite his name, he never held Brogyntyn (Porkington).

OWAIN CYFEILIOG (Owain ap Gruffydd ap Maredudd)
(c.1130-97)

Prince of Powys, son-in-law of **OWAIN Gwynedd**; also a noted poet. He took his name from the commote of Cyfeiliog, which he ruled from 1149; later he ruled all southern Powys. He spent the end of his life at the Cistercian monastery of Ystrad Marchell (Strata Marcella), which he had founded in 1170, having handed over power to his son, **GWENWYNWYN**.

OWAIN GLYNDWR (Owain ap Gruffydd)
(c.1354-1417)

Powys nobleman, descended through his father from **RHYS ap Gruffydd (1)** and through his mother from the royal house of Deheubarth. In 1400, following an unsuccessful appeal to the English Crown and Parliament over a dispute with Lord

GREY* of Ruthin, he proclaimed himself Prince of Wales. With the aid of members of his family, he captured Conway Castle and in the course of several military successes, notably the Battle of Pilleth (1402), captured both Grey and **Edmund MORTIMER**, a claimant to the English throne, who became his son-in-law and ally. They formed alliances with Henry Percy ("Hotspur") and his father, the Earl of Northumberland; in the meantime, Glyndwr held court at Harlech Castle, held Parliaments at Machynlleth and Dolgellau, and was recognised by several foreign governments. Subsequent defeats by the English, commanded by the future **HENRY V**, resulted in his going into hiding in about 1410. His ultimate fate is unknown.

OWAIN GOCH (Owain ap Gruffydd)
(c.1219-82)
Eldest of the four sons of **GRUFFYDD ap Llywelyn (2)** and his wife **SENENA**, nicknamed "Goch" ("red") because of his colouring. After an unsuccessful conflict with his brother **LLYWELYN ap Gruffydd** in 1255, he was imprisoned for over twenty years, until granted a share in his brother's lands by the influence of King **EDWARD I** of England.

OWAIN GWYNEDD (1) (Owain ap Gruffydd ap Cynan; Owain Fawr)
(c.1100-1170)
Prince of Gwynedd, a younger son of **GRUFFYDD ap Cynan**, who ruled Gwynedd from his father's death in 1137 until his own death. His older brother and early ally, **CADWALLON (2)**, had died in 1132. In 1152 he exiled his younger brother, **CADWALADR ap Gruffydd**, after several episodes which revealed the latter's lack of judgment and honesty. Extending his authority to the borders of Powys, Owain gained control of Mold and Yale (Ial), and built his own castle at Buddugre. The accession of

Henry II to the English throne halted these advances, but Henry's attack on Gwynedd in 1157 (with the support of Cadwaladr) failed. Nevertheless, Owain deemed it prudent to make peace with Henry, and was forced to reinstate Cadwaladr. Later, his alliance with **RHYS ap Gruffydd (1)** united most of Wales against the English. On his death, however, bitter rivalry between his children by his two marriages (the second to **CRISTIN**) and other relationships resulted in much bloodshed and the loss of his territorial advantages.

OWAIN LAWGOCH ("Owain of the Red Hand", Owain ap Thomas ap Rhodri)
(c.1330-1378)
A great-grandson of **GRUFFYDD ap Llywelyn (2)** who, financed by the French King, attempted to restore Welsh independence, having been proclaimed Prince of Wales in his home county of Montgomeryshire. He was renowned for his military skills, and known to the French as "Yvain de Galles", but was assassinated by English agents before his mission to conquer Wales had properly begun.

OWEN TUDOR
See **TUDOR, Owen**.

OWEN, Aneurin
(1792-1851)
Scholar, an expert on ancient Welsh law and medieval history, editor of the laws of **HYWEL Dda**, and son of **William OWEN PUGHE**. He served as Assistant Poor Law Commissioner and Commissioner for the Enclosure of Common Lands, but his main activities were cultural.

OWEN, Daniel
(1836-95)
Novelist, one of the first and regarded by many as the greatest in the Welsh language. A tailor and draper by trade, and self-

educated, his works include "Rhys Lewis" (1882), "Enoc Huws" (1891) and "Gwen Tomos" (1894), unsophisticated sketches of rural life. Though his powers of characterisation and description are great, his novels lack structure.

OWEN, David (Dafydd y Garreg Wen; "David of the White Rock")

(1712-41)

Harpist and composer, famous for the tune named after him, which was first published by **Edward JONES (2)** in 1784, and for other airs such as "Codiad yr ehedydd" ("The rising of the lark") and "Difyrrwch gwyr Criccieth".

OWEN, Dorothy

(1751-93)

Quaker leader, of a branch of the **OWEN (3)*** family resident at Dewisbren, Merionethshire. There she built the first Friends Meeting House in the county (1792).

OWEN, Edward Campbell Rich

(1771-1849)

Naval commander, leader of the Walcheren expedition of 1809; knighted in 1815, and made an admiral in 1846.

OWEN, Goronwy (Goronwy Ddu o Fon)

(1723-69)

Clergyman and prolific poet, patronised by the Cymmrodorion Society. His use of the Welsh language paralleled the work of the contemporary Augustan poets in England. His best work, such as "Cywydd y Farn fawr", was written early in his career, when he was master of Donnington school. He lived and worked in America from 1757.

OWEN, Gwilym

(1880-1940)

Physicist, Professor of Physics at the University College of Wales, Aberystwyth 1919-34, Principal 1934-6. He carried out important research in electronics.

OWEN, Hugh (1)

(1538-1618)

Pro-Jesuit Catholic agent, a member of the **OWEN (4)*** family. Trained as a lawyer, he was involved in the Ridolfi Plot (1571) against Elizabeth and the Gunpowder Plot of 1605.

OWEN, Hugh (2)

(1804-81)

Civil servant and educationist, largely responsible for the founding of the University College of Wales at Aberystwyth (1872). In his "Letter to the Welsh people" of 1843, he destroyed the arguments of the "voluntaryists" who did not believe in accepting official funding to pay for improvements in education. He influenced the Conservative government of the time, and helped secure the passing of the Welsh Intermediate Education Act 1889. He was knighted in the year of his death.

OWEN, Herbert Isambard

(1850-1927)

Educationist, named after Isambard K Brunel by his father, an engineer; knighted in 1902. Trained as a physician, he conceived the idea of a new medical university in London and was prominent in the founding of the University of Wales (1894), of which he became Deputy Chancellor.

OWEN, John (1) ("of Clenennau")

(1600-1666)

Royalist commander who stubbornly resisted Parliament throughout the Civil War. He was knighted in 1644, when appointed governor of Conway, and held it until 1647. After his defeat at Llandegai in 1648, he was condemned to death but reprieved, participated in Booth's rebellion, and lived to see the Restoration of the monarchy.

OWEN, John (2)

(1854-1926)

Bishop of St David's 1897-1926, a campaigner for Disestablishment and the creation of the Church in Wales; previously Professor of Welsh at St David's College, Lampeter, 1879-85, and Principal 1892-7. He chaired the Committee which produced the report on "Welsh in education and life" (1927).

OWEN, Lewis
See also **LEWIS, Owen**.

OWEN, Lewis ("Baron")
(c.1500-55)
Judge, who passed the death sentence on eighty men, the "Red bandits of Dinas Mawddwy", and was murdered in retaliation. He was the ancestor of many noble families of Merioneth, including **VAUGHAN (5)*** and **NANNAU***.

OWEN, Margaret ("Peggy")
(1742-1816)
Friend of **Hester THRALE** and Dr Johnson; a member of the **OWEN (5)*** family . Mrs Thrale, a relation, introduced her to Johnson and the Burneys, among others; their correspondence is preserved. Reynolds painted her portrait.

OWEN, Mary (1)
(1737-89)
Prominent Methodist, wife of a John Owen, whom she assisted by riding long distances to find preachers for her home area.

OWEN (née REES), Mary (2)
(1796-1875)
Schoolmistress of Briton Ferry, author of a huge number of hymns, such as "Caed modd i faddau beiau" and "Dyma gariad, pwy a'i traetha".

OWEN, Morfydd Llwyn
(1891-1918)
Singer and composer, whose work was largely inspired by Welsh folk tradition. She

died after a year of troubled marriage to the psychoanalyst **Ernest JONES**. Her best-known works are songs, such as "Slumber song of the Madonna", and the hymn-tune, "William".

OWEN, Nicholas ("Little John")
(c.1550-1606)
Roman Catholic priest and martyr. His skill in the construction of "priest-holes" saved many lives until he was captured at Hindlip Hall following the Gunpowder Plot, and died under torture. [Sometimes incorrectly called John Owen.]

OWEN, Robert (1)
(c.1550-1605)
Roman Catholic diplomat, brother of **Hugh OWEN (1)**. He was involved in the negotiations that brought the Stuarts to the English throne.

OWEN, Robert (2)
(1771-1858)
Founder of the co-operative movement and pioneer of trade unionism. From humble beginnings as a shop assistant in Newtown, Montgomeryshire, he progressed to factory owner, and eventually travelled to Scotland, where he became manager of the Chorlton Twist Company in New Lanark. He set out to improve workers' conditions, providing better housing and schools with no religious instruction. Later, he attempted to establish "Villages of Co-operation" in Britain and America. Though not always successful, his progressive ideas were the basis for much of modern Socialism, but he exhausted his personal fortune in his efforts to obtain justice and equality for working people.

OWEN, Robert (3) (Bob Owen Croesor; Bob Owen Twll Wenci)
(1885-1962)
Genealogist and book collector, a quarry-

man by trade; an expert on the history of Welsh Quakerism and emigration. He amassed a collection of 47,000 books and manuscripts, and was awarded the OBE for his activities. A society of book collectors is named after him.

OWEN, Wilfred
(1893-1918)
Shropshire poet, killed in World War I. His wartime experiences are the subject of many of his poems, only five of which were published in his lifetime.

OWEN, William (1)
(c.1488-1574)
Lawyer, author of "Bregement de toutes les estatuts" (1521), the first book by a Welsh author to be printed in Britain. He married into the **HERBERT (1)*** family, and purchased the barony of Cemais in 1543.

OWEN, William (2)
(1607-70)
Brother of Sir **John OWEN (1)** and heir to the family estate of Porkington (Brogyntyn), Shropshire. A Royalist during the Civil War,

he was Governor of Harlech 1644-7 and the chief patron of the poet, **Huw MORYS**.

OWEN, William (3) David
(1874-1925)
Novelist, best known for "Madame Wen" (1925), a story about a female Robin Hood, possibly based on Margaret Wynne, wife of an eighteenth century Anglesey squire.

OWEN PUGHE, William
(1759-1835)
Scholar and author, a prominent member of London Welsh society from 1776 until 1825. His major work was the "Welsh and English dictionary" of 1803, which uses Welsh literary sources to illustrate its entries. However, the dictionary also showed up shortcomings in his knowledge.

OWENS, John
(1790-1846)
English-born son and partner of a Flintshire textile trader based in Manchester; founder of Owens College (later part of Manchester University), to which he bequeathed much of his family's fortune.

P

PADARN or **PATERNUS**
(6th century; exact dates unknown)
Saint, colleague of St **DAVID**; founder of a monastery in west Wales which still existed at the time of **GERALD of Wales**. *Gave his name to:* Llanbadarn Fawr, Ceredigion.

PADRIG
See **PATRICK**.

PAGET, William
(1768-1854)
Soldier, MP for Caernarfon 1790-6, created Marquess of Anglesey in 1815 after losing a leg in a famous incident at Waterloo.

PARGETER, Edith Mary **(Ellis Peters)**
(1913-95)
Shropshire novelist of Welsh descent, often credited with the invention of the "historical whodunnit"; best known for her series of novels featuring the Welsh monk, Cadfael.

PARKER, John
(1798-1860)
Clergyman and artist, restorer of several churches in mid-Wales. Many of his sketches and water-colour views are held by the National Library of Wales.

PARKER, Mary
(1799-1864)
Artist, sister of **John PARKER**, best known for her sketch of the "Ladies of Llangollen".

PARR, Thomas ("Old Parr")
(16th century; exact dates uncertain)
Man of Middleton, Powys, who reputedly lived from 1483 to 1635, achieving the age of 152. His death occurred after he was received at the court of King **CHARLES I**.

PARRY, Blanche
(c.1508-90)
A favourite attendant of Queen Elizabeth I of England. She nursed the Queen as a child and was appointed keeper of her books and jewels in 1565.

PARRY, David
(c.1682-1714)
Scholar who assisted **Edward LHUYD** in his survey of Wales and succeeded him as director of the Ashmolean Museum, Oxford.

PARRY, John
See also **SALUSBURY, John (2)**.

PARRY, John (1)
(c.1710-82)
Blind harpist, employed by the **WIL-LIAMS-WYNN*** family at Wynnstay; collector of old Welsh airs.

PARRY, John (2)
(1775-1846)
Calvinistic Methodist minister, schoolmaster and author, later a book-seller in Chester. Works on religion and grammar include "Rhodd Mam" (1811), which was used as a children's textbook long after his death.

PARRY, John (3)
(1812-74)
Calvinistic Methodist minister, a tutor at Bala College 1843-74. Brother-in-law to **Thomas GEE**, he edited the latter's encyclopedia, "Y gwyddoniodur".

PARRY, John (4)
(1835-97)
Carpenter and author, leader of the Anti-Tithe Movement from 1886.

PARRY, Joseph
(1841-1903)
Composer, first Professor of Music at the University College of Wales, Aberystwyth. He lived and worked (at a steel-mill) in the USA from 1854 to 1868, returning to Britain with his American wife and children to study music; even while abroad, he was a successful eisteddfod competitor. He is remembered chiefly for an opera, "Blodwen", the hymn-tune, "Aberystwyth", and the song, "Myfanwy". Other works include oratorios, cantatas, and some instrumental pieces.

PARRY, Richard
(1560-1623)
Bishop of St Asaph 1604-23, responsible for the publication of a new Welsh translation of the Bible (1620) and Book of Common Prayer (1621), mainly the work of his brother-in-law, **John DAVIES (2)**.

PARRY, Robert Williams
(1884-1956)
Poet who made his name at the 1910 National Eisteddfod with "Yr haf". As a result of the activities of Plaid Cymru in the 1930s, his poetry took on a more political tone, and he campaigned for the reinstatement of **Saunders LEWIS**.

PARRY, Thomas (1)
(c.1500-60)
Member of the Privy Council of Queen Elizabeth I of England, and "Cofferer" in her household. He was knighted on her accession, after serving her faithfully in troubled times. He was related to the **VAUGHAN (9)*** and **CECIL*** families. [Sometimes wrongly described as the husband or father of **Blanche PARRY**.]

PARRY, Thomas (2)
(1904-85)
Literary critic, knighted in 1978; Librarian of the National Library of Wales 1953-58 and Principal of the University College of Wales, Aberystwyth, 1958-69. His "Hanes llenyddiaeth Gymraeg" (1945) is a comprehensive history of Welsh literature.

PARRY, William (1) (William ap Harry)
(c.1540-85)
Agent of Queen Elizabeth I of England, an associate of **Thomas MORGAN (2)**. He was executed on suspicion of being a Catholic spy and plotting the Queen's assassination.

PARRY, William (2)
(c.1742-91)
Portrait artist, son of **John PARRY (1)**; a pupil of Reynolds. His patrons were the **WILLIAMS-WYNN*** family.

PARRY, William (3) John
(1842-1927)
Liberal politician and author, first Secretary of the North Wales Quarrymen's Union (1914). Works include "The cry of the people" (1906); he was sued for libel by the second Lord Penrhyn, an action which did the workers' cause no harm.

PARRY-WILLIAMS, Thomas Herbert
(1887-1975)
Poet who won the "double" of crown and chair at the National Eisteddfodau of 1912 and 1915; inventor of a style of verse he called "rhigymau" ("rhymings"). A conscientious objector during World War I, his appointment to the new Chair of Welsh Language at the University College of Wales in 1920 aroused controversy, but he held the post until 1952, and was knighted in 1958.

PATERNUS
See **PADARN**.

PATRICK or **PADRIG**
(c.385-462)
Patron saint of Ireland, believed to have

been born in Wales, at a place called Bannavem Taberniae.

PATTI, Adelina ("The Queen of Song")
(1843-1919)
Opera singer, of Italian parentage, who made her home at Craig-y-Nos Castle in the Swansea valley.

PAUL AURELIAN
(5th century; exact dates unknown)
Saint, a pupil of **ILLTUD** and contemporary of **DAVID** and **GILDAS**. He lived as a hermit in Wales until summoned by King Mark to Cornwall, where he preached Christianity.

PAULINUS or PEULIN
(5th century; exact dates unknown)
Saint, teacher of St **DAVID**; the latter was said by **RHIGYFARCH** to have restored Paulinus' sight. An inscribed stone found near Llandovery may mark his grave.

PAYNTER, William Thomas
(1903-84)
Miners' leader, involved in 1930s hunger marches; Secretary of the National Union of Mineworkers 1959-68 and a member of the Arbitration Panel of the Advisory Conciliation and Arbitration Service.

PEACOCK (née GRYFFYDH), Jane
(c.1790-1852)
Wife of the English author, Thomas Love Peacock; depicted in his uncompleted work, "Sir Calidore". Described by Shelley, her husband's friend, as "the white Snowdonian antelope" in a letter of 1820, she married Peacock in the same year, at Eglwys-fach, where her father was vicar. Their son-in-law was the author, George Meredith.

PEATE, Iorwerth
(1901-82)
Poet and scholar, a specialist in Welsh folk studies, largely responsible for the success of the folk museum at St Fagan's, of which he was the first Curator. He was a pacifist, and an early member of Plaid Cymru. His many works include the poems, "Ronsyfal" and "Men ychen", an autobiography, "Rhwng dau fyd" (1976), and "The Welsh house" (1940).

PECHAM, John
(c.1230-92)
Archbishop of Canterbury who acted as an intermediary between **LLYWELYN ap Gruffydd** and King **EDWARD I** of England during the conflict of 1282.

PEDROG or PETROC
(6th century; exact dates unknown)
Saint, possibly of Cornish origin. *Gave his name to:* Llanbedrog, Gwynedd; St Petrox and Verwick, Dyfed.

PELAGIUS
(c.355-420)
British monk, originator of the Pelagian heresy, first preached in Powys around 380.

PENDERYN, Dic (Richard Lewis)
(1808-31)
Labourer, arrested as a ringleader of the Merthyr Riots or Rising of 1831 and accused of wounding a soldier. He was convicted, and hanged at Cardiff, becoming a martyr of the workers' movement.

PENNANT, Richard
(1737-1808)
Industrialist, owner of slate quarries on his Caernarfonshire estate, where he made many improvements. He was Whig MP for Petersfield and Liverpool, and was created Baron Penrhyn (Irish peerage) in 1783.

PENNANT, Thomas
(1726-98)
Naturalist and traveller, author of "Tours in

Wales" (1778, 1781). This illustrated account of journeys in North Wales which he made with his friend, **John LLOYD (2)**, is notable for its detail. He also travelled in other countries, and wrote "Outlines of the globe" in 22 volumes (only four of which were published). His correspondents included Linnaeus, Le Comte de Buffon, and Gronovius of Leiden.

PENRHYN, Baron
See **PENNANT, Richard; DOUGLAS-PENNANT, Edward Gordon**.

PENROSE, Llewellin
See **WILLIAMS, Llewellin**.

PENRY, John
(1563-93)
Martyr for the Puritan cause, the most famous of all Welsh martyrs. Of aristocratic birth, he was well-educated, and published his first work, the "Aequity", in 1587. In further pamphlets produced by a secret press, he argued for Welsh-speaking preachers and the abolition of the episcopal system, and was forced to flee to Scotland. On his return to London, he was captured and executed for treason, in the mistaken belief that he was responsible for the "Martin Marprelate" tracts.

PERIS, Ceridwen
See **JONES, Alice Gray**.

PERROT(T), John
(c.1527-92)
MP for Pembrokeshire, rumoured to be an illegitimate son of King **HENRY VIII** and knighted by King Edward VI. His opposition to Catholicism earned him the favour of Queen Elizabeth I, who appointed him Lord Deputy of Ireland in 1584, but he made many enemies. On his return from Ireland in 1588, he was convicted of treason, and died in prison.

PETER DE LEIA
(c.1130-98)
Unpopular Bishop of St David's 1176-98. He spent little time in the diocese, but was responsible for building work on the cathedral in 1181-2. He excommunicated **RHYS ap Gruffydd (1)**, temporarily preventing his burial at St David's.

PETERS, Ellis
See **PARGETER, Edith**.

PETROC
See **PEDROG**.

PEULIN
See **PAULINUS**.

PFEIFFER (née DAVIS), Emily Jane
(1827-90)
Poet, sometimes likened to Elizabeth Barrett Browning in style. She married a German merchant, and took an interest in women's education, making a bequest to the women's hall of residence at University College, Cardiff.

PHILIP AP RHYS
(early 16th century; exact dates unknown)
Church composer, best known for his organ mass, unique in contemporary British music. Only two other works survive.

PHILIPPS
See **PHILIPS, PHILLIPPS, PHILLIPS**.

PHILIPPS, Erasmus
(c.1620-97)
Third baronet **PHILIPPS***, owner of Picton Castle; MP for Pembrokeshire 1654-5 and 1659; a philanthropist and Commissioner under the Act for the Propagation of the Gospel in Wales.

PHILIPPS, Jenkin Thomas
(c.1680-1755)
Linguist, traveller and teacher, author of "A compendious way of teaching ancient and modern languages" (1723). He was private tutor to the children of King **GEORGE II**.

PHILIPPS, John
(c.1666-1737)
Fourth baronet, son of **Erasmus PHILIPPS**. From its outset, he was heavily involved in the Society for the Promotion of Christian Knowledge (SPCK), which his personal fortune helped support, but was equally involved in other religious and philanthropic movements and was a major influence on **Griffith JONES (1)**, who married his sister, Margaret.

PHILIPPS, Thomas
(c.1470-1520)
Squire of **Henry TUDOR**, a military commander in the French war of 1513, knighted in the same year; founder of both branches of the **PHILIPPS*** or **PHILIPS*** family.

PHILIPS or PHILIPPS, James
(1594-1675)
MP for Cardiganshire and Pembrokeshire at various times between 1653 and 1661, best known as the husband of **Katherine PHILIPS**.

PHILIPS or PHILIPPS (née FOWLER), Katherine ("The Matchless Orinda")
(1631-64)
English-born poet, one of the first British women to have poetry published. She lived in Wales following her mother's remarriage, herself becoming the second wife of **James PHILIPS** of Cardigan Priory. She was a Royalist sympathiser, her husband a staunch Parliamentarian. Her translations of Corneille plays were very successful, and she became the centre of a literary coterie, the "Society of Fellowship", but died of smallpox in London.

PHILLIMORE, Egerton Grenville Bagot
(1856-1937)
English antiquary who learned Welsh and made a study of Welsh history and place-names; founder and editor of "Y Cymmrodor" (1889-91). His collection of manuscripts, sold to Sir **John WILLIAMS (8)** in 1894, is now held by the National Library of Wales.

PHILLIPPS, Thomas
(1792-1872)
Antiquary and collector of books and manuscripts, created a baronet in 1821. His collection, the biggest in Britain, included many important Welsh manuscripts, such as "The book of Aneirin". In 1822, he set up his own press to publish some of the contents.

PHILLIPS, Morgan (1)
(c.1510-70)
Catholic scholar, co-founder of the seminary at Douai (1568) which was attended by many Welsh students; author of "Defence of the honour of Mary Queen of Scotland" (1571).

PHILLIPS, Morgan (2)
(1902-63)
General Secretary of the Labour Party 1944-62.

PHILLIPS, Thomas (1)
(1760-1851)
Naval surgeon, major benefactor of Welsh education; founder of the Welsh Collegiate Institution at Llandovery (1847).

PHILLIPS, Thomas (2)
(1801-67)
Lawyer and author, mayor of Newport at the time of the Chartist march of 1839. He was knighted in 1840 for his part in putting down the riot.

PHYLIP, Rhisiart
(c.1560-1641)
Poet, younger brother of **Sion PHYLIP**; a specialist in "cynghanedd". He wrote elegies to Queen Elizabeth I and to **KATHERYN of Berain**, and was involved in several "bardic controversies", one with his brother.

PHYLIP, Robert
See **PUW, Robert**.

PHYLIP, Sion
(c.1543-1620)
Poet and minstrel, first of the **PHYLIP*** bards of Ardudwy, associated with the **WYNN (1)*** and **NANNAU*** families. His verse, including elegies for Queen Elizabeth I and **Henry STUART**, was notable for its learned tone. Works included awdlau, cywyddau, and englynion.

PICTON, Thomas
(1758-1815)
Soldier, who served as Governor of Trinidad and later Flushing and distinguished himself in the Napoleonic Wars, commanding the "Fighting Division" in the Peninsular campaign; knighted in 1815. He was killed at the Battle of Waterloo, having been seriously wounded at Quatre Bras. He is the only Welshman buried in St Paul's Cathedral.

PIERCY, Benjamin
(1827-88)
Civil engineer, involved in the construction of railway lines throughout mid-Wales. He built bridges over the Severn, Mawddach and Traeth Bychan estuaries. Later he worked in Sardinia, becoming a close friend of Garibaldi, and was honoured by the Italian Crown. After acquiring the Marchwiel Hall estate in 1881, he sponsored the building of railways in North Wales, and also helped construct the Assam railway in India, assisted by his brother, Robert.

PIOZZI, Hester
See **THRALE, Hester**.

POLLITT, Harry
(1890-1960)
English politician, secretary of the British Communist Party 1924-9 and editor of the "Daily Worker". As Communist candidate for Rhondda East, he won 45% of the vote in the 1945 General Election.

PONSONBY, Sarah
(1755-1831)
Irish lady, descendant of the 1st Viscount Duncannon, who lived at Plas Newydd with her companion, **Eleanor BUTLER**, from 1780 to 1829, becoming the centre of a coterie, and gaining renown throughout Britain as "the ladies of Llangollen". Their admirers included Wellington, Wedgwood, Wordsworth, and Queen Charlotte.

PONTYPRIDD, Baron
See **THOMAS, Alfred**.

POWEL, Anthony
(c.1560-1619)
Genealogist, associated with the **MANSEL*** family of Margam; a major subject of the forgeries of **IOLO Morganwg**.

POWEL, David
(c.1552-98)
Historian and topographer, probably the first graduate of Jesus College, Oxford. He was first to record the unlikely story of how King **EDWARD I** of England bestowed the title Prince of Wales upon his new-born son, later King **EDWARD II**, at Caernarfon, after defeating the native princes. In his "Historie of Cambria" (1584), a comprehensive and colourful account of the history of Wales, he traced Elizabeth I's claim to the principality through the **MORTIMER*** ancestry of her grandmother, Elizabeth of York.

POWELL, Griffith
(1561-1620)
Principal of Jesus College, Oxford, 1613-20, responsible for extending its buildings; author of works on Aristotelian philosophy.

POWELL, Philip
(1594-1646)
Benedictine priest and martyr, who missioned in England from 1622, after studying under **David (Augustine) BAKER**. He was arrested while ministering to Catholic families in the West Country, and executed.

POWELL, Rice
(c.1600-65)
Parliamentarian leader during the Civil War, who held Cardigan Castle against **Charles GERARD**. He joined the revolt over non-payment of his troops, and was defeated at the Battle of St Fagans in 1648. Following his capture at Tenby, he was condemned to death, but reprieved.

POWELL, Thomas (1)
(c.1572-1635)
Lawyer, a pioneer in the field of public records; author of numerous works in verse and prose, including "The attorney's almanacke" (1627).

POWELL, Thomas (2)
(c.1779-1863)
Industrialist, proprietor of coal-mines at Tir Founder, Duffryn, and Cwm Pennar, among others. One of the first to exploit South Wales's smokeless steam coal, he was thus able to expand his activities; he co-founded the Newport Coal Association (1833), the first coal "ring" in South Wales. The Powell Duffryn Steam Coal Company was formed after his death to take over his business.

POWELL, Thomas (3)
(early 19th century; exact dates unknown)
Radical leader, involved in the Chartist rioting at Llanidloes in 1639, for which he was imprisoned. He later worked for Henry Hetherington, the London book-seller prosecuted in 1841 for the sale of blasphemous literature.

POWELL, Vavasor
(1617-70)
Nonconformist preacher who supported Parliament during the Civil War, but opposed Cromwell's appointment as Lord Protector in the pamphlet, "A word for God" (1655). In prison following the Restoration, he wrote "The bird in the cage, chirping" and "The sufferer's catechism".

POWYS, John Cowper
(1872-1963)
English-born novelist and philosopher, who prided himself on his Welsh descent and lived for some years in North Wales. Works include the historical romances, "Owen Glendower" (1940) and "Porius" (1951), and a series of essays on Welsh themes entitled "Obstinate Cymric" (1947).

POYER, John
(c.1600-49)
Merchant of Pembroke, who became a Parliamentarian leader during the Civil War, but went over to the Royalists in 1648, following disputes over soldiers' pay. He was among the leaders defeated at the Battle of St Fagans in 1648, and was the only one executed for his part in the rebellion, having drawn lots with his comrades **Rowland LAUGHARNE** and **Rice POWELL**.

PREECE, William Henry
(1834-1913)
Electrical engineer, specialist in wireless telegraphy; knighted in 1899. Though he sent messages across the Bristol Channel in 1892, the significance of the experiment was not recognised.

PRENDERGAST (née WILLIAMS), Anne
(c.1710-70)
Notorious heiress to the **WILLIAMS (4)***
family estate of Marl; a lady-in-waiting to
Queen **CAROLINE of Anspach**, and possibly mistress of the Duke of Cumberland.
She married Sir Thomas Prendergast in
1739, and after his death in 1760, married
his cousin, Terence Prendergast; both marriages were unhappy. After her death, her
estranged husband sold her home, Pant Glas,
to the **MOSTYN (1)*** family.

PRICE
See also **PRYCE, PRYSE**.

PRICE (née TREGELLES), Anna
(1759-1846)
Cornish wife of the manager of the Neath
iron-works, mother of **Joseph Tregelles
PRICE**. A devout Quaker, she moved to
Neath with her family in 1799, and was an
active peace campaigner, a great influence
on her son.

PRICE, Benjamin
(1804-96)
Minister of the "Free Church of England",
founded in 1844. He became its "Bishop" in
1876, consecrated in a special service by a
Canadian bishop of the Reformed Episcopal
Church.

PRICE, Herbert
(c.1600-65)
Extreme Royalist politician, MP for Brecknock, great-grandson of Sir **John PRICE
(1)**. He lived at Brecon Priory, where he
entertained King **CHARLES I** at the height
of the Civil War.

PRICE, Hugh
(c.1495-1574)
Founder and benefactor of Jesus College,
Oxford (1571), traditionally associated with
Welsh students. He was a Doctor of Canon

Law at the university, and Treasurer of St
David's Cathedral.

PRICE, John (1) (John ap Rhys)
(c.1502-55)
Chief notary to King **HENRY VIII**,
probably the author of the second Act of
Union (1543). Secretary to the Council of
Wales and MP for Hereford and Ludlow, he
participated in the dissolution of the monas-
teries, and was knighted in 1547 by King
Edward VI. In the same year, he produced
"Yn y llyfr hwn", a translation of the Creed,
Lord's Prayer and Commandments, the first
printed book in Welsh.

PRICE, John (2) ("Old Price")
(1803-87)
Clergyman, schoolmaster, and naturalist,
close friend of Charles Darwin; author of
works on natural history, and founder of a
periodical, "Old Price's remains" (1863-4).

PRICE, Joseph Tregelles
(1784-1854)
Cornish-born Quaker, manager of Neath
Abbey ironworks from 1818 in succession
to his father. He was a co-founder of the
Peace Society (1816), his pacifist views
leading him to discontinue the manufacture
of arms. One of his many magnanimous acts
was to obtain a temporary reprieve for **Dic
PENDERYN**, but he failed to prevent the
latter's execution.

PRICE, Richard (1)
(1723-91)
Glamorgan preacher, philosopher and
political theorist. He was a prominent supporter of the American and French rev-
olutions, and author of the tract "Obser-
vations on the nature of civil liberty" (1776)
and the sermon "A discourse on the love of
our country" (1789). After facing widespread criticism at home for his views, he
was given an honorary degree by Yale

University and offered American citizenship, which he declined. A cousin of **Ann MADDOCKS**, he was also an associate and correspondent of Priestley, Hume, Smith, Mirabeau, and George Washington.

PRICE, Richard (2) John Lloyd
(1842-1923)
Founder of the Welsh Whisky Distillery at Frongoch, heir to the **PRICE*** family estate of Rhiwlas; probably the inventor of the concept of sheepdog trials.

PRICE, Robert
(1655-1733)
Lawyer and judge, MP for Weobley, an early nationalist. His speeches in opposition to King William III were published in 1702 under the title "Gloria Cambriae".

PRICE, Thomas (1) (Carnhuanawc)
(1787-1847)
Scholar, clergyman, and traveller, founder of Cymdeithas Cymreigyddion y Fenni (a cultural society based in Abergavenny), the Welsh Literary Society of Brecon and Welsh Minstrelsy Society. With Lady **LLANOVER**, he was one of the founding patrons of Llandovery College in 1848. His works include a history of Wales in fourteen parts (1836-42).

PRICE, Thomas (2)
(1820-88)
Baptist minister and author, who encouraged the work of "friendly societies" such as the Oddfellows, took part in local politics, and helped establish the "British School" in Aberdare.

PRICE, Thomas (3)
(1852-1909)
Politician, whose career in public life began when he emigrated to Australia in 1883 with his wife and seven children and there became active as a trade unionist. He served as Prime Minister of South Australia 1905-9.

PRICE, William
(1800-93)
South Wales physician with an eccentric interest in Welsh tradition; also a supporter of Chartism. He anticipated modern practice by refusing to treat smokers, and was a vegetarian. His impromptu cremation of his infant son in 1884 was successfully defended in court, setting an important precedent.

PRICE THOMAS, Clement
(1893-1973)
Thoracic surgeon, knighted 1951; President of the Welsh National School of Medicine 1958-70 and Adviser to the Ministry of Health 1946-63.

PRICHARD, Caradog
(1904-80)
Journalist, poet and novelist. He won the Crown at the National Eisteddfod in three successive years, with "Briodas" (1927), "Penyd" (1928), and "Y gan ni chanwyd" (1929). In later life he also won the Chair. His highly-acclaimed novel, "Un nos ola leuad" (1961), like some of his poems, is semi-autobiographical.

PRICHARD (née PRYSE), Catherine (Buddug)
(1842-1909)
Poet, daughter of **Robert John PRYSE**. She gained her bardic name by defending the female sex in the periodical, "Udgorn Cymru", but is best known for lyrics such as "O na byddai'n haf o hyd" and "Neges y blodeuyn".

PRICHARD, Rhys ("Yr Hen Ficer")
(1579-1644)
Clergyman and poet, author of the "Welshman's Candle" ("Canwyll y Cymry"). As a rural vicar and later Chancellor of St David's, he accumulated material for this collection of simple verses offering religious instruction to the uneducated, but they were

only published in 1659, by **Stephen HUGHES**.

PRICHARD, Thomas Jeffery Llewelyn
(1790-1862)
Poet and author, an actor by profession, best known for his "novel" about the life of Twm Sion Cati (**Thomas JONES (1)**) (1828). Other works included, "Heroines of Welsh history" (1854), researched while he was employed in the library of **Lady LLAN-OVER**, and several travel guides.

PROGER, Edward
(1618-1714)
Royalist, younger brother of Sir **Henry PROGER**. He became a close friend of the future King **CHARLES II** and was exiled with him in France. After the Restoration, he served as MP for Brecknock 1662-79, and remained in the royal service into the reign of Queen Anne.

PRYCE
See also **PRICE, PRYSE**.

PRYCE-JONES (formerly JONES), Pryce Edward
(1834-1920)
Mail-order pioneer, proprietor of Pryce-Jones Ltd, Newtown; also Conservative MP for Montgomery 1885-6 and 1892-5. He was knighted in 1887.

PRYDDERCH, Rhys
(c.1620-99)
Independent minister, master of a famous school at Ystradwallter; author of "Gemau Doethineb", a collection of proverbs.

PRYS, Edmwnd
(1544-1623)
Humanist clergyman and poet, who assisted **William MORGAN (1)** in the translation of the Bible into Welsh. His major work was a metrical translation of the Psalms, "Salmau

Can", published in 1621 – the first Welsh book to include printed music.

PRYS, Elis (Y Doctor Coch)
(c.1512-94)
Corrupt clergyman, son of **ROBERT ap Rhys** and brother-in-law of **William SALESBURY**. A doctor of law and favourite of the Earl of Leicester, he was notorious for his part in the dissolution of the monasteries. He served as MP for Merioneth and a member of the Council of the Marches.

PRYS, Tomos or Thomas
(c.1564-1634)
Soldier and poet, eldest son of **Elis PRYS**. He served under the Earl of Leicester in the Netherlands and other European countries. He turned to piracy in the 1590s, but settled in Denbighshire on inheriting his father's estate at Plas Iolyn. Along with **William MYDDELTON**, he was reputedly the first person to smoke tobacco publicly in Britain. His poetry includes many love lyrics addressed to "Eiddig".

PRYSE
See also **PRICE**.

PRYSE, Carbery
(c.1660-95)
Cardiganshire landowner, 4th baronet Pryse, who established lead- and silver-mining at Esgair Hir on his estate. When he died unmarried, his interests were purchased by Sir **Humphrey MACKWORTH**.

PRYSE, John
(1826-83)
Printer and publisher, based at Llanidloes; founder of the "Llanidloes and Newtown Telegraph" (1859). He reprinted many popular works, as well as producing "Pryse's Welsh interpreter", "Pryse's handbook", etc.

PRYSE, Robert John (Gweirydd ap Rhys)
(1807-89)
Self-educated historian, journalist, editor and translator, author of "Hanes y Brytaniaid a'r Cymry" (1872-4). He made his living as a master weaver until 1857, when he went to work for **Thomas GEE**, and made a substantial contribution to "Y gwyddionadur", the encyclopaedia published by Gee.

PUDDICOMBE (née EVANS), Anne
Adaliza Beynon (**Allen Raine**)
(1836-1908)
Popular novelist, a great-granddaughter of **Daniel ROWLAND**, educated in England. Her works, such as "Torn sails" (1898) and "Garthowen" (1900), are mostly romances set in Wales.

PUGH
See also **PUGHE, PUW**.

PUGH, Edward
(c.1761-1813)
Portrait painter, miniaturist and author, best known for "Cambria Depicta" (1816), an account of his travels in North Wales, accompanied by his own illustrations.

PUGH, Ellis
(1636-1718)
Quaker leader, who emigrated to Pennsylvania in 1687. His book, "Annerch ir Cymru", was published posthumously in 1721, becoming the first Welsh book printed in America.

PUGH, John
(1846-1907)
Calvinistic Methodist minister, founder of the "Forward Movement" (1891). As superintendent of the movement, he opened nearly fifty mission-halls in South Wales.

PUGHE, William Owen
See **OWEN PUGHE, William**.

PUW
See also **PUGH**.

PUW, Huw
(1663-1743)
Legendary athlete, also a priest, reputedly capable of tremendous feats in high jumping and stone-throwing.

PUW or PUGH, Robert (1)
(c.1535-1629)
Member of the famous **PUW*** family who, under the influence of **Robert GWYN**, set up a secret press in Rhiwledyn caves to publish a religious tract, "Y Drych Cristianogawl". After leading a fugitive life, he was imprisoned, but later released and allowed freedom to worship under King James I.

PUW, Robert (2) (Robert Phylip)
(1609-79)
Roman Catholic priest and martyr, grandson of **Robert PUW (1)**. A talented linguist, he served as chaplain to Queen Henrietta Maria in exile, and returned to Britain after the Restoration. He was eventually arrested for supposed involvement in the "Popish Plot", and died in prison.

PYRKE, John
(1755-1834)
English owner of the japannery at Usk between 1814 and 1826. He popularised the chocolate-brown lacquer characteristic of Usk japan-ware.

R

RAINE, Allen
See **PUDDICOMBE, Anne**.

RANDLES, Elizabeth
(c.1801-29)
Harpist and pianist, a musical prodigy, the daughter of a well-known blind harpist of Wrexham, Edward Randles. She and her father played for King **GEORGE III**.

RATHBONE, William
(1819-1902)
Radical MP for Caernarfonshire 1880-95, an opponent of Welsh nationalism. He came of a family of philanthropic Unitarian business people; his own efforts were directed towards the development of further education in Wales.

RAVENSCROFT, Thomas
(c.1592-1635)
Musician, a member of the **RAVENS-CROFT*** family of Hawarden; best known for "Ravenscroft's Psalter", his own setting of the Psalms. His collection of rounds and catches, "Pammelia" (1609), was the first published in Britain.

RECORDE, Robert
(c.1510-58)
Physician who attended both King Edward VI and **Mary TUDOR**, was Comptroller of the Mint (1549) and Surveyor of the Mines and Monies of Ireland (1551). He was also a mathematician, the author of "The grounde of artes" (1540) (in which he invented the "equals" sign) and textbooks on geometry and algebra. Dismissed from his official post for alleged dishonesty, he died in prison.

REES
See also **RHYS**.

REES, Abraham
(1743-1825)
Presbyterian minister and scholar, editor of "Chambers' encyclopaedia" (1781-6) and "The new cyclopaedia" (1802-20; the latter, in 45 volumes, was largely his own work.

REES, Evan (Dyfed)
(1850-1923)
Calvinistic Methodist minister and poet, who also worked as a miner and railwayman; four times winner of the Chair at the National Eisteddfod, also winner of the Chair at the World Fair Eisteddfod of 1893, and Archdruid 1905-23.

REES, Goronwy
(1909-79)
Journalist, academic and novelist, Principal of the University College of Wales, Aberystwyth 1953-7. Works include political studies, novels, and the memoirs, "A bundle of sensations" (1960) and "A chapter of accidents" (1972).

REES, Henry
(1798-1869)
Calvinistic Methodist minister, the most famous of his time, sought after as a preacher throughout Wales. A leading opponent of the Education Bill of 1843, he served as first moderator of the General Assembly in 1864.

REES, Lewis
(1710-1800)
Influential Independent minister of Llanbrynmair, who preached in North Wales and was persecuted for his beliefs; a forerunner of **Howell HARRIS**.

REES, Sarah Jane (Cranogwen)
(1839-1916)
Poet, schoolmistress and musician, editor of the Welsh women's magazine, "Y Frythones", 1878-1901, and founder of the Women's Temperance Movement.

REES, Thomas (Twm Carnabwth)
(c.1806-76)
Leader of one of the first "Rebecca Riots" in 1839, when he and his followers dressed as women in order to attack the toll-gate at Efail-wen.

REES, William (1) (Gwilym Hiraethog)
(1802-83)
Independent minister and author, founder and first editor of "Yr amserau" (1843), one of the first Welsh newspapers, in which he argued for disestablishment of the Church in Wales and other radical causes. Self-educated, he wrote popular novels, plays, poems and hymns in Welsh.

REES, William (2)
(1808-73)
Publisher, founder of a press at Ton (near Llandovery) which became famous for publications such as the periodical, "Y cylchgrawn" (1834-5), the translation of the Mabinogion by Lady **Charlotte GUEST** (1848-49) and the work of his brother, Rice Rees.

REES, William (3) Thomas **(Alaw Ddu)**
(1838-1904)
Composer, precentor of **Lady LLAN-OVER**'s chapel. Works include oratorios such as "Ruth and Naomi" and hymn-tunes such as "Glanrhondda".

REES-WILLIAMS, David Rees
(1903-76)
Labour MP for Croydon 1945-50, Minister of Civil Aviation 1951; created Baron Ogmore 1950.

REICHEL, Henry Rudolf
(1856-1931)
Irish-born scholar, first Principal of the University College of North Wales, Bangor, 1884-1927, also Vice-Chancellor of the University of Wales. He was knighted in 1907 by King **EDWARD VII** on the occasion of the laying of the foundation stone of the new college buildings.

RENDEL, Stuart
(1834-1913)
Liberal MP for Montgomeryshire 1880-94; created 1st Baron Rendel in 1894. Though an Englishman and an Anglican, he won strong support in Welsh-speaking areas, was often referred to as "the member for Wales", and influenced Gladstone, his personal friend, in favour of the University College of Wales at Aberystwyth. He was a prime mover in the passing of the Intermediate Education Act 1889, and sympathised with the campaign for Disestablishment, but opposed nationalism.

RHAYADER, Baron
See **JONES, Leif**.

RHIGYFARCH or **RICEMARCHUS**
(c.1056-99)
Priest and poet, son of **SULIEN**, the author of a Latin manuscript known as the Ricemarch Psalter and of a biography of St **DAVID**.

RHIRID FLAIDD
(12th century; exact dates unknown)
Lord of Gest in Eifionydd, celebrated in contemporary literature, from whom several noble families claimed descent.

RHIWALLON AP CYNFYN
(c.1030-1070)
Co-ruler of Powys 1063-70, with his brother, **BLEDDYN ap Cynfyn**; their rule was tolerated by King Edward the

Confessor. He was killed at the Battle of Mechain.

RHODRI AB OWAIN
(c.1150-95)
Prince of Gwynedd, son of **OWAIN Gwynedd** by **CRISTIN**. He married the daughter of **RHYS ap Gruffydd (1)** to obtain support against his brothers after their father's death, but was eventually defeated by his nephew, **LLYWELYN Fawr**.

RHODRI AP GRUFFYDD
(c.1235-1315)
Prince of Gwynedd, a younger brother of **LLYWELYN ap Gruffydd**. Deprived of his inheritance and temporarily imprisoned by Llywelyn, he sought the patronage of King **EDWARD I** of England, and gave up his inheritance in return for financial compensation. Following the defeat and death of his brothers in 1282-3, he retained his possessions and continued to live as an English nobleman. It is partly through him that the present British royal family claims descent from **LLYWELYN Fawr**.

RHODRI MAWR
(c.820-78)
Ruler of Gwynedd from 844, son of **MERFYN Frych** and **NEST (1)**. By his advantageous marriage to **ANGHARAD (1)**, princess of Seisyllwg, and the inheritance of Powys from his uncle, **CYNGEN**, he came to rule most of Wales by 872, protecting the country with a degree of success against Viking invasions. Shortly before his death in battle against Saxon neighbours, he arranged for the division of his territories between three of his six sons, **ANARAWD ap Rhodri**, **CADELL ap Rhodri** and Merfyn ap Rhodri.

RHONDDA, Viscount
See **THOMAS, David A (3)**.

RHONDDA, Viscountess
See **THOMAS, Margaret Haig**.

RHUN AP MAELGWN (Rhun Hir)
(mid-6th century; exact dates unknown)
King of Gwynedd, son of **MAELGWN Gwynedd**. He is referred to in the Mabinogion, and by **CYNDDELW Brydydd Mawr**, who calls Gwynedd "gwlad Rhun" ("the land of Rhun").

RHYDDERCH HAEL (Rhydderch Hen)
(6th century; exact dates unknown)
Legendary figure, victor of the Battle of Arfderydd (573). His territory was probably in present-day Scotland.

RHYGYFARCH
See **RHIGYFARCH**.

RHYL, Baron
See **BIRCH, Nigel**.

RHYS
See **REES**.

RHYS AB OWAIN
(c.1050-78)
Prince, descendant of **HYWEL Dda**, briefly ruler of Deheubarth. Having driven off and killed **BLEDDYN ap Cynfyn**, he was himself killed in battle by **CARADOG ap Gruffydd**.

RHYS AP GRUFFYDD (1) (" Yr Arglwydd Rhys": "The Lord Rhys")
(1132-97)
Prince of Deheubarth, youngest son of **GRUFFYDD ap Rhys (1)** and **GWENLLIAN (1)**, who succeeded in restoring Welsh supremacy in the South whilst maintaining a peaceful relationship with the English Crown, eventually extending his jurisdiction to Gwent and Glamorgan. A patron of the arts, he held the first recorded eisteddfod at Cardigan in 1176, and

supported the Cistercian order, founding the abbey of Talyllychau (Talley). Family ties with local rulers added to the security of his position. The most powerful ruler in Wales after **OWAIN Gwynedd**, he was given the courtesy title of "Lord" by King Henry II of England.

RHYS AP GRUFFYDD (2)
(c.1240-84)
Grandson of **EDNYFED Fychan**, a supporter of **LLYWELYN ap Gruffydd**. After the Treaty of Aberconwy, he was appointed a royal justice by King **EDWARD I**.

RHYS AP GRUFFYDD (3) ("Syr Rhys")
(c.1290-1356)
Supporter of King **EDWARD II** of England, a descendant of **EDNYFED Fychan**. After some time in exile, he was restored to his offices and estates in Cantref Mawr by King Edward III in 1330. He raised troops for the King, and was himself knighted after the Battle of Crecy in 1346. Marriage to Joan de Somerville brought him extensive possessions in England, making him one of the greatest landowners in Wales.

RHYS AP MAREDUDD
(c.1250-1291)
Lord of Dryslwyn, grandson of **RHYS Gryg**. He was rewarded for his support of King **EDWARD I** against **LLYWELYN ap Gruffydd** with the lordship of Ystrad Tywi that had previously belonged to his cousin, **RHYS Wyndod**, but subsequent unfair treatment caused him to revolt in 1287. He remained a fugitive from the law for four years before being captured and executed.

RHYS AP TEWDWR
(c.1040-93)
Ruler of Deheubarth from 1075, a descendant of **HYWEL Dda** and son-in-law of **RHIWALLON ap Cynfyn**. His position was at first threatened by his Welsh neighbours, notably **CARADOG ap Gruffydd**, causing him to seek aid first from the Vikings of Ireland; later, with **GRUFFYDD ap Cynan** as an ally, he saw off his opponents at the Battle of Llandudoch (1091) and maintained his rule until defeated and killed at Brecon by the Normans.

RHYS AP THOMAS
(1449-1525)
Leading supporter of **Henry TUDOR**, grandson of **GRUFFYDD ap Nicolas**. He was knighted at Bosworth and given large estates in South Wales; he later took a prominent part in the Battle of Blackheath (1497). A Knight of the Garter from 1505, he remained in favour during the reign of King **HENRY VIII**, and spent his later years at Carew Castle.

RHYS FARDD (Y Bardd Bach; Bardd Cwsg)
(mid-15th century; exact dates unknown)
Poet whose works foretell the rise of the **TUDOR*** dynasty and predict great Welsh victories over the English.

RHYS FYCHAN
(c.1250-1302)
Supporter of **LLYWELYN ap Gruffydd** who forfeited his lands in the Treaty of Aberconwy, but was spared after the conquest of 1282. [Sometimes confused with **RHYS Gryg** and with another Rhys Fychan, father of **RHYS Wyndod**.]

RHYS GRYG ("Rhys the Hoarse"; Rhys Fychan)
(c.1170-1234)
Prince of Deheubarth, son of **RHYS ap Gruffydd (1)**. Having fought his brothers, **GRUFFYDD ap Rhys (2)** and **MAELGWN ap Rhys**, for supremacy, he was confirmed as ruler of Dinefwr and Tywi by **LLYWELYN Fawr**, in whose service he was killed. [Sometimes confused with **RHYS Fychan**.]

RHYS WYNDOD
(c.1270-1302)
Lord of Ystrad Tywi, great-grandson of **RHYS Gryg**. He supported **LLYWELYN ap Gruffydd** in the rebellion of 1282, along with his three brothers, and was subsequently imprisoned by King **EDWARD I**, forfeiting his possessions, including Dinefwr Castle.

RHYS, Edward Prosser
(1901-45)
Journalist and poet, editor of "Baner ac amserau Cymru", and founder of the publishing firm of Gwasg Aberystwyth (1928). His best-known poems are "Cymru" and the controversial "Atgof", which won the Crown at the National Eisteddfod of 1924 despite its theme of homosexuality.

RHYS, Ernest ("Mr Everyman")
(1859-1946)
English-born poet and novelist, editor of the Everyman Library published by Dent from 1906 until his death. Some of his works, such as "The whistling maid" (1900), are set in Wales, and he was regarded as a member of the "Celtic Twilight" movement.

RHYS, Jean (Ellen Gwendolen Rees Williams)
(1894-1979)
Novelist, born in the West Indies to a Welsh father and Creole mother. She became recognised only in later life, her best-known work being "Wide Sargasso Sea" (1966).

RHYS, John
(1840-1915)
Philologist and folklorist, Professor of Celtic Literature at Oxford from 1877, Principal of Jesus College 1895-1915, also first President of Cymdeithas **DAFYDD ap Gwilym**. Knighted in 1907, his works included "Lectures in Welsh philology" (1877), "Celtic Britain" (1882), and "The Welsh people"

(1900), on which he collaborated with Sir **David Brynmor JONES (3)**. He was one of the prime movers in the campaign to obtain a charter for the University of Wales.

RHYS, Morgan John (Morgan ab Ioan Rhus)
(1760-1804)
Baptist minister, founder of "Y cylchgrawn Cymraeg", the first Welsh political journal (1793). Emigrating to America in 1794, he established the Welsh colony of Cambria in Pennsylvania and founded "the Church of Christ".

RICE, Griffith
(c.1530-84)
Carmarthenshire landowner, first of the **RICE*** family to take the surname; son of Sir Rhys ap Gruffydd, who was executed for treason in 1531. **Mary TUDOR** and Elizabeth I granted him some of his father's property.

RICE, George
(1724-79)
Whig MP for Carmarthenshire 1754-79; Commissioner of the Board of Trade 1761-70. His marriage, to the daughter of the 1st Earl **TALBOT (2)***, united the **RICE*** and Talbot families.

RICE, Walter
(c.1560-1611)
MP for Carmarthenshire on several occasions, knighted in 1603, son of **Griffith RICE**. His marriage to the daughter of Sir Edward **MANSELL*** united the **RICE*** and Mansell families.

RICEMARCHUS
See **RHIGYFARCH**.

RICHARD II (Richard of Bordeaux)
(1367-1400)
King of England, son of **EDWARD of**

Woodstock and **JOAN (2)** of Kent. He became Prince of Wales after the death of his father in 1367, and succeeded his grandfather, Edward III, as King. An unpopular ruler, he was deposed by his cousin, Henry Bolingbroke, and died a prisoner at Pontefract.

RICHARD, Henry ("the Apostle of Peace")
(1812-88)
Congregational minister; the first Welsh Nonconformist MP, sitting as a Liberal for Merthyr Tydfil 1868-88. He championed the poor and oppressed, and obtained a hearing for the cause of the Welsh language and educational system, his conduct earning him the nickname "the Member for Wales". As secretary of the Peace Society from 1848, he came into contact with Richard Cobden, who became his friend. His works in Welsh and English included "Letters on the social and political condition of Wales" (1866).

RICHARDS, Henry **Brinley**
(1819-85)
Pianist and composer, mainly of songs and piano music, best known for "God bless the Prince of Wales". As Director of the Royal Academy of Music, he initiated its local examination system, and sponsored both **Mary DAVIES** and **Joseph PARRY**.

RICHARDS, Ceri
(1903-71)
Surrealist artist, a close associate of **Dylan THOMAS**, some of whose work he attempted to convey visually. During World War II, he was a war artist; other themes in his work include Welsh rural scenes, the industrial environment, and religious subjects. Much of his work is displayed in his home town of Swansea.

RICHARDS, Richard ("Baron Richards")
(1752-1823)
Judge, Lord Chief Baron of the Exchequer, knighted in 1814. His marriage to Catherine **HUMPHREYS*** united the neighbouring estates of the **RICHARDS*** and Humphreys families.

RICHARDS, Thomas
(1719-90)
Clergyman, author of the historical dictionary, "Thesaurus antiquae linguae Britannicae" (1753), which became a valuable reference work for bards.

ROBERT AP HUW
(1580-1665)
Harpist to King James I of England; author of the Penllyn Manuscript, the key to Welsh medieval harp music.

ROBERT AP RHYS
(c.1470-1534)
Chaplain at the court of **Henry TUDOR**, and later to Cardinal Wolsey. He held large estates in Denbighshire from King **HENRY VIII**, and founded the **PRICE*** dynasty.

ROBERT OF BELLEME
(c.1050-1115)
Norman Earl of Shrewsbury from 1098, in succession to his brother, **HUGH d'Avranches**. Having attempted to placate his Welsh neighbours, including **GRUFFYDD ap Cynan** (whom he tolerated as ruler of Gwynedd), he revolted against King Henry I of England in 1102. His Welsh alliances broken, he was exiled to Normandy.

ROBERT OF GLOUCESTER (Robert of Caen)
(c.1095-1147)
Earl of Gloucester, Lord of Glamorgan and Glynllwg, illegitimate son of King Henry I of England, possibly by **NEST (2)**; son-in-law of **Robert FITZHAMO(N)**. His support for his half-sister Matilda against King Stephen was crucial to the outcome of their war.

ROBERT OF RHUDDLAN (Robert de Tilleul)
(c. 1050-93)
Norman nobleman, deputy of **HUGH d'Avranches**; builder of castles at Rhuddlan and Caernarfon.

ROBERT, Gruffydd
(c.1522-1610)
Catholic Archdeacon of Anglesey, author of an important work on Welsh grammar (1567). Following the death of **Mary TUDOR**, he went into voluntary exile in Italy, where he was influenced by humanist philosophy; all four parts of his great work were published abroad.

ROBERTS, Bartholomew (Barti Ddu, Black Barty)
(c.1682-1722)
The most notorious pirate of his day, whose career began when, as a sailor, his ship was captured by pirates. It lasted only from 1718 till his death at the hands of the Royal Navy.

ROBERTS, Caradog
(1878-1935)
Composer, best known for the hymn-tune "Rachie".

ROBERTS, Evan
(1878-1951)
Calvinistic Methodist minister and mystic evangelical preacher, whose activities caused a religious revival in Wales in 1904-8, centred on his chapel of Moriah in Loughor. At the height of his success, his influence was felt even by the Government.

ROBERTS, Goronwy
See **GORONWY-ROBERTS, Goronwy**.

ROBERTS, Griffith
(1735-1808)
Physician of Dolgellau, a major contributor of manuscripts to what later became the Hengwrt-Peniarth collection.

ROBERTS, Isaac
(1829-1904)
Astronomer, formerly a builder; famous for his photographs of stars and nebulae. He was created a Fellow of the Royal Society in 1890.

ROBERTS, John (1)
(1576-1610)
Benedictine monk and Roman Catholic martyr. He ministered in London during the worst ravages of the plague. After several arrests, he was convicted and executed. He was canonized in 1970.

ROBERTS, John (2)
(1767-1834)
Independent minister and theologian, author of "The Blue Book" (actually titled "Galwad Ddifrifol ..."), in support of the "New System" which attempted to heal the rift between Calvinism and Arminianism. All three of his sons became well-known in the theological and literary fields.

ROBERTS, John (3) ("J.R.")
(1804-84)
Independent minister and author, son of **John ROBERTS (2)**. He became joint minister of his father's former church, along with his brother, **Samuel ROBERTS**, and was long-serving editor of "Y Cronicl".

ROBERTS, John (4) (Alaw Elwy; "Telynor Cymru")
(1816-94)
Harpist, descended through his mother from the **WOOD*** family, into which he married. He played before several kings and queens, and his whole family gave a concert for Queen Victoria in 1889.

ROBERTS, John (5) Henry (Pencerdd Gwynedd)
(1848-1924)
Organist and composer, known for his

hymns and songs, founder of the "Cambrian School of Music" in Liverpool.

ROBERTS, Kate
(1891-1985)
Playwright and novelist, also known for short stories. She was first inspired to write by the effect of World War I on her family. A supporter of Plaid Cymru from its earliest days, she bought the periodical "Y Faner" in 1935, in partnership with her husband, Morris Williams, and used it to further the Nationalist cause. Her best-known works include "Traed mewn cyffion" (1936), "Stryd y glep" (1949), and "Tywyll heno" (1962).

ROBERTS, Lewis
(1596-1640)
Merchant, Governor of the East India Company and author of "The merchantes mappe of commerce" (1638), a reference book, and "The treasure of trafficke" (1640), a work on economics.

ROBERTS, Owen Owen
(1793-1866)
Physician, a specialist in the treatment of cholera, which struck Wales severely in 1830. A Radical, he supported schools and hospitals, and campaigned for electoral reform.

ROBERTS, Richard (1)
(1789-1864)
Prolific inventor, who followed various trades. He was responsible for innovations in textile machinery, engineering, railways, lighthouses and clocks. He spent most of his life in Manchester, where he established a business and was prominent in public affairs.

ROBERTS, Richard (2) (Gruffydd Rhisiart; "G.R.")
(1810-83)
Author, third son of **John ROBERTS (2)**.

He did not go into the ministry like his brothers, but kept the family farm; he is best known for his novel, "Jeffrey Jarman" (1855).

ROBERTS, Robert Davies
(1851-1911)
Scientist and author, a pioneer in adult education. He organised educational activities for adults, and supported universities in setting up specialist departments.

ROBERTS, Samuel ("S.R.")
(1800-85)
Independent minister and social reformer, eldest son of **John ROBERTS (2)**. The founder of "Y cronicl" (1843), in which he championed the rights of the individual, he supported Radical causes such as the Anti-Corn Law League and the Peace Society, and campaigned against slavery, capital punishment, and the Crimean War; he supported the idea of universal suffrage. In 1857, he attempted to found a Welsh colony in Tennessee, but returned to Wales after ten years of hardship and persecution.

ROBERTS, Robert **Silyn**.
(1871-1930)
Calvinistic Methodist minister, translator, lecturer and teacher, Socialist author and poet; a close associate of **W. J. GRUFFYDD**. He collaborated with **Thomas JONES (7)** in the campaign for adult education, and founded the North Wales branch of the Workers' Education Association (1925).

ROBERTS, Thomas (1)
(1760-1811)
Proprietor of the first printing press at Caernarfon (1797).

ROBERTS, Thomas (2)
(c.1766-1841)
Quaker goldsmith, co-founder of the

London Cymreigyddion Society (1796); author of a famous political pamphlet, "Cwyn yn erbyn Gorthrymder" (1798).

ROBERTS, William
(1830-99)
Physician, youngest son of David ROBERTS (1)*; knighted in 1885. He was chief physician at Manchester Royal Infirmary 1855-83 and Professor of Medicine at Owens College 1873-89.

ROBERTSON, Henry
(1816-88)
Scots engineer, who lived and worked in Wales and the border area from 1842. He was responsible for the building of the North Wales Mineral Railway, to serve local industry, and later founded the Brymbo Steel Works (1884). He served as Liberal MP for Shrewsbury 1862-5 and 1874-85.

ROBINSON, John
(1617-81)
Royalist commander in the Civil War, grandson of Nicholas ROBINSON. He defended Holt Castle against Parliamentary forces in 1643, and took part in the Anglesey revolt of 1648. After the Restoration, he was MP for Beaumaris 1661-79. Descendants include the novelist Edward Bulwer-Lytton.

ROBINSON, Nicholas
(c.1530-85)
Bishop of Bangor 1566-85, a member of the Conway branch of the ROBINSON* family. A protege of William CECIL*, he won favour with Queen Elizabeth I and had a wide reputation as a preacher and scholar.

ROLLS, Charles Stewart
(1877-1910)
Welsh-born industrialist and aviator, co-founder of the Rolls Royce car manufacturing firm; son of 1st Baron Llangattock.

ROOS, William
(1808-78)
Portrait painter and engraver, whose subjects included Christmas EVANS and Thomas CHARLES.

ROSS, John
(c.1729-1807)
Publisher, owner of a press at Carmarthen from 1763 to 1807, which produced more Welsh books than all its rivals put together; these included three editions of "Peter WILLIAMS' Bible".

ROWLAND
See also ROWLANDS.

ROWLAND, Daniel
(1713-90)
Methodist clergyman, one of the leaders of the Methodist revival in Wales. With Howell HARRIS, he started societies of converts throughout the country, eventually resulting in the Welsh Presbyterian denomination. He also composed many hymns, and translated the works of Bunyan and Wetherall into Welsh. Later, he criticised Harris in "Ymddiddan rhwng Methodist Uniongred ac un cyfeiliornus" (1749), and their followers split into two groups in about 1752. He then succeeded Harris as effective leader of the Methodists in Wales, tending towards Whitefield rather than Wesley. "Rowland's people" were based at Llangeitho, where his son was minister, from about 1760 to 1769.

ROWLAND, Henry
(1551-1616)
Bishop of Bangor 1598-1616, responsible for repairs to the cathedral. He founded a school at Mellteyrn, almshouses at Bangor, and scholarships to Jesus College, Oxford.

ROWLANDS
See also ROWLAND.

ROWLANDS, John
See **STANLEY, Henry Morton**.

ROWLANDS, William
(1807-66)
Minister and author, founder of the Calvinistic Methodist movement in the USA, where he lived and worked from 1836.

RUMSEY, Walter
(1584-1660)
Judge, Royalist MP for Monmouthshire 1640; inventor of a device known as the "provang", for cleaning the larynx, described in his work, "Organon salutis" (1657).

RUSSELL, Bertrand
(1872-1970)
3rd Earl Russell; philosopher and author, born in Gwent. A pacifist, he lost his academic post and was imprisoned during World War I; but he changed his attitude to war after the rise of Fascism. In the meantime, he visited the USSR and China, earned a living as a journalist, and succeeded to the family title in 1931. He was awarded the Nobel Prize for Literature in 1950. From 1955 until his death, he lived at Plas Penrhyn, Penrhyndeudraeth, Gwynedd, with his fourth wife.

S

SAI
See **SAY**.

SAINT
See under name of individual saint.

SALESBURY
See also **SALUSBURY**.

SALESBURY, Henry
(c.1561-1637)
Author of the Welsh grammar, "Grammatica Britannica" (1593), related to the **SALESBURY (1)*** family of Lleweni.

SALESBURY, William
(c.1520-84)
Protestant scholar who produced numerous printed works in Welsh, including an English-Welsh dictionary (1547). He was a close associate of **GRUFFYDD Hiraethog**, whose collection of proverbs he published in 1547 (the second printed book in Welsh). Having spent the reign of **Mary TUDOR** in hiding, he completed translations of the Book of Common Prayer and New Testament (1567), in partnership with Bishop **Richard DAVIES (1)**, under the Act of Parliament of 1563 which they had instigated.

SALISBURY
See **SALESBURY**, **SALUSBURY**.

SALUSBURY
See also **SALESBURY**.

SALUSBURY, Charles John
(1792-1868)
3rd baronet **SALESBURY (1)***, heir to the Vaun estate of Llanwern through his mother. His correspondence with famous contemporaries is of interest.

SALUSBURY, John (1)
(1567-1612)
Heir to the **SALUSBURY (1)*** estate, younger brother of **Thomas SALUSBURY (1)**. A lawyer and poet, he gained favour with Queen Elizabeth I despite his brother's disgrace, served as MP for Denbighshire and was knighted in 1601. He carried on a feud with the **SALUSBURY (2)*** family of Rug.

SALUSBURY, John (2) (John Parry)
(1575-1625)
Roman Catholic priest, founder of the Jesuit college of St Francis Xavier at Cwm Llanrothal (Llanrhyddol) (1622).

SALUSBURY, Thomas (1)
(c.1564-86)
Catholic nobleman, son of **KATHERYN of Berain**, executed for treason for his part in the Babington Plot of 1586.

SALUSBURY, Thomas (2)
(1612-43)
Poet and translator, MP for Denbighshire 1641-3, who served in the Royalist army during the Civil War, and inherited the **SALUSBURY (1)*** baronetcy and estates in 1632.

SALUSBURY, William ("Hen hosanau gleision", "Old blue stockings")
(c.1580-1660)
Colonel who held Denbigh for the Royalists during the Civil War and served as MP for Merioneth 1620-22. He inherited the **SALUSBURY (2)*** estates from his brother in 1611, and divided them between his two sons.

SALUSBURY, Hester Lynch
See **THRALE, Hester**.

SAMSON

(c.485-565)

Early Christian bishop, a pupil of **ILLTUD**. He spent some time in Ireland, where he is commemorated in place names, and later travelled to Cornwall and Brittany, winning the respect of the Franks and founding a monastery at Dol.

SAMWELL or **SAMUEL, David (Dafydd Ddu Feddyg)**

(1751-98)

Naval surgeon and poet. While a crew member on board the "Discovery", he was an eye-witness to Captain Cook's death.

SANKEY, John

(1866-1948)

English judge who helped draw up the constitution of the Church in Wales following Disestablishment. He also chaired the Commission of 1919 which recommended the nationalisation of the coal industry.

SAUNDERSON, Robert

(1780-1863)

Publisher, a close associate of **Thomas CHARLES**, by whom he was employed at the Chester offices of Charles & Jones. He moved with the business to Bala, and took it over in 1814.

SCOTT (née ROSS), Ann

(1735-1842)

Daughter of **John ROSS**, who carried on her father's printing and publishing business after his death.

SCOTT-ELLIS, Thomas Evelyn (Lord Howard de Walden)

(1880-1946)

English-born author who settled at Chirk Castle, learned Welsh and was a generous patron of the arts. He attempted unsuccessfully to set up a Welsh national drama company.

SCUDAMORE, John

(c.1360-1420)

Knight, of Norman descent, who held Carreg Cennen Castle for the English Crown against **OWAIN Glyndwr**. He later married Owain's daughter, Alice, and became a supporter of his rebellion. Owain was believed to have spent his last days at one of Scudamore's houses, Monnington Straddel.

SEIRIOL

(c.500-550)

Saint, reputedly a grandson of **EINION Yrth**, who converted many of the Scandinavian immigrants in Anglesey, and later retired to the island known as Ynys Seiriol or Priestholm.

SEISYLL AP CLYDOG

(early 8th century; exact dates unknown)

King of Ceredigion and Ystrad Tywi, a descendant of **CUNEDDA**. He gave his name to the kingdom of Seisyllwg, later Deheubarth.

SELYF

(6th-7th century; exact dates unknown)

King of Powys, killed at the Battle of Chester by Northumbrian forces in around 615. **CYNDDELW Brydydd Mawr** coined the phrase "cenawon Selyf" to describe contemporary warriors of Powys.

SENENA

(c.1201-62)

Wife of **GRUFFYDD ap Llywelyn (2)** (1218), mother of **LLYWELYN ap Gruffydd** and his brothers. In 1241, while her husband was a prisoner of the English Crown, she attempted to obtain his freedom by a valuable ransom.

SEWARD, William

(c.1700-42)

Methodist preacher, stoned to death at

Hay-on-Wye, becoming the first "Methodist martyr".

SHADRACH, Azariah ("the Bunyan of Wales")
(1774-1844)
Independent minister, founder of a chapel at Aberystwyth and author of devotional works in Welsh and English.

SHALDEFORD, Henry
(c.1300-45)
Attorney in North Wales for **EDWARD of Woodstock**, who was murdered on his way to take up his appointment. The incident was indicative of anti-English feeling.

SIDDONS (née KEMBLE), Sarah
(1755-1831)
Actress, one of the first women to make a successful and respectable career on the stage. Daughter of the actor-manager Roger Kemble, whose travelling theatre company was based in the Welsh borders, she appeared on stage as a child, and joined the company at fifteen. She married the actor William Siddons in 1773, and they appeared together at Drury Lane in 1776. Under the direction of Garrick, and later Sheridan, she became the most famous actress in Britain, and was painted by Reynolds and Gainsborough. After making her name, she spent little time in Wales, but occasionally visited her friend, **Hester THRALE**.

SIDNEY, Henry
(1529-86)
English nobleman and diplomat, President of the Council of Wales from 1559 until his death. He made his home in Ludlow, and was popular in Wales, of which he said, "a better country to govern Europe holdeth not".

SIDNEY, Mary
(1561-1621)
Scholar, poet and translator, daughter of

Sir **Henry SIDNEY**. She spent her childhood at Ludlow Castle, and later at the court of Queen Elizabeth I. By her marriage to the much older **Henry HERBERT (1)**, she became Countess of Pembroke, and returned to Ludlow when her husband succeeded her father as President of the Council of Wales.

SIDNEY, Robert
(1563-1626)
Earl of Leicester, second son of Sir **Henry SIDNEY**. Following his marriage to **Barbara GAMAGE** in 1584, he served as MP for Glamorgan 1585 and 1592. The **GAMAGE*** estate of Coity passed to their descendants.

SION CENT
(c.1367-1445)
Poet, first to adopt the style of 'cywydd' divided into sections with a refrain. His works, the best known of which are "Cywydd dychan i'r awen gelwyddog" and "I wagedd ac oferedd y byd", are largely concerned with religion.

SION TUDUR
See **TUDUR, Sion**.

SIWAN
See **JOAN (1)**.

SKIDMORE
See **SCUDAMORE**.

SMITH (formerly ASSHETON), Thomas Assheton (1)
(1752-1828)
English industrialist, heir to the Vaenol estate of his uncle; on inheriting, he took the surname Smith. He was MP for Caernarfonshire 1774-80, and developed the slate quarries on the estate. The size of the industry increased four-fold under his management, and he built a new road and harbour at Port Dinorwic.

SMITH, Thomas Assheton (2)

(1776-1858)

Owner of the Vaenol estate, son of **Thomas Assheton SMITH (1)**; Conservative MP for Caernarfonshire 1832-41. Famous as a master of foxhounds, he was nicknamed "the British Nimrod". His developments on the estate included a railway along the banks of Llyn Padarn.

SOMERSET, Charles

(c.1460-1526)

1st Earl of Worcester, illegitimate son of Henry **BEAUFORT***, Duke of Somerset, a leading Lancastrian. His support for **Henry TUDOR** brought him royal favour and offices, including his earldom (1513). Marriage to Elizabeth **HERBERT (1)*** gained him the title Baron Herbert in 1504.

SOMERSET, Edward (1)

(1553-1628)

4th Earl of Worcester, son of **William SOMERSET**; Lord Privy Seal 1616-21. As Lord Lieutenant of Glamorgan and Monmouthshire, he ruled them independently from Raglan, despite being a member of the Council of Wales. His Roman Catholicism did not lose him the favour of Queen Elizabeth I, and he was later involved in anti-Catholic activities.

SOMERSET, Edward (2)

(1601-67)

2nd Marquess of Worcester, son of **Henry SOMERSET (1)**. He was a member of the Council of Wales from 1633, and, like his father, a Roman Catholic and staunch Royalist. He was made General of South Wales (1642) and given the title Earl of Glamorgan (1645), but was forced into exile in France. On his return, he was imprisoned by Parliament, remaining in obscurity after the Restoration.

SOMERSET, Henry (1)

(c.1577-1646)

5th Earl of Worcester, second son of **Edward SOMERSET (1)**. A Roman Catholic and Royalist, he made Raglan a centre for the King's supporters in the Civil War, and was created 1st Marquess of Worcester in 1642. Raglan Castle was under siege for several months in 1646; after surrendering, he died in prison.

SOMERSET, Henry (2)

(1629-1700)

3rd Marquis of Worcester, son of **Edward SOMERSET (2)**, created Duke of Beaufort in 1682. He transferred the family seat to Badminton, but retained vast estates in South Wales. As President of the Council of Wales from 1672 until its dissolution in 1689, he toured all its counties, his itinerary recorded by **Thomas DINELEY**.

SOMERSET, William ("Tew Wilym o Went")

(1526-89)

3rd Earl of Worcester, in royal favour from the reign of King Edward VI onwards, associate of William **CECIL***. He was a member of the Council of Wales, but lost his influence in the principality to the **HERBERT (2)*** Earls of Pembroke.

SPENCER, DIANA

See **DIANA, Princess of Wales**.

SPOONER, Charles Easton

(1818-89)

Railway engineer, Welsh-born son of **James SPOONER**. He succeeded his father as engineer of the Ffestiniog railway, and was an expert on narrow-gauge railways.

SPOONER, James

(1789-1856)

English railway engineer, responsible for

surveying the Ffestiniog Railway, one of the first narrow-gauge railways in the world.

SPRING, Howard
(1889-1965)
Popular novelist, a journalist by profession. His best-known work, "Fame is the spur" (1940), is concerned with the pressures of political life; he was present at Churchill's "Atlantic Charter" meeting with Roosevelt. Other works include "Shabby tiger" (1934), "Rachel Rosing" (1935), children's stories, a play and an autobiography.

SPURRELL, William
(1813-89)
Publisher, who established the **SPURRELL*** family press at Carmarthen in 1840. It produced dictionaries, periodicals, and works of local interest. His son, Walter, followed him into the business.

STANLEY (née TENNANT), Dorothy
(1855-1926)
Artist, granddaughter of **George TENNANT**. In 1890, she married Sir **Henry Morton STANLEY** in Westminster Abbey, and devoted herself to furthering his career. After his death, she completed his unfinished autobiography.

STANLEY, Henry Morton (formerly JOHN ROWLANDS)
(1841-1904)
Journalist and explorer, remembered chiefly for his meeting with the missionary David Livingstone in 1871, which he recorded in "How I found Livingstone" (1872). Born to the Rowlands family of Denbigh, he was abandoned as a child, and spent some years in a workhouse at St Asaph. While working his passage to the USA, he was befriended by the wealthy Henry Stanley, whose name he then adopted. Having travelled the world as a reporter, he embarked on the search for Livingstone on instructions from the "New York Herald", and later carried out two further exploratory visits to Africa, discovering Lake Edward and Mount Ruwenzori. He was made a GCB in 1899, and served as Unionist MP for North Lambeth 1895-1900.

STANTON, Charles Butt
(1873-1946)
Militant miners' leader at Aberdare, fiercely critical of his local Labour MP, **Keir HARDIE**, for opposing war. After Hardie's death in 1915, he himself became MP for Merthyr Boroughs, supporting the Coalition Government and serving until defeated by an official Labour candidate in 1922.

STEELE (née SCURLOCK), Mary ("Prue")
(1678-1718)
Second wife of the essayist, Sir Richard Steele, immortalised by him in his works and correspondence. Their stormy marriage (1707) produced two sons and two daughters, one of whom became Lady **TREVOR***. After his wife's death, Steele himself retired to Wales.

STEPHEN (formerly JONES), Edward (Tanymarian)
(1822-85)
Congregational minister, poet and composer. Works include hymn-tunes, of which the best-known is "Tanymarian", anthems, songs, and the oratorio, "Ystorm Tiberias" (1852).

STEWART
See also **STUART**.

STEWART, Malcolm Percy
(1872-1951)
English industrialist and philanthropist. As Ramsay MacDonald's Special Commissioner for Wales 1934-6, he devised schemes for reducing unemployment, and was

created 1st baronet Stewart of Stewartby (1937).

STRADLING or STRADLYNG, Edward (1)
(c.1290-1355)
Head of the **STRADLING*** family in Glamorgan and Somerset, a patron of Neath Abbey, knighted in 1327. He married into the **CLARE*** family, and benefited from the fall of the **DESPENSER*** dynasty in 1330.

STRADLING, Edward (2)
(1529-1609)
Scholar, son and heir of **Thomas STRADLING**, knighted in 1573. The author of a history of Norman Wales in which the story of the "Twelve Knights" of Glamorgan was popularised, he was also a patron of the arts and education, and improved the buildings and estate of St Donat's.

STRADLING, Edward (3)
(1601-44)
2nd baronet **STRADLING***, son of Sir **John STRADLING**. He was MP for Glamorgan in 1640, and married into the **MANSEL*** family of Margam. He died a prisoner of war, having served as a Royalist commander at the Battle of Edgehill.

STRADLING, John
(c.1570-1637)
Poet and author, adopted son and heir of Sir **Edward STRADLING (2)**, created a baronet in 1611. He was MP for Glamorgan 1625-6, and founded Cowbridge Grammar School.

STRADLING, Thomas
(c.1520-73)
Heir to the **STRADLING*** estate, knighted in 1549. A Roman Catholic, he was imprisoned under Queen Elizabeth I. He married into the **GAMAGE*** family.

STUART, Charles
See **CHARLES I, CHARLES II**

STUART, Charles Edward Louis Philip Casimir (**"Bonnie Prince Charlie"; "The Young Pretender"**)
(1720-88)
Born in France, son of **James Francis Edward STUART**, he was given the unofficial title Prince of Wales by Jacobite supporters, who recognised his father as King James III of England. After an unsuccessful attempt to invade England in 1745 (the "Second Jacobite Rebellion"), he returned to his father in Italy, and eventually died in squalor, leaving one illegitimate daughter.

STUART, Henry (Henry of Stirling)
(1594-1612)
Elder son of King James I of England (James VI of Scotland); Prince of Wales from 1610, after his father's accession had united the kingdoms of England and Scotland. The titles of High Steward of Scotland, Duke of Rothesay, Earl of Carrick, Lord of the Isles, and Baron of Renfrew were added to those of the Prince of Wales at this time. He died without becoming King, and his titles passed to his younger brother, later King **CHARLES I**.

STUART, James Francis Edward ("The Old Pretender")
(1688-1766)
Prince of Wales, son of King James II/VII, born only months before his father was deposed in favour of the Protestant William of Orange and his wife Mary, half-sister to the Prince. He had been given the title at his christening, perhaps in anticipation of an attempt to overthrow the King. He lived in exile in France until 1715, when he made an unsuccessful attempt to raise a Scottish army and take the throne (the "First Jacobite Rebellion").

SUETONIUS PAULINUS, Gaius
(1st century AD; exact dates unknown)
Roman governor of Britain 58-62 AD, who
invaded Anglesey (Mona) in 61 A.D., and
massacred the druids.

SULIEN (Sulgenus)
(c.1010-91)
Bishop of St David's 1073-78 and 1080-85,
sometimes called "the wise", founder of an
ecclesiastical dynasty. It was through his

activities and influence that the monastery of
Llanbadarn Fawr became known as a centre
of learning.

SYPYN CYFEILIOG
(c.1340-90)
Poet, best known for the "one night's
awdl" he addressed to one Dafydd ap
Cadwaladr, which appears in the Red Book
of Hergest. He was also associated with
the **SALESBURY (1)*** family of Lleweni.

T

TALBOT, Charles
(1685-1737)

1st Baron **TALBOT (2)*** of Hensol (1733); MP for various constituencies, appointed Lord Chancellor in 1733. He became connected with Wales through marriage into the **MATHEW*** family, his wife Cecil being the granddaughter and heiress of judge David Jenkins of Hensol. There he built a Tudor-style castle as the family residence.

TALBOT, Emily Charlotte
(1840- 1918)

Unmarried daughter of Christopher Rice Mansel Talbot; last member of the **TALBOT (1)*** family to live at Margam Castle. She commissioned the cataloguing of the Margam and Penricc muniments by Walter de Gray Birch.

TALIESIN
(c.515-90)

Poet, mentioned by **NENNIUS**, who gained recognition at the court of Cynan Garwyn, king of Powys, and later composed works in honour of **MAELGWN Gwynedd** and **URIEN Rheged**. Only one of his poems, the "Hengerdd", survives, but the manuscript of the "Llyfr Taliesin", dating from around 1275, contains poetry attributed to him. He is also the subject of the folk-tale known as "Hanes Taliesin", the written version of which dates from the sixteenth century.

TALLIS, John Fox
(1854-1925)

Engineer and surveyor, employed by the Ocean Coal Company and Ebbw Vale Company to work in the South Wales coalfield. He introduced electric lighting underground, and encouraged the Ebbw Vale working miners during the strike of 1893. *Gave his name to:* Tallistown, a district of Ebbw Vale.

TANGWYSTL GOCH
(12th century; exact dates unknown)

Red-headed concubine of **LLYWELYN Fawr** and mother of **GRUFFYDD ap Llywelyn (2)**.

TANY, Luke (de)
(13th-14th century; exact dates unknown)

Norman knight entrusted by King **EDWARD I** of England with the task of invading Anglesey in 1282. His attempt to cross to the mainland by means of a pontoon bridge failed.

TEILO or ELIUD
(6th century; exact dates unknown)

Patron saint of Llandaff. A contemporary of St **DAVID**, with whom he probably travelled to Jerusalem, he is believed to have been bishop of St David's. He founded a monastery at Llandeilo, and is also associated with Brittany.

TELFORD, Thomas
(1757-1834)

Scots engineer responsible for many public works in Wales, mostly associated with the development of the canal system. The most impressive of these is the Pontycysyllte aqueduct project, completed in the period 1795-1805. In later years, he returned to Wales and designed the Menai suspension bridge, built in the years 1819-25.

TENBY, Viscount
See **LLOYD GEORGE, Gwilym.**

TENNANT, Dorothy
See **STANLEY, Dorothy**.

TENNANT, George
(1765-1832)
English lawyer, developer of the Tennant
Canal (1824). He planned the tidal harbour
at the Swansea end of the canal. *Gave his
name to:* Port Tennant, a district of Swansea.

TEWDWR
See also **Tudor**.

THELWALL, Ambrose
(1570-1652)
Court official, brother of **Eubule THEL-
WALL** and **Bevis THELWALL**. He served
Sir Francis Bacon and was later appointed
Yeoman of the Robes to King James I/VI,
King **CHARLES I**, and the Prince of Wales
(later King **CHARLES II**).

THELWALL, Bevis
(c.1572-1650)
London merchant, brother of **Ambrose
THELWALL** and **Eubule THELWALL**.
A personal friend of King James I/VI, he
was knighted and appointed Clerk of the
Great Wardrobe.

THELWALL, Eubule
(1562-1630)
Lawyer, a member of the Bathafarn branch
of the **THELWALL*** family; MP for Denbigh in 1624, 1626 and 1628-9, knighted in
1619. He was Principal of Jesus College,
Oxford, 1621-30, and financed renovations
to the College.

THELWALL, Simon
(1526-86)
Lawyer, linguist and poet, heir to the Plas
y Ward estate of the **THELWALL***
family. He was MP for Denbigh on several
occasions between 1553 and 1571. As a
judge, he sentenced **Richard GWYN** to
death in 1584.

THIRLWALL, Connop
(1797-1875)
English Bishop of St David's 1840-74.
Accepting criticism of his appointment, he
learned Welsh for use in church services. His
energetic efforts did not prevent him from
being accused by Sir **Benjamin HALL (2)**
of misappropriation of the revenues of
Christ College, Brecon. Despite his liberal
views, he failed to assist **Rowland WIL-
LIAMS**.

**THOMAS OF MONMOUTH (Thomas
Monumentensis)**
(c.1120-72)
Benedictine monk, author of a life of St
Thomas of Norwich, in Latin, which sup-
ported anti-Jewish feeling in England.

THOMAS WALLENSIS (1)
(c.1200-55)
Bishop of St David's 1247-55; a Grey Friar,
associated with Oxford and known to Roger
Bacon.

**THOMAS WALLENSIS (2) (Thomas
Waleys)**
(c.1300-50)
Dominican friar and author, imprisoned for
heresy by Pope John XXII; his views were
later adopted as part of mainstream belief.

THOMAS, Alban
(1686-1771)
Scholar and physician who assisted **Edward
LHUYD** in the production of his "Glossography" (1707). He was forced to leave
London because of his Jacobite associations,
and assisted **Moses WILLIAMS** in the
preservation and publication of old Welsh
manuscripts.

THOMAS, Alfred
(1840-1927)
Liberal MP for East Glamorgan 1885-
1910, author of the National Institutions

Bill of 1891, which proposed an elected assembly for Wales. He was chairman of the Welsh Parliamentary party 1897-1910, was knighted in 1902 and created Baron Pontypridd in 1912.

THOMAS (née FISON), Anna (Morfydd Eryri)
(1839-1920)
English wife of a Welsh clergyman, who settled in Wales in 1871, learned the Welsh language, and was a leading member of the eisteddfod reform movement. She arranged evening classes to educate local quarry-workers.

THOMAS, Ben Bowen
(1899-1977)
Academic, first Warden of Coleg Harlech (1927); knighted 1950. A member of the Crowther/Kilbrandon Commission on the Constitution (1969-73), he reported in favour of a legislative assembly for Wales.

THOMAS, Clement Price
See **PRICE THOMAS, Clement**.

THOMAS, Daniel Lleufer
(1863-1940)
Lawyer and biographer, co-founder of Cymdeithas **DAFYDD ap Gwilym** at Oxford (1886). He served as secretary and chairman of various public bodies, and helped found the University College and National Library of Wales. As a magistrate, he was praised for his handling of the Tonypandy Riots of 1910.

THOMAS, David Wynne
See **WYNNE, David**.

THOMAS, David (1) (Dafydd Ddu Eryri)
(1759-1822)
Poet, founder of several literary societies through which he gained a reputation as a teacher of bardic tradition, though he had

himself received a minimal education. His pupils were known as "Cywion Dafydd Ddu".

THOMAS, David (2)
(1794-1882)
Industrialist, inventor of a "hot blast" process for the production of iron using anthracite coal, which brought rapid industrialisation to parts of West Wales. From 1839, he lived and worked in the USA, encouraging large-scale emigration from Wales to the towns of Scranton and Wilkes Barre in Pennsylvania.

THOMAS, David (3) Alfred
(1856-1918)
Industrialist, Liberal MP for Merthyr Tydfil 1888-1910. An early supporter of the Cymru Fydd movement, he nevertheless opposed its integration with the South Wales Liberal Federation, making an enemy of **David LLOYD GEORGE**. Having made a fortune as a coal-owner, he was created Viscount Rhondda in 1915, but was excluded from political office until 1916, when he became President of the Local Government Board. As Food Controller during the latter part of World War I, he was very successful.

THOMAS, David (4) John (Afan)
(1881-1928)
Composer, conductor and organist, known for hymn-tunes and songs such as "Drosom ni" and "Cymru fach i mi". Other works include a cantata, "Merch y llyn", and a choral work, "He fell among thieves", with words by Sir Henry Newbolt.

THOMAS, Dylan Marlais
(1914-53)
English-speaking poet whose revolutionary use of the language brought him worldwide fame. His most famous work, the radio play, "Under Milk Wood", was first broadcast in 1954. Other works included short stories

and the autobiographical "Portrait of the artist as a young dog" (1940). His best-known poems include "Fern Hill", "And death shall have no dominion", and "Poem in October". In 1949 he retired to the Boat House at Laugharne, where he made his home, but did not give up his heavy drinking, which brought about his death in the USA during one of his lecture tours.
Gave his name to: Dylan Thomas Theatre, Swansea; etc.

THOMAS, Ebenezer (Eben Fardd; Cybi o Eifion)
(1802-63)
Poet and hymnist who emerged from a poor background to become a schoolmaster in a Methodist academy at Clynnog. He won the Chair at the National Eisteddfod three times (1824, 1840, 1858), becoming one of the most important literary figures of his time. His best-known poems include "Dinystr Jerusalem" and "Y flwyddyn".

THOMAS, Edmund
(1712-67)
3rd baronet **THOMAS (3)***, MP for Glamorgan 1761-7. A personal friend of **FREDERICK Lewis Augustus**, Prince of Wales, he was groom of the bedchamber 1742-51, and on the Prince's death became Treasurer of the Princess's household in 1757. He sold the family estate of Wenvoe in 1765.

THOMAS, Edward (1) William
(1814-92)
Violinist and composer, best known for "Can bugail Morgannwg" (1861) and a violin concerto dedicated to Joseph Joachim.

THOMAS, Edward (2) (Cochfarf)
(1853-1912)
Cardiff local politician, founder of the "Cymmrodorion Caerdydd" society at a coffee house run by him in Custom House

Street. His second wife, Madame Hughes-Thomas, toured the world with her ladies' choir, accompanied by her husband, who helped organise an eisteddfod in the USA.

THOMAS, Philip Edward (3)
(1878-1917)
Poet of the "Anglo-Welsh" school, born in London. Works include a novel, "The happy-go-lucky Morgans" (1913) and several books about natural history, such as "Beautiful Wales" (1905). He died in action at Arras during World War I. Most of his poetry was composed under the influence of Robert Frost and published after his death, under the pseudonym Edward Eastaway.

THOMAS, Edward (4) ('Eddie')
(1927-1997)
Boxing champion and manager, awarded the MBE for his services to the sport. An ex-miner, he was forced to resign as Mayor of his home town of Merthyr Tydfil in 1994 after being declared bankrupt, but remained a local hero.

THOMAS, Evan
(1804-84)
Bone-setter, member of the renowned **THOMAS (4)*** family. He practised in Liverpool from about 1835, and his ideas on the treatment of bone disease achieved a degree of success in preventing amputations.

THOMAS, Frederick Hall (Freddie Welsh)
(1886-1927)
Lightweight boxing champion of the world (1914), an outstandingly successful competitor who retired to the USA.

THOMAS, Thomas George
(1909-97)
Labour politician and statesman; MP for Cardiff Central 1945-83. A deeply reli-

gious man and a former teacher, he was one of the first on the scene of the Aberfan disaster, which occurred while he was a Minister at the Welsh Office. As Secretary of State for Wales 1968-70, he presided over the Prince of Wales' Investuture arrangements of 1969. During his term of office as Speaker of the House of Commons (1976-83), the first broadcasting of Parliament proceedings brought him unprecedented public attention, but he proved more impartial than party colleagues had expected. In 1983, he was created Viscount Tonypandy. Always an anti-Nationalist, one of his final political acts was his public opposition to the devolution proposals of 1997.

THOMAS, Gwyn
(1913-81)
Novelist and playwright, much of whose work is based on life in the South Wales industrial valleys where he grew up, the son of a coal-miner. His works include "All things betray thee" (1949), "Jackie the jumper" (1963), and the collection of essays entitled "A Welsh eye" (1964).

THOMAS, Hugh (1)
(1673-1720)
Historian and genealogist, author of a history of Brecknock (1698); deputy to the Garter King-at-Arms. His collection of pedigrees and manuscripts passed into the hands of **Robert HARLEY**.

THOMAS, Hugh (2) Owen
(1834-91)
Orthopaedic surgeon, son of **Evan THOMAS**. He practised in Liverpool, at first in partnership with his father. He was one of the best-known and most successful surgeons in Britain, pioneered new methods, and wrote several books on the subject. The "Thomas calliper", his own invention, came into widespread use.

THOMAS, James (1) Lewis
(1825-1904)
Architect, brother of **John THOMAS (3)**. He designed the military hospital at Netley, and was Treasurer of the Society of Ancient Britons.

THOMAS, James (2) Henry ("Jimmy")
(1874-1949)
Labour politician, MP for Derby 1910-36. He was instrumental in the formation of the National Union of Railwaymen (1917), of which he served as general secretary, and served as Colonial Secretary 1924-9 and 1935-6, Lord Privy Seal 1929-30, and Dominions Secretary 1930-35. His career ended when he was found guilty of leaking Budget information in 1936.

THOMAS, Jennie
(1898-1979)
Co-author of "Llyfr mawr y plant" (1931), a children's book in which the popular characters, Sion Blewyn Coch and Wil Cwac Cwac, first appeared.

THOMAS, John (1)
(c.1730-1804)
Congregational minister and hymnist, author of "Rhad ras" (1810), sometimes called "the first Welsh autobiography".

THOMAS, John (2) William (**Arfonwyson**)
(1805-40)
Mathematician and author, largely self-educated. While working as a schoolmaster, he wrote "Elfennau rhifyddiaeth", published in three parts between 1830 and 1832. He later edited the periodical, "Tywysog Cymru", and published an English-Welsh dictionary (1833). In London, he worked for William Cobbett and obtained a post at Greenwich Observatory, where he produced Welsh almanacs.

THOMAS, John (3) Evan
(1810-73)
Sculptor, known particularly for his statues in Brecon Cathedral and the statue of the Duke of Wellington at Brecon, his native town; brother of **James THOMAS (1)**. His success allowed the purchase of the mansion of Penisha'r Pentre in 1857. Another brother, William Meredith Thomas, was his assistant and completed some of his unfinished works.

THOMAS, John (4) (Pencerdd Gwalia)
(1826-1913)
Harpist to Queen Victoria, appointed in 1871; also a composer of music for the harp. He founded the London Welsh Choral Union (1871); its Royal Academy scholarship was named after him.

THOMAS, John (5)
(1838-1905)
Photographer, proprietor of the "Cambrian Gallery" in Liverpool. He was famous for his portraits of Welsh celebrities, including the best-known preachers of the period, but also photographed Welsh landscapes, churches and ancient monuments.

THOMAS, John (6)
(1886-1933)
Chemist, a researcher first at the National Physical Laboratory and later at Nobel's Explosives Co. He became managing director of Solway Dyes Ltd, and his major contributions were in the discovery of new dyes. He ended his career in a senior position with ICI.

THOMAS, Lewis
(1832-1913)
Industrialist, who lived and worked in Australia from 1859. There he opened the Aberdare colliery and established a Welsh community at Blackstone in Queensland. He served as MP for Bundamba 1894-99 and was subsequently a member of the Legislative Council.

THOMAS, Lucy ("Mother of the Welsh Coal Trade")
(1781-1847)
Widow of a coal-owner, who established a family tradition in the industry. She opened the first seam for the mining of coal for household purposes at Abercanaid in 1828, and with her son, William Thomas, sold it in London.

THOMAS, Margaret Haig
(1883-1958)
Publisher, daughter of **David A THOMAS (3)**, Viscount Rhondda. She became her father's business partner after a career as a suffragette. On his death in 1918, she succeeded to the title and unsuccessfully attempted to attend the House of Lords as Viscountess Rhondda. She founded the periodical, "Time and tide" (1920), which she edited herself and subsidised from her own funds.

THOMAS, Noah
(1720-92)
Physician to King George III, knighted in 1775; an early member of the Society of Cymmrodorion in London.

THOMAS, Owen
(1858-1923)
World War I General, a friend of **David LLOYD GEORGE**; Labour MP for Anglesey 1918-23. He retained interests in South Africa, where he had served during the Boer War.

THOMAS, Percy Edward
(1883-1969)
Architect, designer of the Guildhall, Swansea (1934) and Temple of Peace, Cardiff (1938); knighted 1946.

THOMAS, Rachel
(1905-95)

Actress, known for her film, stage and television work. One of her first appearances was opposite Paul Robeson in "The proud valley". She continued her career into old age, and gained new popularity for her role in the Welsh-language television series, "Pobol y Cwm".

THOMAS, Richard
(1838-1916)

English industrialist, owner of tin plate works throughout South Wales, having expanded from Gloucestershire. The firm he founded later merged with Baldwin's and was the basis of the Steel Company of Wales (1947).

THOMAS, Sidney Gilchrist
(1850-85)

English-born metallurgist, inventor of a method of dc-phosphorizing pig-iron which revolutionised the steel industry world wide. The fortune he made as a consequence was left to his sister, Lilian Gilchrist Thomas, to be used for philanthropic purposes.

THOMAS, Thomas
(1880-1911)

Sportsman, first winner of the British middleweight boxing championship (1909). His training programme consisted of bareback horse-riding and sparring with a bull.

THOMAS, Trevor
(1907-93)

Art historian and author; campaigner for homosexual equality. After periods as Director of Leicester Museum and Art Gallery 1940-6 and Director of the Crafts Centre of Great Britain 1946-8, he was Professor of Art and Art History at universities in New York State, USA, 1957-60.

THOMAS, James William Tudor
(1893-1976)

Ophthalmic surgeon, based in Cardiff hospitals from 1920 to 1960, President of the Ophthalmological Society of the UK 1966-8; knighted 1956.

THOMAS, William ap
See WILIAM ap Tomos.

THOMAS, William (1)
(c.1500-54)

Scholar, political adviser to King Edward VI of England and Clerk of the Privy Council 1550-53. He lost preferment on the accession of **Mary TUDOR**, and was executed for his support of Wyatt's rebellion.

THOMAS, William (2)
(1572-1634)

Heir to the **THOMAS (1)*** estates. In 1605, he acquired Coed Helen for the family. A close associate of Sir **John WYNN**, he was knighted in 1603 and was a member of the Council of Wales (1617). He built the house known as Pen-y-bryn at Aber in around 1600.

THOMAS, William (3) (Islwyn)
(1832-78)

Calvinistic Methodist minister and poet, a prolific eisteddfod competitor; often regarded as the founder of the "Bardd Newydd" school. He was heavily influenced by the death of his fiancée, Ann Bowen, in 1853, at the age of twenty, which was the inspiration for his two best-known poems, both entitled "Y storm". These are not typical of his work, and he later married Martha Davies, Ann's step-sister. He edited several periodicals, and was associated with **Lady LLANOVER**, who is supposed to have suggested his bardic name.

THOMAS, William (4) (Gwilym Marles)
(1834-79)

Unitarian minister, Radical politician,

schoolmaster, novelist and poet; possibly the inspiration for the character of the Reverend Eli Jenkins, created by his great-nephew, **Dylan THOMAS**.

THOMAS, William (5) James
(1867-1945)
Industrialist and philanthropist, founder of the Bedwas Navigation colliery; knighted in 1914, and created a baronet in 1919. *Gave his name to:* Trethomas, Glamorgan.

THOMPSON, David
(1770-1857)
English-born explorer, who spent most of his life in North America, at first in the service of the Hudson Bay company and North-Western Company. *Gave his name to:* Thompson River, British Columbia

THRALE (née SALUSBURY), Hester
(1740-1821)
Long-standing friend and confidante of Samuel Johnson, in whose company he visited Wales on several occasions. An offshoot of the wealthy **SALUSBURY (1)*** family, she married Thrale in 1761 and was introduced to London society. Following his death in 1780, she married Piozzi, an Italian music teacher. Her diaries and correspondence, written in a colloquial style, are an interesting source of information about Johnson himself and about contemporary manners.

TIBBOT, John
(c.1757-1820)
Clock-maker, related to the **TIBBOTT*** family. He invented new types of clock and watch mechanism, possibly including the free pendulum.

TIBETOT, Robert (de)
(c.1230-98)
Justiciar of West Wales 1281-98. One of King **EDWARD I**'s most trusted men, he played a leading role in the successful campaign of 1282, and effectively ruled South Wales during the period immediately following, putting down the rebellion of 1287-8 and executing **RHYS ap Maredudd**.

TILLEUL, Robert de
See **ROBERT of Rhuddlan**.

TOMKINS, Thomas
(1572-1656)
Composer born in St David's, where his father was organist. He composed music for the coronation of King **CHARLES I**.

TONYPANDY, Viscount
See **THOMAS**, Thomas **George**

TOY, Humphrey (1)
(c.1510-75)
Merchant and tanner of Carmarthen, mayor of the town in 1557, probable associate of **William SALESBURY**.

TOY, Humphrey (2)
(16th century; exact dates unknown)
London bookseller and printer, nephew of **Humphrey TOY (1)**. He and/or his uncle helped finance the translation of the New Testament into Welsh (1567) by **William SALESBURY**, whose earlier works he had also published.

TRAHAERN AB IEUAN AP MEURIG
(c.1430-63)
Agent for the **HERBERT (1)*** family, supporter of King Edward IV; patron of the arts and owner of a copy of the "Seint Greal" (Holy Grail).

TRAHAERN AP CARADOG
(c.1050-81)
Ruler of Arwystli, and later of part of Powys, following the death of his kinsman, **BLEDDYN ap Cynfyn**. He invaded Gwynedd in 1075, but was killed at the Battle of

Mynydd Carn, where he fought against **GRUFFYDD ap Cynan**. His descendants retained Arwystli, and his granddaughter, Gwladus, married **OWAIN Gwynedd**, becoming the mother of **IORWERTH Drwyndwn**.

TRAHAERN FYCHAN
(12th century; exact dates unknown)
Kinsman of **RHYS ap Gruffydd (1)**, summarily executed at Brecon by **William de BRAOSE (1)** in 1197, an incident which caused tension between the Welsh and Normans in Deheubarth.

TREDEGAR, Viscount and Baron
See **MORGAN, Charles (2)**.

TREFOR or TREVOR, John or Sion
(c.1360-1410)
Bishop of St Asaph 1395-1410; having deserted King **RICHARD II** and served the Prince of Wales (later **HENRY V**), he became a leading supporter of **OWAIN Glyndwr**. He is thought to be the author of "Tractatus de armis", a work on heraldry which he probably also translated into Welsh.

TREVITHICK, Richard
(1771-1833)
English engineer and inventor, employed by the **HOMFRAY*** family at the Penydarren Ironworks from 1803. In 1804, he successfully demonstrated a steam locomotive on rails, built at Penydarren for use on the tramway there.

TREVOR
See also **TREFOR**.

TREVOR, Arthur
(c.1605-66)
Lawyer and judge, son of **Edward TREVOR**. A Royalist, he wrote eye-witness accounts of the early Civil War campaigns.

His first military involvement in 1645-6 resulted in his capture and imprisonment, but he was able to resume his legal practice after the War.

TREVOR, Edward
(c.1580-1642)
Soldier, founder of the **TREVOR*** family fortunes. While serving in Ireland, he acquired the "Rostrevor" estate in County Down by marriage. Knighted in 1617, he built the mansion of Brynkynallt on his family estate near Chirk in 1619. He served as MP for Newtown 1634, but died following his imprisonment by Irish rebels in 1641-2.

TREVOR, John (1)
(1563-1630)
Politician, brother of **Richard TREVOR** and, like him, in the service of Lord Howard of Effingham, whose pocket boroughs he represented as MP from 1592 to 1614; Surveyor of the Queen's Ships (1598) and knighted in 1603.

TREVOR, John (2)
(c.1590-1673)
Politician, son of Sir **John TREVOR (1)**; MP for Flintshire, Denbighshire, and Howard pocket boroughs. Knighted in 1619, on his marriage to the daughter of Sir Edmund Hampden, he represented North Wales on several Parliamentary committees and commissions during the Civil War and Commonwealth, but was pardoned at the Restoration.

TREVOR, John (3)
(1626-72)
Diplomat, Secretary of State under King **CHARLES II**, son of **John TREVOR (2)**; MP for Flintshire 1646-8, and owner of the Trevalun estate. He married the daughter of John Hampden, and supported Cromwell, but backed Monck on the Restoration, and was knighted in 1668.

TREVOR, John (4)

(1638-1717)

Judge, grandson of Sir **Edward TREVOR** and nephew of **Arthur TREVOR**, who undertook his legal training. He took part in an embassy to France with a relation, Sir **John TREVOR (3)** of Trevalun. Knighted in 1671, he was MP for several English boroughs 1673-81, Denbighshire and Denbigh 1687-8, and inherited the family estate at Brynkynallt on the death of his brother in 1681. A supporter of his cousin, **George JEFFREYS**, he became Speaker of the House of Commons and Master of the Rolls in 1685. Despite his staunch Protestantism, he was loyal to King James II, but temporarily regained his former offices under William III.

TREVOR, Marcus

(1618-70)

Soldier, Irish-born son of Sir **Edward TREVOR** and half-brother of **Arthur TREVOR**. He changed sides several times during the Civil War. For his role in obtaining Irish support for the Restoration, he was created Viscount Dungannon and Baron **TREVOR*** in 1662. The title later passed to the sons of his second wife.

TREVOR, Richard

(1558-1638)

Soldier and politician, heir to the **TREVOR*** family estate at Trevalun. He was knighted in Ireland in 1597, and gained the patronage of Lord Howard of Effingham, becoming a member of the Council of Wales (1602) and vice-admiral in North Wales 1596-1626. In the meantime, he fought legal battles with neighbouring families, including the **SALUSBURY (1)*** family, traditional enemies of the Trevors.

TREVOR, Sackville

(c.1565-1633)

Sea captain, brother of Sir **Richard TREVOR** and Sir **John TREVOR (1)**; MP for Anglesey 1625. He served successfully under Lord Howard 1596-1603, was knighted in 1604, and took part in the 1627 expedition to La Rochelle. Chosen to accompany the Prince of Wales, later **CHARLES I**, to Spain in 1623, he saved him from drowning in Cadiz harbour.

TREVOR, Thomas (1)

(1572-1656)

Judge, brother of Sir **John TREVOR (1)**, Sir **Richard TREVOR** and **Sackville TREVOR**; MP for Howard pocket boroughs 1601-25, solicitor to the Prince of Wales (later King **CHARLES I**), knighted in 1619. As Baron of the Exchequer (1625), he played a part in the "ship money" controversy. Though impeached by Parliament in 1641, he continued to serve as a judge throughout the Civil War.

TREVOR, Thomas (3)

(1658-1750)

Judge, son of Sir **John TREVOR (3)**; Solicitor-General 1692-5 and Attorney-General 1695-1701. He was created 1st Baron Trevor of Bromham in 1712, but lost favour under King George I until 1726, when he was made Lord Privy Seal.

TUDFUL
See **TYDFIL**.

TUDOR
See also **TEWDWR, TUDUR**.

TUDOR, Arthur

(1486-1502)

Elder son of **Henry TUDOR**, he became Prince of Wales in 1490 and married **KATHERINE of Aragon** in 1501. The question of whether that marriage was ever consummated turned out to be of great significance for the political and religious future of the country. Arthur "governed"

Wales from Ludlow, where he died, probably of influenza.

TUDOR, Edmund
(c.1430-56)
Son of **Owen TUDOR** and **KATHERINE of Valois**. Created Earl of Richmond by his half-brother, King Henry VI of England, he married the heiress Margaret Beaufort, who by virtue of her descent from Edward III was the major Lancastrian claimant to the English throne. He died before the birth of his son, **Henry TUDOR**.

TUDOR, Henry (King Henry VII)
(1457-1509)
King of England, son of **Edmund TUDOR** and Margaret Beaufort, born in Pembroke Castle. His claim to the English throne (through his mother) was weak, but with assistance from France, he invaded England in 1485. After defeating the usurper Richard III at the Battle of Bosworth, he strengthened his hold on the country by marrying Elizabeth of York, eldest remaining child of King Edward IV. Though he took little interest in Wales after his accession, he revived the Council of Wales and the Marches, making his elder son, **Arthur TUDOR**, its President. He was succeeded by his second son, as King **HENRY VIII**.

TUDOR, Jasper
(c.1431-95)
Son of **Owen TUDOR** and **KATHERINE of Valois**, created Earl of Pembroke by his half-brother, King Henry VI of England. Exiled in France as a result of his support for the Lancastrian cause, he was the military mastermind behind the successful invasion of England in 1485 by his nephew, **Henry TUDOR**. Following Henry's accession to the throne, he became Duke of Bedford and Lord of Glamorgan.

TUDOR, Katheryn
See **KATHERYN of Berain**.

TUDOR, Mary (Queen Mary I; "Bloody Mary")
(1516-58)
Queen of England, daughter of King **HENRY VIII** and **KATHERINE of Aragon**. In the absence of a male heir eligible to become Prince of Wales, she was given the title of Governor of Wales from 1525 to 1533 and presided over the Council of Wales, but lost her status when she was declared illegitimate. Following the death of her brother, King Edward VI, she ruled England 1553-8, but her attempts to restore Roman Catholicism as the official religion were unsuccessful in the long term.

TUDOR, Owen or Owain
(c.1400-61)
Courtier who secretly married the widowed Queen of England, **KATHERINE of Valois**, in 1428, after the death of King **HENRY V**. Following her death in 1436, he was victimised by the regent, the Duke of Gloucester, and deprived of the custody of his five children, but restored to favour on the coming of age of King Henry VI. He was loyal to the King when the Wars of the Roses broke out, and was executed following the Lancastrian defeat at Mortimer's Cross.

TUDUR
See also **TUDOR**.

TUDUR AP GORONWY
(14th century; exact dates unknown)
One of the murderers of **Henry de SHALDEFORD**, attorney to **EDWARD of Woodstock**, in 1345, along with his brother, **HYWEL ap Goronwy**.

TUDUR, Sion
(c.1522-1602)
Poet and satirist, who served as a Yeoman

of the Crown, protecting the future King Edward VI. His home at Wicwair (Wigfair) in Flintshire became a centre for other poets, of whom he was a patron, but he was also a travelling bard.

TURBERVILLE, Edward
(c.1648-81)
Criminal and Protestant convert, involved in the concoction of the "Popish Plot".

TURNER, Llewelyn
(1823-1903)
Industrialist and philanthropist, founder of the Royal Welsh Yacht Club (1846); knighted in 1870.

TWISLETON, George
(1618-67)
Soldier, MP for Anglesey 1654-6 and 1659, a leading Parliamentary campaigner in the Civil War; a member of the High Court of Justice which tried King **CHARLES I**.

TYDECHO
(6th century; exact dates unknown)
Saint, possibly of Breton origin, subject of a 15th-century work by **Dafydd LLWYD**. The churches named after him are mostly in the Mawddwy area of mid-Wales.

TYDFIL
(late 5th century; exact dates unknown)
Saint, daughter of **BRYCHAN**; possibly a martyr. *Gave her name to:* Merthyr Tydfil.

TYSILIO
(7th century; exact dates unknown)
Saint, possibly a prince of Powys; also identified with St Suliac of Brittany. *Gave his name to:* Llandysilio, Anglesey.

TYSUL
(6th century; exact dates unknown)
Saint, possibly a cousin of St **DAVID**. *Gave his name to:* Llandysul.

U

URIEN RHEGED
(c.550-90)
Ruler of the Celtic kingdom of Rheged, referred to by **NENNIUS** and celebrated in the poetry of **TALIESIN**. His base was probably in the north of present-day England, but he successfully opposed the invading Angles until killed in battle at Lindisfarne.

USK, Adam of
See **ADAM of Usk**.

V

VALENTINE, Lewis Edward
(1893-1986)
Clergyman and leading politician, a participant in the arson attack on the Penrhos aerodrome in 1936, with **Saunders LEWIS** and **D**(avid) **J WILLIAMS (5)**. As President of Plaid Cymru, he was the party's first election candidate (1929).

VAUGHAN, Arthur Owen (Owen Rhoscomyl)
(c.1863-1919)
Soldier and popular novelist, famous for his adventures with "Rimington's Guides" in the Boer War. Works include "The jewel of Ynys Galon" (1895) and "The white rose of Arno" (1897).

VAUGHAN, Edward
(c.1630-83)
MP for Cardigan 1679-81, a Lord of the Admiralty; son of Sir **John VAUGHAN (3)**, whose "Reports" he edited, and heir to the **VAUGHAN (10)*** estate of Trawsgoed.

VAUGHAN, Gruffydd
(c.1390-1447)
Knight of Montgomeryshire, possibly present at Agincourt (though he belonged to a family which supported **OWAIN Glyndwr**) and involved in the capture of Sir John Oldcastle in 1417. Outlawed for killing Sir Christopher Talbot in 1443, he was captured and executed at Powys Castle.

VAUGHAN, Gwyneth
See **HUGHES, Anne Harriet**.

VAUGHAN, Henry (1)
(c.1587-1659)
MP for Carmarthenshire 1621-9 and 1640, brother of **John VAUGHAN (2)**. He was

knighted in 1643 and commanded the Royalist forces in Pembrokeshire. After the Battle of Naseby 1645, he was imprisoned in the Tower of London.

VAUGHAN, Henry (2)
(1621-95)
Royalist physician, poet of the "Metaphysical" school, and translator; twin brother of **Thomas VAUGHAN (4)**. One of the **VAUGHAN (9)*** family of Tretower, his relationship to the **HERBERT (2)*** family is also apparent in works such as "Silex scintillans" (1650). He called himself a 'Silurist'.

VAUGHAN, John (1)
(16th century; exact dates unknown)
One of three commissioners appointed in 1535 to preside over the dissolution of the monasteries in Wales, along with **Elis PRYS**.

VAUGHAN, John (2)
(1572-1634)
Soldier, heir to the **VAUGHAN (3)*** estate of Golden Grove; MP for Carmarthen 1601 and 1620-22, and Comptroller of the Household to the Prince of Wales (later King **CHARLES I**), who created him Baron Vaughan of Mullingar and Earl of Carbery in the Irish peerage.

VAUGHAN, John (3)
(1603-74)
Royalist judge and politician, of the **VAUGHAN (10)*** family; MP for Cardigan 1640, knighted 1668. An opponent of Clarendon, he was famous for his decision in a case involving **Thomas BUSHELL**, and supported the independence of the Welsh courts.

VAUGHAN, John (4)
(1640-1713)

3rd Earl of Carbery, second son of **Richard VAUGHAN (2)**, knighted in 1661; MP for Carmarthen 1661-79 and Carmarthenshire 1679-81 and 1685-7. As Governor of Jamaica 1674-8, he came into conflict with Sir **Henry MORGAN**, his deputy. An associate of Pepys, he was President of the Royal Society 1686-9 and a member of the Kit Kat Club.

VAUGHAN, John (5)
(1663-1722)

Social reformer and religious leader, a patron of free libraries, related to the **VAUGHAN (3)*** family of Golden Grove. An associate of Sir **John PHILIPPS (1)**, he acted as a schools' inspector on behalf of the SPCK, and was the father of **Bridget BEVAN**.

VAUGHAN, Richard (1)
(c.1550-1607)

Bishop of Bangor 1595-7, Chester 1597-1604, and London 1604-7. He may have assisted **William MORGAN (1)** in the Welsh translation of the Bible.

VAUGHAN, Richard (2)
(c.1600-86)

2nd Earl of Carbery, son of **John VAUGHAN (2)**; Royalist commander in South Wales in the early part of the Civil War. He was knighted in 1625, and served as MP for Carmarthenshire 1624-9, President of the Council of Wales 1660-72. His secretary, Samuel Butler, wrote "Hudibras" while in his service at Ludlow.

VAUGHAN, Richard (3)
(1653-1724)

Lawyer, brother of **John VAUGHAN (5)** and brother-in-law of **Griffith JONES (1)**; MP for Carmarthen 1685-1724 and Chief Justice of Carmarthenshire, Cardiganshire and Pembrokeshire.

VAUGHAN, Robert (1) Powell
(c.1592-1667)

Antiquarian, of a Merionethshire branch of **VAUGHAN (3)***. He acquired the Hengwrt estate through his mother's family, the Owens. A close associate of **Rhys CAIN** and **Sion CAIN**, his collection of Welsh manuscripts (the Hengwrt-Peniarth collection) is held by the National Library of Wales.

VAUGHAN, Robert (2) Williames
(1768-1843)

MP for Merioneth 1792-1836, in whose honour the "Vaughan scholarship" was founded (1841).

VAUGHAN, Roger
(c.1410-71)

Founder of the **VAUGHAN (9)*** family, younger brother of **Thomas ap Roger VAUGHAN (1)**. On acquiring the Tretower estate, possibly a gift from his half-brother, **William HERBERT (1)**, he enlarged and altered the house. A Yorkist, he was knighted in 1465 and appointed Constable of Cardigan Castle 1470; but following the Battle of Tewkesbury, he was captured and executed by **Jasper TUDOR**. Bards such as **GUTO'R Glyn** and **LEWIS Glyn Cothi** sang his praises.

VAUGHAN, Rowland (1)
(c.1580-1629)

Herefordshire gentleman, a member of the **VAUGHAN (1)*** family of Bredwardine, brought up under the patronage of his great-aunt, **Blanche PARRY**. His attempts to irrigate his estate of New Court are recorded in a book, "Most approved and long experienced waterworkes" (1610).

VAUGHAN, Rowland (2)
(c.1587-1667)

Royalist soldier, poet and translator, descended from the **VAUGHAN (6)*** family of Llwydiarth. He probably fought at Naseby; his home at Caer-gai, in Merionethshire, was destroyed by Parliamentary forces in 1645, he himself being imprisoned at Chester. His works include topical "englynion" and translations of the works of **Lewis BAYLY**.

VAUGHAN, Thomas (1) ap Roger
(c.1415-69)

Founder of the **VAUGHAN (2)*** family of Hergest, son of **Gwladus GAM**. Holder of stewardships under King Henry VI, he turned Yorkist, was probably killed at the Battle of Edgecote, and was proclaimed a hero by **LEWIS Glyn Cothi**.

VAUGHAN, Thomas (2)
(c.1410-83)

Soldier and diplomat. Despite his association with **Jasper TUDOR**, he was a Yorkist, but was Keeper of the King's Wardrobe to King Henry VI. Later he was ambassador to King Louis XI of France and Charles of Burgundy on behalf of King Edward IV, becoming household treasurer in 1465. He was appointed chamberlain to the Prince of Wales (later King **EDWARD V**) in 1470, and knighted in 1475, on the day of the Prince's investiture, but was arrested and executed by the future King Richard III after the Prince's accession.

VAUGHAN, Thomas (3)
(c.1440-1500)

Only legitimate son of **Roger VAUGHAN**; heir to the **VAUGHAN (9)*** estate of Tretower. He supported King Richard III against **Henry TUDOR**, but was pardoned in 1486. He improved Tretower Court, and was a patron of bards.

VAUGHAN, Thomas (4)
(1621-66)

Royalist clergyman and philosopher, twin brother of **Henry VAUGHAN (2)**.

VAUGHAN, William (1)
(1575-1641)

Founder of the colony of Cambriol or "New Wales" in Newfoundland, which lasted from 1617 to 1637; knighted in 1628. He was the brother of **John VAUGHAN (2)** and Sir **Henry VAUGHAN (1)** of Golden Grove, after which he named one of his books (1600).

VAUGHAN, William (2)
(1707-75)

MP for Merioneth 1734-68, a member of the **VAUGHAN (5)*** family of Corsygedol; first president of the Cymmrodorion Society (1751).

VAUGHAN-THOMAS, Wynford
(1908-87)

Writer and broadcaster. As BBC War Correspondent during the Second World War, he covered the air raids on Berlin and the Anzio landing, and was awarded the Croix de Guerre in 1945. He was associated with HTV and the Council for the Preservation of Rural Wales, and was an executor of the **Dylan THOMAS** Literary Estate.

VELVILLE, Roland de
(15th-16th century; exact dates unknown)

Constable of Beaumaris Castle; an illegitimate son of **Henry TUDOR**.

VERNEY (née HAY WILLIAMS), Margaret
(1844-1930)

English-born educationist and author, daughter of the 2nd baronet Hay Williams of Bodelwyddan and wife of Sir Edmund Hope Verney. Her interest in education was stimulated by visits to schools on the Continent. She began a scheme for lending pictures to schools, and was a member of the Statutory Council of the University of Wales 1894-1922.

VINCENT, William Henry Hoare
(1866-1941)
Civil servant, knighted in 1913. A member of the Council of India 1923-31, he also represented India at the League of Nations in 1926, and was later Treasurer of the University of Wales 1932-41.

VIVIAN, Henry Hussey
(1821-94)
Industrialist, son of **John Henry VIVIAN**; MP for Glamorgan 1857-9 and Swansea 1885-93. He developed a range of by-products from the copper-smelting business founded by his father, and introduced the "sliding scale" of miners' wages after the strike of 1889. It was largely due to his efforts that Swansea became a major industrial centre. He was created a baronet in 1882 and Baron Swansea in 1893.

VIVIAN, John Henry
(1785-1855)
Merchant and industrialist, owner of the Hafod copper smelting works; the first MP for Swansea 1832-55.

VORTIGERN
See **GWRTHEYRN**.

VULLIAMY, Colwyn Edward (Anthony Rolls; Twm Teg)
(1886-1971)
Author and translator, of Italian ancestry, who produced works on subjects such as history and anthropology as well as many biographies and novels. Some of the latter, such as "The proud walkers" (1955), are set in Wales. He was very successful as a writer of murder mysteries.

W

WAITHMAN, Robert
(1764-1833)
Merchant, who made his fortune in London; MP for the City 1818-33, Lord Mayor in 1823.

WALEYS, Thomas
See **THOMAS Wallensis (2)**.

WALLACE, Alfred Russel
(1823-1913)
Naturalist who travelled in Asia and South America, and collaborated with Charles Darwin, whose theory of natural selection matched the view he had reached as a result of his own research. His own "Contributions to the theory of natural selection" (1870) was only one of his many works on zoo-geography and associated subjects.

WALTER, Lucy ("Mrs Barlow")
(c.1630-58)
Welsh-born mistress of King **CHARLES II** (possibly his wife), mother of the Duke of Monmouth. The child was taken from her when her indiscreet conduct became an embarrassment to the exiled royal family, and she was sent to England and Holland, eventually dying in poverty.

WARD, John
(1856-1922)
Archaeologist, curator of Cardiff municipal museum, which merged with the National Museum of Wales in 1912. He excavated the Roman fort at Gelligaer and the tumulus at St Nicholas, and was author of "The Roman era in Britain" (1911).

WARING, Anna Laetitia
(1823-1910)
Hymnist, Welsh-born daughter of **Elijah**

WARING. Her first collection, "Hymns and meditations" (1850) included the favourites, "In heavenly love abiding" and "Father, I know that all my life".

WARING, Elijah
(c.1788-1857)
English-born Quaker who lived in Wales from 1810 and became founder and editor of "The Cambrian visitor", published in Swansea (1813), intended for English readers. He was a friend of **IOLO Morganwg**, whose biography (1850) he wrote.

WATKINS
See also **WATKYNS**.

WATTS, Edmund Hannay
(1830-1902)
English industrialist, founder of the firm of Watts, Watts & Co, leading ship-brokers and coal exporters operating in London, Cardiff and Newport. *Gave his name to:* Wattstown, Rhondda; Wattsville, Sirhowy.

WAYNE, Matthew
(c.1780-1853)
Industrialist, partner of **Joseph BAILEY** at Nant-y-glo and later owner of an ironworks at Gadlys, Aberdare (1827), becoming the first to export coal and iron from Aberdare via the port of Cardiff.

WELCH, Ronald
See **FENTON, Ronald**.

WESLEY (née GWYNNE), Sarah
(1726-1822)
Daughter of **Marmaduke GWYNNE**, wife of Charles Wesley. She married the great preacher and hymn-writer in 1749, and accompanied him on his journeys around the country until he ceased to travel in 1756.

WEST, Daniel Granville
(1904-84)
Labour MP for Pontypool 1946-58; first Welsh life peer (1958) as Baron Granville-West.

WHELDON, Huw Prys
(1916-86)
Broadcaster, managing director of the BBC 1968-75; knighted 1976. He was best known as presenter of the early arts programme, "Monitor".

WHITE, Rawlins
(c.1485-1555)
Illiterate fisherman, one of three Protestant martyrs in Wales during the reign of **Mary TUDOR**. Resisting the sympathetic attempts of Bishop **Anthony KITCHIN** to persuade him to recant, he was burned at Cardiff.

WHITE, Richard
See **GWYN, Richard**.

WHITFORD, Richard
(c.1475-1542)
Priest and scholar, friend of Sir Thomas More and of Erasmus, whom he brought to England in 1499. He served as chaplain to Richard Foxe, Bishop of Winchester, retiring in 1506 to the monastery of Sion House, where he translated the work of Thomas a Kempis.

WILFRE or WILFREDUS
(c.1050-1115)
Bishop of St David's 1085-1115, an opponent of the Norman invasions of West Wales; for this he was excommunicated by Anselm, Archbishop of Canterbury. He later obtained Anselm's support against the local Norman lords, but his diocese lost its independence.

WILIAM
See **WILLIAM, WILLIAMS**.

WILIAM AP SION EDWART
(early 16th century; exact dates unknown)
Constable of Chirk Castle, honoured by King **HENRY VIII** for his service at the siege of Tournai (1513), following which he earned the motto "A fynno Duw derfydd".

WILIAM AP TOMOS (Y Marchog Glas o Went, "The Blue Knight of Gwent")
(c.1390-1446)
Knight whose distinguished military service in the Hundred Years War, along with two advantageous marriages, brought him property at Raglan Castle (to which he added the Yellow Tower), Llandeilo, and various other places in South Wales.

WILIEMS, Thomas
(c.1545-1622)
Physician, genealogist and collector of manuscripts, author of an unpublished Latin-Welsh dictionary used by Dr **John DAVIES (2)** as the basis of his "Antiquae linguae Britannicae dictionarium duplex" (1632).

WILKINSON, John
(1728-1808)
English-born industrialist, brother-in-law of Joseph Priestley. He expanded the ironworks at Bersham, Flintshire, founded by his father, Isaac, in 1753, which had made Wrexham the biggest town in Wales. In 1792, he acquired the Brymbo Hall estate, where he founded another works and employed advanced agricultural techniques. He was a pioneer of the steam engine and an investor in canals, but was accused of arms dealing with France.

WILLIAM
See also **WILIAM, WILLIAMS**.

WILLIAM AP GRIFFITH
(c.1450-1500)
Supporter of **Henry TUDOR** who fought at the Battle of Bosworth and was sub-

sequently appointed Sheriff of Caernarfon-shire for life; founder of the **WILLIAMS (6)*** family of Cochwillan.

WILLIAM(S), Lewis
(1774-1862)
Self-educated schoolmaster, employed by **Thomas CHARLES** in circulating schools; remembered as the teacher of **Mary JONES**.

WILLIAMS
See **WILLIAM**; **WILIEMS**.

WILLIAMS, Alice (Alis Mallt Williams)
(1867-1950)
Novelist, an early feminist and supporter of Plaid Cymru. Her two major works, "One of the royal Celts" (1889) and "A maid of Cymru" (1901) were written in partnership with her sister Gwenffreda, under the name "The Dau Wynne".

WILLIAMS, Anna
(1706-83)
Poet and author, daughter of **Zachariah WILLIAMS**. She became blind in her early twenties, and consequently had to give up writing, but became a close friend of Dr Johnson.

WILLIAMS, Arthur (1) Wynn
(1819-86)
Physician, author of "Cancer of the uterus and other parts" (1868). He promoted the use of iodine as an antiseptic.

WILLIAMS, Arthur (2) John
(1834-1911)
Lawyer and politician, youngest of the **WILLIAMS (5)*** brothers and sisters of the Rhondda; Liberal MP for South Glamorgan 1885-95 and co-founder of the National Liberal Club (1882). He married Rose **CRAWSHAY***.

WILLIAMS, Caroline Elizabeth
(1823-1908)
Philanthropist, joint executrix of the will of **Walter COFFIN**, along with her three brothers; founder of the Dinas Institute (1893). Her book, "A Welsh family", describes the history of the **WILLIAMS (5)*** family of the Rhondda.

WILLIAMS, Charles (1)
(1633-1720)
Merchant, who made a fortune in Turkey after being forced into exile by a duel in which he killed his cousin. The influence of **John HANBURY** allowed him to return to Britain and make substantial bequests to his home town of Caerleon.

WILLIAMS, Charles (2) Hanbury
(1708-59)
Verse satirist, politician and diplomat, son of **John HANBURY** of Pontypool; heir to an estate at Caerleon as a result of his father's association with **Charles WILLIAMS (1)**. He served as Liberal MP for Monmouth-shire 1734-47, and was knighted in 1746.

WILLIAMS, Charles (3) James Watkin
(1828-84)
Surgeon, lawyer, and author, Liberal MP for Denbigh 1868-80 and Caernarfonshire 1880-84; a campaigner for Disestablishment of the Church in Wales.

WILLIAMS, Christopher David
(1873-1934)
Portrait and landscape painter, who travelled throughout Europe; best known for his pictures of the Investiture of the Prince of Wales (the future **EDWARD VIII**) in 1911 and the Charge of the Welsh Division at Mametz Wood 1916.

WILLIAMS, Daniel (1)
(c.1643-1716)
Controversial Presbyterian minister, author

of "The vanity of childhood and youth" (1691). He left most of his estate to charity, resulting eventually in the founding of "Dr Williams' School" at Dolgellau and the Dr Williams Library in London.

WILLIAMS, Daniel (2) Thomas **(Tydfylyn)**
(1820-76)
Congregational minister, poet and musician, who wrote the words for several of the works of **Joseph PARRY**.

WILLIAMS, David (1)
(c.1536-1613)
Judge, MP for Brecon 1584-93 and 1597-1604, knighted by King James I/VI; owner of the Gwernyfed estate.

WILLIAMS, David (2)
(1738-1816)
Deist philosopher and politician, a forerunner of the Chartists. An associate of Benjamin Franklin, with whom he founded the "Thirteen Club", his "Letters on political liberty" (1782) was a defence of the American revolutionaries. He also supported the French Revolution and visited France in 1792-3, returning there to represent Britain after the Peace of Amiens 1802. His other works include "A treatise on education" (1774) and "History of Monmouthshire" (1796). He founded the Royal Literary Fund (1790) to support struggling authors.

WILLIAMS, David (3) (Dewi Heli)
(1799-1869)
Lawyer, Liberal MP for Merioneth 1868-9. He established the **WILLIAMS (2)*** family at Castell Deudraeth.

WILLIAMS, David (4) (Alaw Goch; "Abercynon")
(1809-63)
Industrialist, founder of coal-mines at Aberdare and Mountain Ash. Sympathetic to the plight of the working classes, he was

a benefactor to the local community and a leading figure in the eisteddfod movement; the village of Trealaw in the Rhondda valley was named in his honour.

WILLIAMS, David (5) John
(1885-1970)
Author, co-founder of Plaid Cymru; one of the three saboteurs involved in the 1936 attack on the Penrhos aerodrome, along with **Lewis VALENTINE** and **Saunders LEWIS**. His literary output, consisting mainly of short stories, draws heavily upon his Carmarthenshire background.

WILLIAMS, David (6)
(1900-78)
Historian, Professor of Welsh History at the University College of Wales 1945-67; author of "History of Modern Wales" (1950).

WILLIAMS, Edward
See **IOLO Morganwg**.

WILLIAMS, Edward (1)
(c.1650-1721)
MP for Brecknock 1697-8 and 1705-21, younger son of **Thomas WILLIAMS (1)**. He acquired the Gwernyfed estate through marriage to Elizabeth **WILLIAMS (3)***.

WILLIAMS, Edward (2)
(c.1730-1804)
5th baronet **WILLIAMS (3)***, co-founder of the pioneering Brecknock Agricultural Society (1755). On his death without a male heir, the Gwernyfed estate passed by marriage to the Wood family, originally of Middlesex.

WILLIAMS, Edward (3)
(1750-1813)
Independent minister, author and schoolmaster; co-founder of the London Missionary Society (1795). Best known for his influential book, "An essay on the equity of

Divine government" (1813), he was among the greatest Welsh religious leaders of the 19th century.

WILLIAMS, Edward (4)
(1826-86)
Industrialist, son of **Taliesin WILLIAMS**. He worked for the Dowlais Company in London, beginning a career which culminated in ownership of the Linthorpe iron-works at Middlesbrough (1879), where he became prominent in public life. He was the first secretary of the South Wales Institute of Engineers 1857-64 and President 1881-3.

WILLIAMS, Elizabeth (The Maid of Sker)
(c.1747-76)
Legendary figure, whose tragic romance with a harpist, Thomas Evans, became a popular story when recorded by **Jane WILLIAMS**, and was the basis of a novel by **Isaac HUGHES**.

WILLIAMS, Emlyn
(1905-87)
Playwright, best known for "Night must fall" (1935) and "The corn is green" (1938). He wrote for television, film and stage, and was also an actor, often taking the lead in his own plays and touring in a one-man show about Charles Dickens. In addition, he produced two volumes of autobiography, "George" (1961) and "Emlyn" (1973).

WILLIAM(S), Evan (1)
(c.1706-70)
Harpist and composer. Tunes written by him in **Edmwnd PRYS**'s "New Measure" were the first music by a Welsh composer ever published.

WILLIAMS, Evan (2)
(1719-48)
Congregational minister, a prominent figure in the "revival" led by **Howell HARRIS**. An itinerant preacher, he is remembered for the persecution he suffered during his travels in Caernarfonshire.

WILLIAMS, Evan (3)
(1749-1835)
Publisher and bookseller, one of four brothers of **John WILLIAMS (5)**. He set up a bookshop in the Strand, London, in partnership with another brother, **Thomas WILLIAMS (3)**, and was associated with the London Welsh societies. His long career resulted in the publication of many books in Welsh or about Wales, such as the works of **William OWEN PUGHE** and **Edward RICHARD**.

WILLIAMS, Grace
(1906-77)
Composer, whose works include an opera, "The parlour" (1961), symphonies, concertos, and a Latin mass on which she collaborated with **Saunders LEWIS**, as well as the popular "Fantasia on Welsh nursery tunes" (1940) and "Sea sketches" (1944). Many of her works have a Welsh flavour.

WILLIAMS, Griffith
(c.1600-63)
Lawyer, heir to the **WILLIAMS (6)*** family estate at Cochwillan; nephew of Archbishop **John WILLIAMS (2)**, whose political allegiances he followed. He married into the **BODWRDA*** family, and was created a baronet by Cromwell in 1658 and also by King **CHARLES II** in 1661.

WILLIAMS, Gwilym ("Miskin")
(1839-1906)
Judge, son of **David WILLIAMS (4)**, appointed to the Mid-Wales Circuit in 1884 as a direct result of the "Homersham-Cox" incident, the outcry over the appointment of non-Welsh-speaking county court judges. A leading figure in the eisteddfod movement,

he helped his father launch the "Cambria daily leader", the first daily newspaper in Wales.

WILLIAMS, Henry (Ysgafell)
(1624-84)

Baptist leader, a follower of **Vavasor POWELL**. Following the Restoration, his family were continually persecuted for their religious activities; their farm at Ysgafell became famous for a "miracle" which took place there.

WILLIAMS, Hugh
(1796-1874)

Chartist lawyer and poet, brother-in-law of Richard Cobden (who married his sister, Catherine). He defended several members of the "Rebecca" movement, and was rumoured to be its secret leader. His "National songs and poetical pieces" (1840) was a collection of Radical poetry.

WILLIAMS, Isaac (1)
(1802-65)

Clergyman and poet, a leader of the "Oxford Movement" in the Anglican church; author of the controversial "Tract 80" ("Reserve in communicating religious knowledge"), and many other theological works in English. His best-known poems include "The baptistery" and "The altar" (1842).

WILLIAMS, Isaac (2) John
(1874-1939)

First Keeper of the Department of Art at the National Museum of Wales (1914). The Isaac and Annie Williams Bequest was left to the museum by him and his first wife.

WILLIAMS, Jane (Ysgafell)
(1806-85)

English-born author, poet, translator, historian, educationist and musician, a descendant of **Henry WILLIAMS**. She learned Welsh under the influence of **Lady LLAN-OVER**, but wrote mainly in English. Works include the authoritative "A history of Wales derived from authentic sources" (1869), and biographies of **Thomas PRICE (1)** and **Elizabeth DAVIES**.

WILLIAMS, John (1) (Baron Williams of Thame)
(c.1500-59)

Keeper of the Jewels to King **HENRY VIII**. He was created a baron in reward for his support of **Mary TUDOR**, and was President of the Council of Wales under Elizabeth I. [Sometimes confused with **John WILLIAMS (3)**.]

WILLIAMS, John (2)
(1582-1650)

Moderate Bishop of Lincoln 1621-41 and Keeper of the Great Seal 1621-5, who opposed the Catholic tendencies of Archbishop Laud and was imprisoned as a result. After Laud's execution, he became Archbishop of York, and held Conway Castle for the King until 1645, but was turned out by his own party and went over to the Parliamentary cause. He was responsible for the Library building at St John's College, Cambridge.

WILLIAMS, John (3)
(c.1584-1627)

Goldsmith to King James I of England; founder of the free school at Llanrwst (c.1608). He became very influential as a result of the debts owed him by prominent figures. [Often confused with his son, John Williams (c.1600-37) and with **John WILLIAMS (1)**.]

WILLIAMS, John (4)
(1727-98)

Independent minister, Keeper of Dr Williams' Library in London 1777-82; author of numerous works of Biblical scholarship.

WILLIAMS, John (5) ("Yr Hen Syr", "The Old Sir")
(1746-1818)
Clergyman, brother of **Evan WILLIAMS (3)** and **Thomas WILLIAMS (3)**; head of the school at Ystrad Meurig 1777-1818, where he had been taught by his predecessor, **Edward RICHARD**.

WILLIAMS, John (6)
(1754-1828)
Methodist minister, Principal of the Countess of Huntingdon's College 1786-91; son of **William WILLIAMS (2)**, whose hymns he edited and translated.

WILLIAMS, John (7) (Ab Ithel)
(1811-62)
Clergyman and translator, associate of **IOLO Morganwg** and organiser of the Llangollen Eisteddfod of 1858. He founded and edited "The Cambrian Journal" (1853), and edited texts on behalf of the Welsh Manuscripts Society, but his work was plagiaristic and uncritical.

WILLIAMS, John (8)
(1840-1926)
Physician to Queen Victoria, created a baronet in 1894. His chief contribution to Welsh culture was his legacy to the newly-founded National Library of Wales of his great manuscript collection, including the Llansteffan and Peniarth manuscripts. He helped found the Welsh Hospital in South Africa during the Boer War, and campaigned for the eradication of tuberculosis in Wales.

WILLIAMS, John (9)
(1856-1917)
Musician and choirmaster, known for his work with the Royal Eryri male voice choir, which performed at the investiture of the Prince of Wales in 1911.

WILLIAMS, John (10) Ellis
(1901-75)
Novelist and playwright, whose works included the Hopkyn and Parri detective series, and children's books.

WILLIAMS, Llewellin (Llewellin Penrose)
(c.1725-1800)
Sailor and adventurer, who lived in America among the Indians for several years; also a painter, an influence on the artist Benjamin West, whom he met during his travels. His account of his adventures was published in 1815 as "The journal of Llewellin Penrose, a seaman".

WILLIAMS, William Llewelyn
(1867-1922)
Lawyer and judge, historian and author; first editor of the "South Wales Post" and Liberal MP for Carmarthen 1905-18. A campaigner for the disestablishment of the Church in Wales, he opposed **David LLOYD GEORGE** when the latter abandoned the cause of Welsh home rule, and stood unsuccessfully against the official Liberal candidate at Cardiganshire in 1921. Works include "The making of modern Wales" (1924), poetry, novels and short stories.

WILLIAMS, Maria Jane (Llinos; Aberpergwm)
(1795-1873)
Accomplished musician, a singer, guitarist and harpist; a member of the **WILLIAMS (1)*** family of Aberpergwm. Her collection of Welsh airs, published as "The ancient national airs of Gwent and Morgannwg", won a prize sponsored by **Lady LLANOVER**. She also contributed to the work of **John THOMAS (4)**.

WILLIAMS, Matthew
(c.1750-1801)
Actor, manager of the Richmond theatre and proprietor of the Shakespeare Coffee House in Bow Street, London.

WILLIAMS, Morgan (1)
(1808-83)

Chartist leader, supplier of uniforms for the movement in Merthyr from his own textile factory, who published a Chartist newspaper, "Udgorn Cymru".

WILLIAMS, Morgan (2) Bransby
(1825-1914)

Engineer, eldest of the **WILLIAMS (5)*** brothers of the Rhondda. He worked throughout Europe, and was largely responsible for the railway systems linking the Baltic provinces of Russia, where he married Constance, Baroness von Wulf.

WILLIAMS, Morris (Nicander)
(1809-74)

Clergyman, poet, essayist and hymnist; adaptor of psalms, fables, and homilies. He contributed to the revision of the Welsh version of the Book of Common Prayer.

WILLIAMS, Moses
(1685-1742)

Clergyman, scholar and translator, son of **Samuel WILLIAMS**. While working at the Ashmolean Museum and Bodleian Library at Oxford, he assisted **Edward LHUYD** in the research for his "Glossography" (1707). He also edited works by **William BAXTER** and **David POWEL**. He was the originator of the Shirburn Castle collection of printed books and Llansteffan collection of manuscripts, the result of tireless efforts to preserve and record important works.

WILLIAMS, Peter
(1723-96)

Methodist leader, poet, author and hymnist, an associate of **Howell HARRIS**. The most important of his many works was an annotated edition of the Welsh Bible (1770), popularly known as "Beibl Peter Williams".

WILLIAMS, Raymond
(1921-1988)

Influential academic, novelist and critic, Professor of Drama at Cambridge 1974-83. His books included "People of the Black Mountains", a semi-fictional history, and the trilogy of novels, "Border country" (1960), "Second generation" (1964), and "The fight for Manod" (1979), as well as studies in social history, politics, and communications.

WILLIAMS, Richard (Dic Dywyll; Bardd Gwagedd)
(c.1790-1862)

Blind poet and ballad-singer, active during the period of social unrest which included the Merthyr Rising and Rebecca Riots. One of his ballads, "The workhouse", was said to have been instrumental in preventing the building of such an institution at Merthyr.

WILLIAMS, Robert
(c.1781-1821)

Composer, famous for the popular hymn-tune, "Llanfair" (1817).

WILLIAMS, Roger
(c.1537-95)

Soldier of fortune, who fought in the Netherlands on behalf of William the Silent, Prince of Orange, and apprehended his assassin, Balthasar Gerard. Knighted after the Battle of Zutphen in 1586 by the Earl of Leicester, he accompanied Francis Drake to Portugal, and later fought on behalf of the French Huguenots. He is supposedly the model for the character of Fluellen in Shakespeare's "Henry V". Recognised as an expert on military matters by his contemporaries, he wrote "A brief discourse of war" (1590).

WILLIAMS, Rowland (Hwfa Môn)
(1823-1905)

Independent minister and poet, three times winner of the Chair and once of the Crown at the National Eisteddfod; Archdruid 1894-1905.

WILLIAMS, Samuel
(c.1660-1722)
Clergyman, poet and translator, believed to have been a major influence on **William WILLIAMS (2)**. His main importance is as a collector and copier of Welsh manuscripts.

WILLIAMS, Taliesin (Taliesin ab Iolo)
(1787-1847)
Poet and author in English and Welsh, son of Edward Williams (**IOLO Morganwg**). He published much of his father's work, but accepted it uncritically.

WILLIAMS, Thomas (1)
(1604-1712)
Physician, a member of the **WILLIAMS (3)*** family, who attended Kings **CHARLES II** and James II, and held many royal offices. He was created a baronet in 1674.

WILLIAMS, Thomas (2) ("Twm Chwarae Teg"; "The Copper King")
(1737-1802)
Lawyer and industrialist, pioneer of the copper-mining industry in North Wales; MP for Great Marlow 1790-1802. He also had interests in Cornwall and Birmingham; by 1800 half the British copper industry was within his control. Active in local politics, he was closely associated with the **BULKELEY*** family.

WILLIAMS, Thomas (3)
(1755-1839)
Banker and publisher, at first a partner in the publishing and bookselling business of his brother, **Evan WILLIAMS (3)**, and later a partner in Banc y Llong (the "Ship Bank") at Aberystwyth.

WILLIAMS, Thomas (4)
(1818-65)
Physician and scientist, lecturer in anatomy at Guy's Hospital. He later worked in Swansea, studying the effects on health of pollution from the copper industry.

WILLIAMS, Thomas (5) Marchant (The Acid Drop)
(1845-1914)
Liberal lawyer, teacher, author and poet, knighted in 1904 for his role in the foundation of the National Eisteddfod Society. He was editor of "The Nationalist" 1907-12. Works include "The Welsh Members of Parliament" (1894).

WILLIAMS, Waldo
(1904-71)
Nationalist poet, generally regarded as the greatest of the twentieth century in the Welsh language. His social conscience was troubled by the events of World War II, and he went to prison in 1950 for refusing to pay income tax in protest at the Korean War. He stood unsuccessfully as a Parliamentary candidate for Plaid Cymru in 1959.

WILLIAMS, William Llewelyn
See **WILLIAMS, Llewelyn**.

WILLIAMS, William (1)
(1634-1700)
Lawyer, MP for Chester 1675 and Beaumaris 1695-1700, Speaker of the House of Commons 1680-6, and critic of King James II. He was later appointed Solicitor-General after a dispute with **George JEFFREYS**, and was knighted in 1687 and created a baronet in 1688. He helped to draft the Declaration of Rights.

WILLIAMS, William (2) (Pantycelyn)
(1717-91)
Poet, author and hymnist in English and Welsh, one of the leaders of the Methodist movement in Wales. Sometimes critical of his mentor, **Howell HARRIS**, he nevertheless played a major role in the movement, travelling throughout Wales to preach and convert; his hymns played a large part in the success of Methodism. His best-known works include the long poem, "Bywyd a

Marwolaeth Theomemphus" (1764), and hymns such as "Now the shadows flee and vanish". He also earned the nickname "Y Pêr Ganiedydd" ("The Sweet Singer").

WILLIAMS, William (3) ("of Wern")
(1781-1840)

Independent minister, one of the "three giants of the Welsh pulpit" (along with **John ELIAS** and **Christmas EVANS**). He promoted the "General Union" movement of 1834, and founded several new churches in North Wales.

WILLIAMS, William (4)
(1788-1865)

London-based businessman, Radical MP for Coventry 1835-47 and Lambeth 1850-65. He was critical of the state of Welsh education and instigated the Commission which made its controversial report in 1847. His own bequest was used to promote university education in Wales.

WILLIAMS, William (5)
(1832-1900)

Veterinary surgeon, founder of the New Veterinary College in Edinburgh (1871) and author of several standard works.

WILLIAMS, William (6) Crwys (Crwys)
(1875-1968)

Poet, three times winner of the Crown at the National Eisteddfod and later Archdruid (1939-47). His best-known works include "Ednyfed Fychan" (1910) and "Dysgub y Dail".

WILLIAMS, Zachariah
(1673-1755)

Physician and inventor; his works include "The mariners compass compleated" (1740).

WILLIAMS, Zephaniah
(1795-1874)

Chartist leader, an inn-keeper by trade, founder of the humanist organisation, Dyneiddwyr Nantyglo. Sentenced to death along with **John FROST** for his part in the march on Newport in 1839, he was reprieved and transported to Australia. In exile, he discovered coal on the island of Tasmania, and made his fortune.

WILLIAMS-ELLIS (née STRACHEY), Amabel
(1894-1984)

Novelist, sister of Lytton Strachey and wife of Sir **Clough WILLIAMS-ELLIS**. She collaborated with her husband in the novel, "Headlong down the years", which expressed their opposition to the siting of a power station in North Wales.

WILLIAMS-ELLIS, Clough
(1883-1978)

English-born architect and environmentalist who designed the Italian-style village of Portmeirion in North Wales, used as the set of many films and television programmes. He was knighted in 1972.

WILLIAMS-WYNN, Charles Watkin
(1775-1850)

Politician, brother of **Watkin WILLIAMS-WYNN (3)**; MP for Montgomeryshire 1799-1850, and Secretary of State for War 1830-1.

WILLIAMS-WYNN, Charlotte
(1807-69)

Scholar and diarist, daughter of **Charles Watkin WILLIAMS-WYNN**. She travelled extensively, and was a friend of Carlyle, Bunsen, and Baron Varnhagen von Ense, with whom she corresponded.

WILLIAMS-WYNN, Watkin (1)
(1693-1749)

Third baronet Williams, who took the surname Wynn from his mother's family. He was MP for Denbighshire 1716-49, and married into the **VAUGHAN (6)*** family of Llwyddiarth, adding to the family estates. A leading Jacobite sympathiser, founder of the "Circle of the White Rose" (c.1723), he played no active part in the rebellion of 1745.

WILLIAMS-WYNN, Watkin (2)
(1748-96)
Baronet, son of **Watkin WILLIAMS-WYNN (1)**; MP for Denbighshire 1774-89. A patron of the arts, he was President of the Cymmrodorion Society and a personal friend of Garrick, Handel and Reynolds.

WILLIAMS-WYNN, Watkin (3)
(1772-1840)
MP for Beaumaris 1794-6 and Denbighshire 1796-1840; son of **Watkin WILLIAMS-WYNN (2)**.

WILSON, Richard
(1713-82)
Landscape and portrait painter, a relation of **Thomas PENNANT**. His most famous painting was "The destruction of the children of Niobe", but his landscapes, often with a Welsh setting, were his most influential works. He travelled in Italy in 1750-57 and later lived in London, becoming Librarian of the Royal Academy.

WINGFIELD, Walter Clopton
(1833-1912)
Soldier, owner of Rhysnant Hall, Montgomeryshire; originator of the game of lawn tennis, first played at Nantclwyd in 1873.

WINIFRED or **WINEFRIDE (Gwenfrewi)**
(7th century; exact dates unknown)
Saint associated with Holywell, daughter of Tevyth. After being beheaded by a would-be rapist, she was reputedly brought back to life by her uncle, St **BEUNO**, and went on to become Abbess of Gwytherin. Her cult became popular after her remains were acquired by Shrewsbury Abbey in 1138.

WINSTONE, James
(1863-1921)
Miners' leader and politician, co-founder of the South Wales Miners Federation, of which he was President 1915-21.

WOGAN, Thomas
(c.1620-69)
MP for Cardigan 1646-53, a younger son of the **WOGAN*** family of Wiston, one of only two Welshmen who signed the death warrant of King **CHARLES I**. He escaped from prison after the Restoration, and spent the remainder of his life in exile.

WOOLO (St)
See **GWYNLLYW**.

WROTH, William
(1576-1641)
Puritan preacher, co-founder of Wales' first Independent church at Llanfaches in about 1630. An associate of **William ERBERY** and **Walter CRADOC**, he submitted to Archbishop Laud and swore obedience to the Church in 1638.

WYNN
See **GWYN, WYNNE**.

WYNN, Hugh
(1620-74)
Royalist colonel in the Civil War, a member of the **WYNN (2)*** family of Berth-ddu. He married three times, making alliances with the **BODVEL***, **VAUGHAN (5)*** and **BULKELEY*** families.

WYNN, John
(1553-1627)
Lawyer, politician and industrialist, owner of the **WYNN (1)*** estate of Gwydir. Knighted in 1606 and later created first baronet Wynn (1611), he is best known as the author of the "History of the Gwydir family" (published in 1770); he had twelve

children of his own. A patron of schools and the arts, he served as MP for Caernarfonshire 1586-7 and a member of the Council of Wales 1608, and was the leading public figure in Caernarfonshire.

WYNN, Richard (1)
(1588-1649)

Second of the ten sons of Sir **John WYNN**; he succeeded his father as 2nd baronet in 1627. He held office in the royal household from 1617, serving as MP for Caernarfonshire in 1614 and for several English constituencies in later years. His electoral defeat in 1620 marked the end of his family's ascendancy in the county.

WYNN, Richard (2)
(c.1625-74)

MP for Caernarfonshire 1647-53, nephew of **Richard WYNN (1)**. He succeeded his father as 4th baronet **WYNN (1)*** in 1660, but had been implicated in Booth's rebellion of 1659. On his death, the Gwydir estate passed to his son-in-law, the Marquis of Lindsey, and the baronetcy to a cousin.

WYNNE
See **GWYN, WYNN**.

WYNNE, David (David Wynne Thomas)
(1900-85)

Composer, formerly a collier. His works, mainly chamber music, include three string quartets, a popular sonata for violin and piano (1948), and a "Sequence of six bagatelles" for the harp (1951).

WYNNE, Sarah Edith (Eos Cymru, "The Welsh Nightingale")
(1842-97)

Singer and actress, well known for her appearances at the National Eisteddfod, and also popular in the USA. She was the subject of a bust (1874) by **Joseph EDWARDS**,

presented to her by the London Welsh Choral Union, of which her brother was Secretary, but retired from the concert platform on her marriage in 1875.

WYNNE, Ellis
(1670-1734)

Clergyman, author of "Gweledigaethau y bardd cwsc" ("Visions of the sleeping bard") (1703), a work of Puritan morality. He is also known for the hymn, "Myfi yw'r Adgyfodiad mawr".

WYNNE, John (1)
(1650-1714)

Industrialist, developer of the village of Trelawnyd in Flintshire into a centre of the lead industry. He renamed it Newmarket in 1710, founding a school, chapel, and other public buildings.

WYNNE, John (2)
(1667-1743)

Principal of Jesus College, Oxford, 1712-20 and Bishop of St Asaph 1715-27; cousin of **John WYNNE (1)**. He repaired the cathedral and palace at his own expense. When subsequently appointed Bishop of Bath and Wells 1727-43, he lived mostly at Soughton in Flintshire.

WYNNE, William Watkin Edward
(1801-80)

Historian, heir to the Hengwrt estate and manuscript collection of the **VAUGHAN (5)*** family as well as the **WYNNE (1)*** family estates. As Conservative MP for Merioneth 1852-65, he narrowly defeated a Nonconformist candidate at the 1859 General Election, the close contest being attributed to his support for the "Oxford Movement". He was President of the Cambrian Archaeological Association in 1850, and works include "A guide to Harlech Castle" (1878) and "History of the parish of Llanegryn" (1879).

Y

YALE, David
(c.1550-1626)
Clergyman, Chancellor of Chester 1587-1626, who acquired Plas Grono from the **EDISBURY*** family in about 1598.

YALE, Elihu
(1649-1721)
American-born merchant, great-grandson of **David YALE**. He became a governor of the East India Company in 1687 and lived in London and at Plas Grono. He was benefactor of a college at his birthplace of New Haven. After his death, Plas Grono reverted to the Erthig (Erddig) estate. *Gave his name to:* Yale University.

YONGE or **YOUNG, Gruffydd**
(c.1370-1435)
Bishop of Bangor and St Davis's 1407. He became the Chancellor of **OWAIN Glyn-dwr**, whose cause he had espoused in 1403, after long enjoying the patronage of Anne of Bohemia, queen of **RICHARD II**. His "Pennal policy" caused the Welsh church to transfer its allegiance from Rome to Avignon.

YOUNG, John
See **MORGAN, John (2)**.

YORKE, Philip
(1743-1804)
Lawyer and antiquary, author of "Royal tribes of Wales" (1799). He inherited the Erddig estate in Denbighshire, which had been purchased by his family from the **EDISBURY*** family. He made many improvements and was prominent in the social and political life of the area, gradually developing an interest in genealogy as a result of investigating his wife's ancestry.

Z

ZOUCHE, Alan la
Justice of Chester 1251-54, whose arrogant
conduct contributed to the Welsh revolt of
1256-57.

FAMILIES
AND
PEERAGES

A

ALLGOOD
Quaker family of Pontypool and Usk, who discovered a secret method of lacquering wood; prominent c.1650-1850.

ALMER
Family of Denbighshire, prominent c.1500-1600; descended from Ithel ab Eunydd.

ANGLESEY, Marquess of
See **PAGET**.

ANWYL
Family of Merionethshire, including several High Sheriffs of the county.

ARNOLD
Leading Protestant and Whig family of Monmouthshire, c.1500-1700, originally called Arnallt; descended from Gwilym ap Meurig.

AUBREY
Family of Llantriddyd, Glamorgan (originally Brecon), prominent in the 17th century; connected by marriage with **MANSEL***.

AUDLEY
Norman lords of Glynllwg (Newport) 1327-47; connected by marriage with **CLARE***.

B

BACON
Family of iron-masters and mine-owners, prominent in South-East Wales, c.1750-1850.

BAILEY
Family of iron-masters and mine-owners, prominent in Nant-y-glo and Aberaman, 1800-1900; another branch existed at Brecon.

BARHAM
Family of Trecwn, Pembrokeshire, prominent c.1750-1900; also called Foster-Barham.

BARKER
Family of artists, prominent in Pontypool, Glamorgan, c.1750-1850.

BASSETT
Family of Beaupre, Llantriddyd, Bonvilston and Miskin, Glamorgan; connected with **MANSEL***.

BAWDRIP(P)
Family of Splott, Glamorgan, patrons of the arts, c.1500-1700.

BEAUCHAMP
Norman lords of Gŵyr (Gower) 1354-97 and Elfael 1309-15.

BEAUFORT, Duke of
See **SOMERSET**.

BEAUMONT
Norman lords of Gŵyr (Gower) 1107-84. Henry de Beaumont, Earl of Warwick, was granted the right to conquer this region, and built a castle at Swansea.

BIGOD
Norman family prominent in South Wales, c.1250-1300.

BODVEL or BODWELL
Family of Bodvel, Caernarfonshire, prominent c.1550-1700, claiming descent from Collwyn ap Tangno; originally called Gwyn.

BODWRDA or BODURDA
Family of Bodwrda, Caernarfonshire, prominent c.1600-1700, claiming descent from Trahaern Goch; originally called Gwyn.

BOHUN (de)
Norman lords of Brecon (1241-1373) and

Haverford (1245-89). Earls of Essex 1258-1373; also sometime Earls of Northampton and Hereford. Humphrey de Bohun (d.1220) was created Earl of Hereford in 1200.

BONVILLE (de)
Family of Norman origin, prominent in the Cydweli (Kidwelly) area, 12th century. Simon de Bonville gave his name to the village of Bonvilston.

BOSANQUET
Family of Dingestow Court, Monmouthshire, prominent c.1800-1925, descended from Huguenot immigrants; owners of valuable Welsh manuscripts.

BOWEN
Family of Llyngwair, Pembrokeshire, prominent c.1600 onwards; descended from Gwynfardd Dyfed (11th century).

BRAOSE or BREOS (de)
Norman Lords of Builth, Elfael and Radnor c.1100-1230, and of Gŵyr (Gower) 1203-1322.

BRIAN (de)
Norman lords of Talacharn (Laugharne) c.1100-1390.

BROSTER
Family of printers, prominent in the Chester and Bangor area, 1783-1807.

BROUGHTON
Family of Denbighshire, prominent c.1550-1750.

BUCKLEY
Family of Dinas Mawddwy, Gwynedd, prominent 1856-76; the Buckley Arms and Buckley Otterhounds were named after them.

BULKELEY
Family of Anglesey, prominent c.1400-1850; local Members of Parliament for most of the period. Viscounts 1644-1822. See also **WILLIAMS-BULKELEY***.

BURGHLEY, Lords
See **CECIL***.

BUTE, Marquesses of (CRICHTON-STUART)
Family prominent in Cardiff, 18th century onwards; originally Scottish, their Welsh association began when the granddaughter of the 7th **HERBERT (2)*** Earl of Pembroke married Lord Mountstuart, son of the 3rd Earl of Bute, in 1766. They were Marquesses 1796 to date; the 5th Marquess handed Cardiff Castle into the ownership of the city.

BUTTON
Family of Dyffryn House, Glamorgan, originally from Wiltshire, prominent c.1550-1650.

C

CAMVILLE (de)
Norman lords of Llansteffan 1190-1338.

CANTILUPE
Norman lords of Abergavenny 1240-73; the name survives in the site of their castle at Candleston (Cantilupeston).

CAREW
Norman lords, descended from **Arnulf de MONTGOMERY**. They built Carew Castle c.1200 and sold it c.1480 to Sir **RHYS ap Thomas**.

CARNE
Family of Parc Newydd, Gwent, claiming descent from "Ynir Vachan", Prince of Gwent; prominent c.1400-1950. The surname was originally taken from Pencarn,

Gwent, but the district of Carnetown is named after them. Branches existed at Ewenni and Nash in Glamorgan. They were connected by marriage with **KEMEYS***, **MANSEL***, **STRADLING***, and **NICHOLL***.

CARTER
Family of Kinmel, Denbighshire, prominent c.1647-1729.

CECIL or **SITSYLL**
Family of Allt-yr-ynys, Herefordshire, prominent c.1100-1500; descended from a follower of **Robert FITZHAMO(N)**. They were the ancestors of the Lords of Burghley, later Marquesses of Salisbury.

CHARLTON or **CHERLETON**
Norman lords of Powys 1309-1421; they obtained the title by direct descent from the original Welsh ruling family, via the marriage of **HAWYS Gadarn**.

CLARE (de)
Norman lords of Caerleon and Usk 1245-1360 and Glamorgan 1217-1314, (the name was taken from their lands in Suffolk); sometime earls of Hertford, Gloucester and Pembroke. On the death of **Gilbert de CLARE (4)** in 1314, their lands passed by marriage to other families, including **AUDLEY*** and **STAFFORD***.

CLARK
Family of Monmouthshire, prominent c.1800-1910, printers and publishers of local newspapers for the Chepstow and Usk areas.

CLIFFORD
Norman lords of Cantref Bychan c.1110-1282.

CLIVE
Family who took the **HERBERT (2)***

surname in 1807, in order to inherit the earldom of Powis.

CLOUGH
Family of Denbighshire, originally English, prominent c.1550-1850; patrons of bards. Several members were associated with Oxford and Cambridge universities.

COLE
See **MATHIAS***.

CONWAY
Family of Bodrhyddan, Flintshire, prominent c.1400-1721. They were baronets 1660-1721, and distantly related to the Viscounts Conway.

CORBET
Norman lords of Caus (named after their home area of Caux), c.1085-1322.

CORY
Two distinct families of shipping entrepreneurs, prominent in Cardiff, 19th century. The baronetage was created in 1919 for Sir **James CORY**.

CRAWSHAY
Family of Glamorgan, originally from Yorkshire, prominent c.1790-1900; they owned the Cyfarthfa ironworks and built Cyfarthfa Castle (1825).

CRICHTON-STUART
See **BUTE***, **Marquesses of**.

D

DAULBIN
See **DOLBEN***.

DAVIES
Family of wrought-iron workers of Wrexham, 18th century. The brothers Robert

and John Davies, who worked on Chirk Castle, Castell Coch, and churches in Wrexham, Ruthin, and Oswestry.

DAVIES-COOKE
Family of Gwysaney, Flintshire, prominent in the 17th and 18th centuries; after this, the original Davies family married into the Cooke family. They claimed descent from **MADOG ap Maredudd**.

DAVIS
Family of coal-owners, prominent in Gwent, c.1840-1920.

DE
Norman/French prefix. See under second part of surname, eg. **BRAOSE***for **de Braose**.

DESPENSER
Norman lords of Denbigh 1322-26, Blaen-llyfni 1322-26, Caerleon and Usk 1322-26, Gŵyr (Gower) 1322-6, Morgannwg (Glamorgan) 1317-26, Gwynllwg (Newport) 1318-26, Iscennen 1322-26, and Ewyas Lacy (after 1369).

DEVEREUX
Norman family with extensive estates in South and Mid Wales; Viscounts Hereford 1542 to date, Earls of Essex 1572-1646. Leading Protestants in the 16th century.

DILLWYN or DILLWYN-LLEWELYN
Family of Herefordshire, Brecon and Swansea, prominent c.1600-1900.

DINORBEN, Barons
See **HUGHES**.

DOLBEN or DOULBEN
Family of Denbighshire and Pembrokeshire, prominent c.1600-1750.

DOUGLAS-PENNANT
Barons Penrhyn 1866 to date. See also **PENNANT***.

E

EDISBURY
Family of Denbighshire, prominent c.1550-1700.

EDMONDES
Family of Cowbridge, Glamorgan, prominent c.1700-1900; Edmondstown, Rhondda, was built on their property.

EDWARDES or EDWARDS
Family of Denbighshire and Pembrokeshire, prominent c.1500 onwards. Barons Kensington 1776 to date.

EDWARDS (1)
Family of Cilhendre and Plas Iolyn, Welsh Borders, prominent c.1600-1700.

EDWARDS (2)
Family of Stansty, Denbighshire, prominent 1317-1783.

EDWIN
Family of Llanfihangel, Glamorgan, prominent c.1700-1800; they married into the Wyndham family of Dunraven Castle (see **WYNDHAM-QUIN***).

ESSEX, Earls of
See **BOHUN***; **DEVEREUX***.

EVANS (1)
Family of Tan-y-Bwlch, Merionethshire, descended from Robert ab Ifan (d.1541); the inheritance passed through marriage to the Griffith family c.1700.

EVANS (2)
Family of Machynlleth; printers and

publishers of Bibles and the periodical, "Seren Gomer".

EVANS (3)

Family of The Gnoll, Neath, prominent c.1500-1700; the estate passed by marriage to Sir **Humphrey MACKWORTH**. They were descended from David Evans (d.1567), who made a fortune in the salt trade; this was increased when they obtained the rights for the working of coal in the district in 1620.

EVANS-BEVAN

Family of industrialists of Neath, Glamorgan, prominent in the 19th century; originally Bevan. Baronets since 1958.

F

FITZALAN

Norman lords of Bromfield and Yale 1347-97, Chirkland 1322-26 and 1332-97, Clun 1150-1397, and Oswestry 1100-1397, Earls of Arundel from 1243. The titles passed into the Howard family (Earls of Norfolk) by marriage.

FITZGILBERT

Original surname of the Norman family later known as **CLARE***.

FITZHERBERT

Norman lords of Blaenllyfni 1190-1310.

FITZMARTIN

Norman lords of Cemais 1115-1326.

FITZWARIN

Norman lords based in Shropshire, prominent c.1150-1420.

FORT

Family of Norman origin, burgesses of Llansteffan, prominent in the 14th century.

FOTHERGILL

Family of iron-masters, based in South Wales (originally from Cumbria), prominent c.1800-1900.

G

GAMAGE

Norman family of Coity, Glamorgan, descended from Godfrey de Gamached (d. 1176). They held Coity c.1411-1584; having inherited it from Sir Laurence Berkerolles. Their property passed to the Sidney family with the marriage of **Barbara GAMAGE**.

GAMES

Family of Brecon, prominent c.1400-1650, with branches at Aberbran, Tre-gaer, Buckland and Penderyn; descended from **Dafydd GAM**.

GIFFARD

Norman lords of Cantref Bychan 1283-99.

GLYN(NE) (1)

Family of Glynllifon, Caernarfonshire, prominent c.800-1700; their inheritance passed to the **WYNN***(7) family.

GLYNNE (2)

Family of Hawarden (castle and manor), Flintshire, descended from **GLYNNE (1)***, via **John GLYNNE**; prominent 1654 to 1874. Baronets 1662-1874.

GRAY or GREY

Norman lords of Dyffryn Clwyd 1282-1323; founders of the town of Ruthin. Barons Grey de Ruthyn 1324-1963. Sir John Grey obtained the lordship of Powis through marriage into the **CHERLETON*** family c.1421; in 1587, it was sold to the **HERBERT (2)*** family.

GRIFFITH (1)

Family of Cefn Amwlch in Llyn, descended from **RHYS ap Tewdwr**; prominent c.1500-1800.

GRIFFITH (2)

Family of Carreg Lwyd, Anglesey, descended from **EDNYFED Fychan**; prominent c.1550-1650. They were related to **GRIFFITH (4)***.

GRIFFITH (3)

Family of Garn and Plasnewydd, Denbighshire, prominent c.1500-1850; descended from Edwin of Tegeingl.

GRIFFITH (4) or GRUFFYDD (of Penrhyn)

One of the best-known Welsh families, based at Penrhyn and Cochwillan, Caernarfonshire, prominent c.1300-1600; descended from **EDNYFED Fychan**.

GWYN

See **BODVEL**; **BODWRDA**; **GWYNNE**; **WYNN**; **WYNNE**.

GWYNNE (1)

Family of Llanelwedd, Radnorshire, prominent c.1600-1725; originally called Gwyn.

GWYNNE (2)

Family of Garth, Brecon, prominent c.1650-1780; connected with **GWYNNE (1)** after 1700. **Marmaduke GWYNNE** and his family were closely associated with the Wesley brothers.

GWYNNE-EVANS

Family of Gogerddan, Cardiganshire, prominent in the 20th century; related to **GWYNNE*** and **PRYSE***. Baronets since 1913; the current line is named Evans-Tipping.

H

HANMER

Family of Flintshire and Shropshire, prominent c.1350-1850; owners of the Hanmer, Halton, Bettisfield and Fens estatates. Baronets 1620-1746 and 1774 to date; Barons Hanmer and Flint 1872-81. Sir **David HANMER** and his family were closely associated with **OWAIN Glyndwr**.

HARLECH, Barons
See **ORMSBY-GORE**.

HARLEY

Family of Herefordshire, Brecknock and Radnorshire, prominent c.1400-1800. Originally vassals of the **MORTIMER*** family, their great rivals were the **LEWIS (1)*** family. Earls of Oxford 1711-1853; they acquired Wigmore Castle in 1601, and founded the Harleian Manuscript Collection held by the British Museum.

HERBERT (1)

Family of Montgomeryshire, prominent c.1500-1700. Lords of Cherbury from 1553, Earls of Pembroke 1468-79, Earls of Huntingdon 1479-91.

HERBERT (2)

Family of South Wales, illegitimately descended from **HERBERT (1)***; prominent c.1500 onwards. Earls of Pembroke 1551 to date, Earls of Montgomery 1605 to date, Earls of Powis 1804 to date (via the **CLIVE*** family), Earls of Carnarvon 1793 to date, Barons Hemingford 1943 to date.

HILL

Family of iron-masters of Merthyr Tydfil, prominent c.1780-1860.

HILL-TREVOR
See **TREVOR***.

HILLS-JOHNES
See **JOHNES***.

HOLLAND
Family of Lancashire origin, with several branches in North Wales, eg. Conway and Berw, Anglesey; prominent c.1500-1750.

HOMFRAY
Family of Merthyr Tydfil, prominent early 19th century; proprietors of Penydarren ironworks.

HUGHES
Family of Kinmel, Flintshire, prominent c.1800-1900. Barons Dinorben 1831-52.

HUMPHREY
Family of Llwyn-du, Merionethshire; an offshoot of **LEWIS (3)***.

HUMPHREYS
Family of Caerynwch, Merionethshire, prominent 18th century; closely associated with the neighbouring **RICHARDS** family.

I

INGLIS-JONES
Family of Derry Ormond, Cardiganshire, prominent in 19th century.

J

JOHNES
See also **JONES***.

JOHNES
Family of Dolaucothi, Cardiganshire, with a traditiion in the legal profession. The estate passed to the Hills-Johnes branch in 1883.

JONES
See also **JOHNES***.

JONES (1)
Leading Nonconformist family, of Llwyn-Rhys, Cardiganshire, c.1650-1750.

JONES (2)
Family of Fonmon, Glamorgan, prominent c.1650-1800. They claimed descent from Maenarch, legendary lord of Brycheiniog, and Einion ap Collwyn. Colonel **Philip JONES** purchased the Fonmon estate to add to his own at Pen-y-Waun.

K

KEMEYS and **KEMEYS-TYNTE**
Family of Cefnmabli, Glamorgan, c.1450-1704; they then married into the Tynte family of Somerset. Baronets 1642-1735; owners of Llanfair Castle. They were descended from Stephen de Kemys (possibly an anglicisation of Cemais), who owned estates in Glamorgan and Gwent from the 13th century.

KENRICK
Family of Denbighshire and Merioneth; both branches of the family were associated with the Methodist and Presbyterian churches from c.1700. They were descended from Cynwrig ap Rhiwallon, lord of Bromfield (d. 1074).

KENSINGTON, Barons
See **EDWARDES**.

KENYON
Family of Gredington, Flintshire (originally from Lancashire); the Welsh branch was founded c.1700. Barons 1788 to date.

KNIGHT
Family of Tythegston, Glamorgan, (originally from Bristol); they gained the manors of Sker, Tythegston and Newton Nottage in 1708.

L

LACY (de)
Norman lords of Ewyas Lacy 1086-1241 and Denbigh 1282-1311, also of Weobley and Ludlow (originally from Lassy in Normandy). Constables of Chester. Earls of Lincoln by marriage in the 13th century; the inheritance passed to **MORTIMER*** during the 14th century.

LANGFORD
Family of Gresford, Flintshire; they obtained the estate of Allington by marriage c.1500. The original line died out c.1700, but the name continued. Constables of Ruthin Castle in the 15th century.

LESTRANGE
Norman family of Shropshire, 13th century; they intermarried with Welsh families to increase their influence. From one such union, **OWAIN Glyndwr** was descended.

LEWIS (1)
Family of Harpton, Radnorshire, political rivals of the **HARLEY*** family.

LEWIS (2)
Family of Y Fan, Glamorgan, major land-owners in the county, c.1550-1730; descended from Edward Lewis (d.1570).

LEWIS (3)
Quaker family of Dolgellau; a branch of the family emigrated to America in the 17th century. They were descended from Lewis, son of John Gruffydd ap Hywel ap Gruffydd of Derwas. Some generations took the surname **OWEN (3)***; the **HUMPHREY*** family was also descended from them.

LEWIS (4)
Family of Llanilar, Cardiganshire, an off-shoot of an older family of Llandyssul;

connected with the Oxford Movement of the 19th century Anglican church.

LISBURNE, Earls and Viscounts
See **VAUGHAN (6)***.

LLOYD (1)
Family of Bodidris, Denbighshire, prominent c.1550-1700. Baronets 1647-1700.

LLOYD (2)
Quaker family of Dolobran, Montgomeryshire, prominent c.1550 onwards; ironmasters and founders of Lloyds Bank.

LLOYD (3)
Family of Leighton, Montgomeryshire, prominent c.1450-1750, with branches at Marrington and later Moel-y-Garth. Baronets 1661-1743.

LLOYD (4)
Family of Maesyfelin, Cardiganshire, prominent c.1600-1750. Baronets 1708-50.

LLOYD (5)
Family of Peterwell, Cardiganshire, 1700-70; an offshoot of **LLOYD (4)***, from whom they acquired the Maesyfelin estate in 1750. Baronets 1763-69.

LLOYD (6)
Family of Plas Rhiwaedog, Bala, Merionethshire, prominent c.1400 onwards; descended from **OWAIN Gwynedd**.

LLOYD (7)
Family of Dinas, Brecon, prominent c.1750 onwards.

LLOYD MOSTYN
See **MOSTYN***.

LORT
Family of Stackpole, Pembrokeshire, 1600-1775; after this, the family name became

Lort Phillips. Baronets 1662-98; the estate then passed to Campbell of Cawdor.

M

MADRYN
Family of Madryn, Llyn, original owners of the estate, c.1550 to 1700; it was then sold to **Owen HUGHES**, later passing to the **PARRY*** family.

MANSEL
Family of Margam, Penrice and Oxwich, Glamorgan, prominent c.1600-1750; descended from Henry Mansel, who came to Gower c. 1300. Baronets c.1630-1711, Barons Mansel(l) 1711-50. They married into **TALBOT (1)***.

MARSHAL or MARSHALL
Norman lords of Pembroke, Caerleon and Usk 1189-1245. The direct line died out on the death without heir of the last of the five sons of the original **William MARSHAL (1)**, whose daughters married into other Norman families including **BIGOD*** and **BRAOSE***. The earldom passed to the **VALENCE*** family and the office of marshal to the Bigod family.

MATHEW
Family of Llandaff, Radyr, and Castell y Mynach, Glamorgan; they became established as stewards to absentee landlords in the thirteenth century. Earls of Llandaff 1797-1833.

MATHIAS
Family of Pembrokeshire, prominent c.1600-1850; originally called Cole.

MAURICE ("of Clenennau")
Family prominent in North Wales, c.1550-1650; descended from Morris ap John ap Meredydd, founder of the estate at Clenennau c.1485.

MERRICK or MEYRICK
Family of Cotrel in Glamorgan, prominent in the 16th and 17th centuries; patrons of bards.

MEYRICK
Family of Bodorgan, Anglesey, prominent 15th century, with branches in Merionethshire and Pembrokeshire; descended from Cadafael, lord of Cedewain.

MONTAGUE
Norman lords of Hawarden and Moldsdale and Denbigh 1337-54.

MORGAN (1)
Family of Tredegar Park, Gwent, prominent c.1350 onwards, with branches at Langstone, St Pierre, and Llantarnam; descended from Cadifor Fawr (d.1089). Baronets 1642-1727 and 1792-1859, Barons 1859-1962, and Viscounts Tredegar 1905-13.

MORGAN (2)
Family of Vaynor, Glamorgan, prominent 18th and 19th centuries; the community of Morgantown was built on their estate at Gwaelod-y-Garth in Merthyr Tydfil.

MORTIMER (de)
Norman lords of Wigmore in South Wales, and Chirk in North Wales (two distinct branches), 1100-1500; descended from Ralph de Mortimer. They held Blaenllynfi for three separate periods in the 14th century, Maelienydd 1100-1322, Ceri and Cedewain from 1279, Chirkland 1282-1322 and 1327-30, Denbigh 1327-30, Ewyas Lacy from 1314, Caerleon and Usk from 1368, and Radnor from 1230.

MOSTYN (1)
Family of Mostyn Hall, Flintshire, and Gloddaeth, Caernarfonshire, c.1450-1830; they took the surname c.1500. Baronets 1660-1831. The title of Baron Mostyn was

conferred on the Lloyd family from 1831. (Now Lloyd Mostyn.)

MOSTYN (2)
Family of Talacre, Flintshire, a branch of **MOSTYN (1)***. Baronets 1670 to date.

MOWBRAY
Norman lords of Chepstow from 1399. Barons 1448 to date.

MYDDELTON or MYDDLETON
Family of Chirk, prominent c.1500-1800; branches in Denbighshire and Essex. Baronets 1622-1828.

N

NANNAU or NANNEY
Family of Merionethshire, prominent c.1600-1700; patrons of the arts. Their estate passed through marriage to **VAUGHAN (5)*** in 1719.

NICHOLL
Family of Llanmaes and Llantwit Major, Glamorgan; prominent 17th to 19th centuries.

O

OAKELEY
Family of Tan-y-Bwlch, Merionethshire, prominent in 19th century. They came into possession of the estate by marrying into the owning Griffith family c.1780.

ORMSBY-GORE
Anglo-Irish family of Porkington (Brogyntyn), which they obtained by marriage into **OWEN (5)***. Barons Harlech 1876 to date.

OWEN (1)
Family of Bodeon or Bodowen, Anglesey, and Orielton, Pembrokeshire, c.1600-1850; descended from Owen ap Hugh (16th century). Orielton was acquired through marriage into the Wirriot family in 1577. They were Baronets 1641-1851. Another baronetcy was created in 1813 for John Lord (Owen), the heir of an earlier baronet.

OWEN (2)
Family of Llangurig and later Berriw, Montgomeryshire, prominent c.1750-1850.

OWEN (3)
Family of Peniarth, Merioneth, prominent c.1600-1800; descended from **Lewis OWEN** of Dolgellau. The estate passed by marriage to **WYNNE(1)***.

OWEN (4)
Leading Roman Catholic family of Plasdu, Caernarfonshire, c.1550-1600; descended from Collwyn ap Tangno.

OWEN (5)
Family of Glyn, Merionethshire, and Brogyntyn, prominent c.1650-1800; originally called Wynn.

P

PAGET
Family of Plas Newydd, Llanedwen, prominent 18th century onwards; descended from Thomas, Lord Paget, of Staffordshire. Baronets 1730 to date, Earls of Uxbridge 1714 to date, Marquesses of Anglesey 1815 to date.

PAINTER
Family of printers, prominent in Wrexham c.1795-1855. Works printed by them include **Philip YORKE**'s "Royal tribes of Wales" (1799) and a translation of the Family Bible (1813).

PARRY
Family of Madryn, Llyn. Geoffrey Parry
(d.1658), a Parliamentary officer during the
Civil War, acquired the estate by marriage to
a descendant of **Owen HUGHES**.

PENNANT
Family of Penrhyn, Llandegai, Caernarfonshire. Their wealth came from the ownership
of sugar cane plantations in Jamaica. In
1765, they married into the Warburton
family, owners of the old estate of **GRIF-
FITH (4)***, to whom the Pennants claimed
to be related. The estate passed into the
Douglas family of Scotland in 1841. See
also **DOUGLAS-PENNANT***.

PENRHYN, Baron
See **PENNANT*** and **DOUGLAS-PEN-
NANT***.

PHILIPPS
Family of Picton Castle, Pembrokeshire,
1500 onwards;descended from Sir **Thomas
PHILIPPS** of Kilsant. Baronets 1621 to
date, Barons Milford 1776-1823 and 1847 to
date.

PHILIPS or PHILIPPS
Family of Tregybi, Cardigan, and later
Cardigan Priory, c.1600-1700; descended
from Sir **Thomas PHILIPPS** of Kilsant.
The estate passed to **PRYSE*** c.1740.

PHILLIPS
See **LORT***.

PHYLIP ("Phylipiad Ardudwy")
Dynasty of poets of Ardudwy, c.1550-1678.

PICARD
Norman vassals of the Lord of Brecon,
responsible for the building of Tretower
(Blaenllynfi) Castle in the late 11th century.

POWEL
Family of Tir Iarll, Glamorgan, with
branches at Llwydarth and Pen-y-fai; descended from **EINION ap Collwyn**. The
family was founded by **Anthony POWEL**
and was prominent c.1600-1700.

POWELL
Family of Nanteos in Cardiganshire, prominent c.1650-1930, including several MPs
for Cardigan and Cardiganshire; descended
from Dafydd ap Philip ap Hywel.

POWIS, Lords of
See **CHARLTON***, **GREY***, **HERBERT
(2)***.

POWIS, Earls of
See **CLIVE***, **HERBERT(2)***.

PRICE
Family of Rhiwlas, Merionethshire, promi-
nent 16th century onwards; descended from
Rhys Fawr, an adherent of **Henry TUDOR**.

PRICHARD
Family of Llancaiach, Glamorgan, prominent 17th century. Colonel Edward Prichard
was a leading Royalist until 1645. The
family home is now a museum of the Civil
War.

PRITCHETT
Clergy family of Pembrokeshire (orig-
inally Herefordshire), prominent c.1700-
1800, associated with St David's and St
Petrox. They were descended from the
Norman Delabere family.

PROGER or PROGERS
Royalist and Roman Catholic family of
Wern-ddu, Gwent, c.1500-1780, and Gwernvale, Crickhowell, Brecknockshire, c.1550-
1717; the Gwernvale estate passed through
marriage into the hands of the English
writer, Samuel Croxall. They were descended from William Proger (c.1500).

PRYCE
Family of Newtown Hall, Montgomery-shire, prominent c.1500-1800. Baronets 1628-1721.

PRYSE
Family of Cardiganshire, prominent c.1550-1950; Plas Gogerddan now belongs to the University College of Wales, Aberystwyth. Baronets Pryse of Gogerddan 1641-95. See also **GWYNNE-EVANS***.

PUGH
Family of Mathafarn, Montgomeryshire, prominent in the legal profession c.1600-1750; descended from a 16th century magistrate, John ap Hugh. The male line died out c.1750, and the estate was sold to **WILLIAMS-WYNN***.

PULESTON or PULESDEN
Family of Ystrad Tywi, with branches in Wrexham (from c.1450) and Caernarfon (16th century). The family was descended from Roger de Puleston, **EDWARD I**'s Sheriff of Anglesey 1284-95, but flourished under the **TUDOR*** monarchs. Baronets 1813-90, owners of the Emral estate c.1300-1890.

PUW or PUE
Leading Roman Catholic family of Caer-narfonshire, 17th century.

Q

QUARRELL
Leading Puritan family of Mid-Wales, 17th century.

R

RAGLAN, Barons
See **SOMERSET***.

RAVENSCROFT
Family of Hawarden, Flintshire (originally from Cheshire), including several MPs for the county; prominent c.1300-1700. The estate passed by marriage into the family of **Catherine GLADSTONE**.

REES
Family of Ton, Llandovery, prominent c.1800-1850.

RELLY
Family of Pembrokeshire, mid-18th century; associated with the Whitefieldian and Mor-avian sects.

RHYS
Family of Montgomeryshire, late 18th century. Two brothers, David and Thomas, and a sister, Mary, were minstrels.

RICE
Family of Newton and Dynevor, Carmar-thenshire, prominent c.1500-1900; descended from **GRUFFYDD ap Nicolas**.

RICHARDS
Family of Coed, Merionethshire, prominent c.1750-1900. They were closely associated with **HUMPHREYS*** of Caerynwch, to whom they were allied by marriage in 1785.

ROBERTS (1)
Family of Beaumaris, Anglesey, prominent c.1400-1650.

ROBERTS (2)
Leading Methodist familiy of Mynydd-y-gof farm at Bodedern, Anglesey, 1800-1900.

ROBINSON
Family of Caernarfonshire, Anglesey and Denbighshire, prominent c.1500-1700; de-scended from Sir William Norris of Cheshire, who married the sister of **Owain TUDOR**.

S

SALESBURY or SALUSBURY (1)
Family of Lleweni and later Bachygraig, Clwyd, (originally from Herefordshire), prominent c.1300-1800; supporters of the **TUDOR*** monarchs. They married into the **CLOUGH*** family c.1300. Baronets 1619-84.

SALESBURY or SALUSBURY (2)
Family of Rug and Bachymbyd, Denbighshire, 1500-1750; an offshoot of **SALESBURY (1)***.

SALISBURY, Marquesses of
See **CECIL***.

SAY or SAI (de)
Norman Marcher family, Elfael, 12th century.

SCUDAMORE or SKIDMORE
Family of Norman origin, prominent in Herefordshire, 13th century onwards. They were supporters of **OWAIN Glyndwr** and the **TUDOR*** dynasty.

SHEFFIELD, Baron
See **STANLEY***.

SHREWSBURY AND WATERFORD, Earl of
See **TALBOT (2)**.

SKIDMORE
See **SCUDAMORE***.

SOMERSET
Family of South Wales and Gloucestershire, prominent c.1500 onwards. **Charles SOMERSET** married the heiress of **HERBERT (1)*** and inherited their titles and properties (1504). Earls of Worcester 1513 to date, Marquesses of Worcester 1642 to date, Dukes of Beaufort 1682 to date, Barons Raglan 1852 to date.

SOMERY
Norman lords of Dinas Powys, sometime Barons of Dudley.

SPURRELL
Family of printers, originally from Bath, prominent in Carmarthen, 1800-1930.

STAFFORD
Norman lords of Glynllwg (Newport) from 1347.

STANLEY
Family of Penrhos, Anglesey; 1763 onwards; descended from Sir John Stanley of Cheshire. They were heavily involved in the development of the port of Holyhead. Barons from 1839; the 4th baron was created Baron Sheffield and Stanley (1909).

STEPNEY or STEPNETH
Family of Pembrokeshire, prominent c.1600-1850; descended from Alban Stepney, a Hertfordshire lawyer who settled in Wales c.1560, marrying the heiress to the Prendergast estate. They were baronets 1621-1825, and individual members included several MPs, George Stepney (poet), and Lady Catherine Stepney (novelist).

STRADLING
Owners of St Donat's Castle from the late 13th century until 1738, baronets 1611-1738; traditionally descended from d'Esterling, one of the "Twelve Knights" of Glamorgan.

STUART
See **CRICHTON-STUART**.

SULLY (de)
Norman owners of the manor of Sully, 13th century; traditionally descended from one of the "Twelve Knights" of Glamorgan.

SWANSEA, Baron
See **VIVIAN**.

SYMMONS
Family of Llanstinan, Pembrokeshire, prominent c.1700-1800.

T

TALBOT (1)
Family of Margam and Penrice, Glamorgan; the town of Port Talbot was named after them. Descended from the Talbots of Lacock Abbey, Wiltshire, they acquired the estates through marriage into the **MANSEL*** family c.1750.

TALBOT (2)
Family of Hensol, Glamorgan, prominent c.1700 onwards; descended from **Charles TALBOT**. Barons Talbot 1733 to date, Earls 1761-82 and 1784 to date.

THELWALL
Family of Norman origin, owners of Plas y Ward, Denbigh, 1380-1650; also Plas Coch, Llanbedr and Bathafarn.

THEODORE
Family of Penmynydd, Anglesey, prominent from c.1450 (when they adopted the surname) to 1700.
See also **TUDOR***.

THOMAS (1)
Family of Caernarfonshire, prominent c.1550 onwards; they added the family seat of Coed Helen (or Coed Alun) to their estates in the 17th century. They were descended from Rice Thomas, who acquired the manors of Aber and Cemaes in 1551, and were closely associated with the **BULKELEY*** family.

THOMAS (2)
Family of Llanfihangel and Betws, Glamorgan, prominent c.1500 onwards.

THOMAS (3)
Family of Wenvoe, Glamorgan, prominent c.1700-1850; descended from the Harpway family of Herefordshire. Baronets 1694 to date.

THOMAS (4)
Family of bone-setters, of Anglesey and later Liverpool, 19th century. They were traditionally the descendants of a Spanish orphan adopted by an Anglesey couple in the 18th century.

TIBBOT(T)
Leading Methodist family of Llanbrynmair, Montgomeryshire, c.1740-1820.

TOMKINS
Family of Pembrokeshire (originally from Cornwall), prominent church musicians of the 16th and 17th centuries. Thomas Tomkins (c.1565-1627) was choir-master at St David's Cathedral.

TONY
Norman lords of Elfael 1233-1309.

TOSNY
See **Tony**.

TREDEGAR, Viscounts
See **MORGAN (1)***.

TREVOR
Family of Brynkynallt and Trevalun, Denbighshire, prominent 17th century onwards; descended from Tudor Trevor, son-in-law of **HYWEL Dda**. Barons 1662-1706 and 1880 to date. After the death of Sir **John TREVOR (4)** in 1717, the Brynkynallt estate and title passed to the Hill family, who took the name Hill-Trevor.

TUDOR
Family of Penmynydd, Anglesey, descended from **EDNYFED Fychan**, via his great-great-grandson, Tudur ap Goronwy; a branch became the ruling dynasty of England and Wales in 1485 through **Henry TUDOR**. The surname was changed to **THEODORE*** in the 15th century. The estate passed by marriage to **BULKELEY*** in the 18th century.

TURBERVILLE (de) (1)
Norman lords of Coity c.1120-1350; they played a leading role in the conquest of Glamorgan, and were patrons of the Cistercian abbey at Neath.

TURBERVILLE (de) (2)
Norman lords of Crickhowell c.1120-1293.

TYNTE
See **KEMEYS***.

V

VALENCE (de)
Norman lords of Pembroke 1247-1324 and Haverford 1308-24.

VAUGHAN (1)
Family of Bredwardine, Herefordshire, prominent c.1400-1650. They acquired Dunraven by marriage c.1550, selling it in the 17th century. Another branch succeeded to the Bredwardine estate in the late 16th century, adding it to their own estate of Moccas. Bredwardine Castle was rebuilt by them in 1639-40. The family claimed descent from the native lords of Brycheiniog. The first to take the name Vaughan was Roger Vaughan (late 14th century), who married **Gwladys GAM**.

VAUGHAN (2)
Family of Hergest, Kington, Herefordshire,

c.1460-1700; a branch of **VAUGHAN (1)***, descended from the marriage of Roger Vaughan and **Gwladys GAM**. Their home became a haven for Welsh bards, where the Red Book of Hergest and White Book of Hergest were preserved. Another branch grew up at Clyro, Radnorshire, in the 15th century, remaining there until c.1610.

VAUGHAN (3)
Family of Golden Grove, Carmarthenshire, claiming descent from **BLEDDYN ap Cynfyn**. Earls of Carbery c.1600-1713.

VAUGHAN (4)
Roman Catholic family of Courtfield, Herefordshire, prominent c.1600 onwards, especially in the church; Jacobite supporters.

VAUGHAN (5)
Family of Corsygedol, Llanddwywe, Merionethshire, prominent 13th century onwards. They supported the **TUDOR*** invasion of England, holding offices in Merioneth and Caernarfonshire throughout the period 1500-1800, and were noted patrons of the arts, especially associated with the **PHYLIP*** family of bards.

VAUGHAN (6)
Family of Llwydiarth, Montgomeryshire, prominent c.1400-1700, descended from Gruffydd Vaughan, a supporter of **OWAIN Glyndwr**. Their estates passed by marriage to **WYNN (8)*** in the late 17th century. Viscounts Lisburne 1695-1776; Earls of Lisburne 1776 to date.

VAUGHAN (7)
Family of Pant Glas (Ysbyty Ifan), prominent c.1550-1700. They were absorbed by marriage into **WILLIAMS (4)*** c.1700.

VAUGHAN (8)
Family of Porthaml, Talgarth, Brecknockshire, with branches at Tregunter

and Moccas. They were descended from **VAUGHAN (9)***, with whom they intermarried; they also intermarried with the original **VAUGHAN (1)*** family.

VAUGHAN (9)
Family of Tretower Court, Brecon, prominent c.1400-1783, founded by **Roger VAUGHAN**.

VAUGHAN (10)
Family of Trawsgoed (Crosswood), Cardiganshire, prominent c.1200-1947; descended from Adda ap Llewelyn Fychan. They included several MPs for Cardigan.

VENABLES-LLEWELYN
Family of Radnorshire, prominent 19th century onwards. They were descended from Richard Venables (1809-94), vicar of Clyro, whose daughter married into the **DILLWYN-LLEWELYN*** family.

VINCENT
Family prominent in the Bangor area of Gwynedd, 1700-1900, including several leading Anglican churchmen.They were descended from **CORBET*** of Ynys-y-maengwyn through Thomas Vincent (1677-1738), son of Vincent Corbet.

VIVIAN
Family of Swansea (originally from Cornwall), prominent in the 19th century and associated with the copper industry. Baronets 1882-93; Barons Swansea 1893 to date.

W

WARENNE (de)
Norman lords of Bromfield and Yale 1282-1347.

WAYNE
Family of industrialists, prominent in Glamorgan c.1800-70.

WILKINS
Family of Llandough, Glamorgan, prominent c.1600-1830; they then assumed the surname "de Winton", claiming descent from the Norman family of de Wintona. Individual members included clergymen, lawyers, and the founders of "Brecon Old Bank", later merged with Lloyds.

WILLIAMS (1)
Family of Aberpergwm, Glamorgan, prominent c.1500-1800 in local industry and the arts; descended from **MORGAN Fychan**.

WILLIAMS (2)
Family of Bron Eryri (Castell Deudraeth), Merionethshire, c.1800-1940.

WILLIAMS (3)
Family of Gwernyfed, Glasbury, Brecknockshire, prominent c.1600-1800; descended from Sir **David WILLIAMS (1)**. Baronets 1644-1798 and 1674-1804.

WILLIAMS (4)
Family of Marl, Conway, descended from William ap William of Cochwillan (d.1589). The family mansion was built in the mid-17th century. Baronets 1661-1745; the title afterwards passed to **WILLIAMS-BULKELEY***, and the estate by marriage to the Prendergasts, an Irish family.

WILLIAMS (5)
Family of Rhondda, prominent in the 19th century; they inherited the estates of **Walter COFFIN**, where they built industrial housing (Williamstown), later residing at Plas Coed-y-Mwstwr, Bridgend. They were linked by marriage with **CRAWSHAY***, the heir to the family estates taking the name Crawshay-Williams in the late 19th century.

WILLIAMS (6)
Family of Cochwillan, Caernarfonshire, prominent c.1500-1700; descended from Robin

ap Griffith (founder of the **GRIFFITH (4)*** family. Baronets 1658-84; the title afterwards passed into the **WILLIAMS (4)*** family.

WILLIAMS-BULKELEY
Family of Anglesey, prominent 19th century, claiming descent from **EDNYFED Fychan**. Sir Richard Bulkeley Williams assumed the name Bulkeley in 1826 when he inherited the estate of Viscount **BULKELEY***. Baronets 1661 to date.

WILLIAMS-WYNN
Family of Ruabon, Denbighshire, c.1650 onwards; an offshoot of **WYNN***, descended from Sir **William WILLIAMS (1)**. Baronets from 1688, they acquired the estate of Wynnstay by marriage around the same time. The forename Watkin was borne by successive baronets from 1693 onwards, ("uncrowned kings of North Wales"). Wynnstay now houses a college, and the family mansion at Glanllyn, near Bala, passed to Urdd Gobaith Cymru in 1951.

WINTON or WINTONA, de
See **WILKINS**.

WOGAN
Family of Pembrokeshire, with branches at Picton, Wiston, Boulston, Llanstinan and Stonehall, 1200-1800; descended from Gwgan ap Bleddyn, a native lord of Brecon. The surname was introduced to Ireland by Welsh adherents of **Richard de CLARE**.

WOOD
Gypsy family, famous as musicians, descended from an eighteenth-century immigrant, Abram Wood. As a result Welsh gypsies became generally known as "Teulu Abram Wood". The name of one individual, Alabaina Wood, became synonymous with "gypsy".

WYN
See **GWYNNE**; **WYNN**; **WYNNE**.

WYNDHAM-QUIN
Earls of Dunraven; on their Glamorgan estate the Wyndham colliery and the village of Wyndham grew up in the late 19th century.

WYNN
See also **OWEN (5)***; **WILLIAMS-WYNN***; **WYNNE***.

WYNN (1)
Family of Gwydir, Caernarfonshire, prominent c.1500-1700; descended from **OWAIN Gwynedd**. Baronets 1611-1719. Sir **John WYNN** wrote the family history.

WYNN (2)
Family of Berth-ddu and Bodysgallen, Caernarfonshire; a branch of **WYNN (1)***. Descended from the marriage of Griffith Wynn with an heiress of **SALUSBURY (2)*** in the 16th century, they were associated with St John's College, Cambridge.

WYNN (3) or WYNNE
Family of Bodewryd, Anglesey, claiming descent from Gweirydd ap Rhys, founder of one of the "Fifteen Tribes" of Wales; they took the surname Wynn c.1600. The estate passed by marriage to **STANLEY*** in the 18th century.

WYNN (4)
Family of Cesail Gyfarch, Caernarfonshire, prominent in the 16th to 18th centuries. The estate passed by marriage to descendants of Bishop **William LLOYD (1)**.

WYNN(E) (5)
Family of Glyn, Merionethshire, prominent 17th century onwards; associated by marriage with **OWEN (5)***.

WYNN (6)

Family of Maesyneuadd, Merionethshire, prominent c.1650-1750; descended from **OSBWRN Wyddel**. They later assumed the surname **NANNEY*** after a marriage into the Nanney family of Maes-y-pandy.

WYNN (7)

Family of Merionethshire and Caernarfonshire, originally from Boduan or Bodfean, prominent 16th century onwards. Bardsey Island was given to a member of the family, John Wynn, as a reward for his support of King Edward VI.

WYNN (8)

Family of Llanforda, Ruabon, prominent c.1675-1800. They were descended from Sir **William WILLIAMS (1)**, who purchased the estate in 1675. His son married the granddaughter of Sir **John WYNN**, and their son was the first Sir **Watkin WILLIAMS-WYNN (1)**, who adopted the surname Wynn c.1740 and inherited the Wynnstay estate. See also **WILLIAMS-WYNN***.

WYNN (9)

Family of Ynysmaengwyn, Merionethshire, prominent in the 16th century. See also **CORBET***, **NANNEY***, and **PRYSE***.

WYNNE

See also **WYNNE**.

WYNNE (1)

Family of Peniarth, Merionethshire, prominent c.1700-1900; descended from Robert Wynn (d. 1670). The head of the family bore the forename William in succession from the seventeenth century until the death of the seventh William Wynne in 1909.

WYNNE (2)

Family of Denbighshire; they owned the Voelas estate from 1546 into the 20th century and inherited Cefn Amwlch through marriage into the **GRIFFITH (1)*** family. They were descended from Sir **ROBERT ap Rhys** via Cadwaladr Wynne, High Sheriff of the county in 1548.

Y

YALE

Family of Denbighshire, prominent c.1500-1700, descended from **OSBWRN Wyddel**; they acquired the estate of Allt Llwyn Dragon c.1500, renaming it Plas yn Ial, and later acquired Plas Grono at Wrexham.

BIBLIOGRAPHY

I conceived the idea for this work under the false impression that there was no one book to which those like myself could go when faced with a reference to an unfamiliar name, perhaps confusingly similar to some other. After beginning my research, I discovered the existence of the **Dictionary of Welsh Biography**, edited by J. E. Lloyd and R. T. Jenkins, first published in 1959 by the Honourable Society of Cymmrodorion, and updated in 1970. This caused me to consider abandoning the idea of compiling my own list. However, as anyone familiar with that great volume will know, it is more of an encyclopaedia than a quick-reference work, and consequently aims at a slightly different audience. The Editors, in their introduction, note that they initially favoured a multi-volume work, in order to include all those they felt merited it. Later, they suggested to their sponsors that they might omit certain less eminent individuals in order to reduce the number of pages, a suggestion which was dismissed (and to think that I regarded the present work as a mammoth undertaking!)

Another important difference between **Who's who in Welsh history** and the **Dictionary of Welsh Biography** is that the latter claims to include only persons of Welsh birth or descent (though in fact it does not follow this rule strictly). Thus it leaves out people like Eleanor de Montfort and Thomas Bushell, whom I consider to be major figures in the history of Wales. Moreover, it is already a little out of date. The biographies contained in it are detailed and sometimes obscure, whereas those in this book pick out the salient facts about each subject in such a way as to distinguish them from one another. Nevertheless, I must acknowledge the debt I owe to the compilers, the discovery of whose work guided and greatly simplified my own research.

Other biographical dictionaries and similar works which the reader may find of interest include those listed below.

EVANS, Gwynfor. *Welsh nation builders*. Gomer Press, 1988.

EYERS, Michael. *The masters of the coalfield*. Village Publishing, 1991.

HUGHES, Thomas. 'Great Welshmen of modern days'. *Western Mail & Echo*, 1931.

PARRY, John H. *The Cambrian Plutarch*. Simpkin & Marshall, 1834.

STEPHENS, Meic (ed.). Oxford companion to the literature of Wales. OUP, 1986.

VAUGHAN THOMAS, Wynford *The princes of Wales*. Kaye & Ward, 1982.